AILING NATION

LESSONS FROM THE BEDSIDE FOR AMERICA'S LEADERS

NATE LINK, MD

outskirts press

The Ailing Nation
Lessons From the Bedside for America's Leaders

v4.0 r1.2

Outskirts Press, Inc.
http://www.outskirtspress.com

ISBN: 978-1-9772-2498-9

PRINTED IN THE UNITED STATES OF AMERICA

PART ONE: LESSONS IN LEADERSHIP

PART TWO: THE AILING NATION

Prelude

Let us go then, you and I,
When the evening is spread out against the sky
Like a patient etherized upon a table;
Let us go, through certain half-deserted streets,
The muttering retreats
Of restless nights in one-night cheap hotels...
To lead you to an overwhelming question.
Oh, do not ask, "What is it?"
Let us go and make our visit.

From *The Love Song of J. Alfred Prufrock*, T.S Eliot, 1920

America has enjoyed an enviable life. Born in the eighteenth century as the first modern democracy, we shed our British parentage, expanded swiftly across the continent, grew into a major power, led the allies to triumph in two world wars, flexed our economic might, and advanced the cause of freedom across the globe. Surely our nation has had a storybook existence.

Okay, but not exactly a *fairy-tale*. At least not for *everyone.* For nearly two centuries, our narrative embraced abhorrent storylines on enslavement of Black Americans, oppression of Native Americans, subjugation of women, neglect of the elderly, mistreatment of the working class, and despoilment of the environment – to name a few.

Yet, by the late 1960s, we were rapidly advancing on all fronts: civil rights, health care, social security, ecological stewardship, economic growth, and middle-class prosperity.[1] The moon landing itself was a metaphor for a nation that could set sights on distant horizons and carve a path to the stars.

Then...something happened. We fell off our trajectory. We retreated. We lost our mojo. In recent years, our economic progress has slipped from its once-blistering pace, our ability to shape world events has been checked, and our vaunted democratic institutions have begun to collapse around us. In our current state, political parties lock horns, national elections swing back and forth like a pendulum, and Supreme Court vacancies provoke mortal combat.

The worsening fracture of the voting public along racial, religious, and regional fault lines impedes efforts to address obvious threats to our well-being: growing income inequality, a disenchanted work force, a massive federal deficit, and the globe-menacing triple-threat of terrorism, nuclear proliferation, and climate change. Intergroup hostilities, tedious disputes, and a bipartisan aversion to compromise all heighten our sense that we are slipping into an advanced and incurable stage of illness.

America is ailing.

Not in the sense of the acute, noisy, surmountable pandemic of COVID-19, but in the form of something much worse: a chronic, silent, relentless condition that is dragging us down, day by day, step by step, in a silent progression – like AIDS or cancer. A deadly undertow. The three questions that follow are: Why is America ailing? Is the illness curable? If so, what is the treatment? The purpose of this book is to answer these three questions.

I am a physician. I have spent my life in a profession dedicated to identifying signs and symptoms of illness, gathering facts to make a diagnosis, and selecting a treatment to match the ailment. I am also a leader. For the past eight years, I have served as medical director of a large urban hospital using modern tools of governance.

My workshop is Bellevue Hospital, one of eleven facilities in *New York City Health and Hospitals*, the legendary public health system that spans New York's five boroughs.[2] I first came to Bellevue 37 years ago as a lowly intern to begin training in my specialty, Internal Medicine – to learn from the bedside.

Bedside learning has an exalted standing in medical education. Unlike learning from a textbook, training at the bedside introduces the human element. It is, by far, the best place to hone our craft and the wellspring of our most cherished lessons, which reinforce my love for this hospital and remind me of the duality of my profession.

In truth, the practice of Medicine is both an art and a science. Poetry and numbers. The art of Medicine has a soft, squishy center: trust, compassion, and human relationships. The science of Medicine has hard, straight edges: evidence, analysis, and objective decisions.

Like a golden braid, the art is woven tightly into the science, and the two are mutually reinforcing. A worthy physician is master of both.[3] As it turns out, the same qualities define great leadership, which, too, is an art and a science. The marriage of art and science is a core theme of this book.

In my assessment of America's ailments, I am struck by remarkable similarities to a chronically ill patient: a bewildering array of symptoms, the insidious advance of physical signs, a gradual ebbing of strength, and the evolving stages of denial, dysfunction, and decline.

This subjective assessment is supported by objective data spanning four decades. While real economic output per person has nearly doubled and corporate profits have more than tripled, median wages per worker have barely budged – to the discontent of the middle-class. While global temperatures have risen by nearly two degrees and polar ice caps have begun to melt, elected officials continue to deny the truth – to the detriment of the planet.

And while surveys show most Americans seek the middle ground about our most divisive topics – health care, abortion, and gun control – national leaders staunchly resist any form of compromise – to the dismay of the electorate. This striking disparity between what voters want and what their leaders do is pathognomonic (proof positive) of a democracy in decline.

As I review the history of this disease, I recognize it is not an acute disorder – to be cured by a single election. It is a *chronic* condition, one that long predates Donald Trump, our most prominent recent symptom. This slowly growing cancer has been silently spreading for decades.

As I rummage through my doctor's bag, I realize the medical profession has much to offer our nation's leaders: A culture of excellence. Intellectual tools to diagnose and treat difficult problems. A systematic approach that guides almost everything we say and do, and yet is seldom employed in the chambers of government.

However, as I begin to delve into the complexities of this perplexing case, I realize the answers are not readily apparent. It will take a fair amount of detective work to get to the correct diagnosis, and from there to the proper treatment. Only then will it be clear whether our democracy is a life that can be saved.

One might question how I, a physician leader in a safety-net hospital, have the standing to comment on national leadership culture. On *politics*. It is a valid question. My answer is that a fresh perspective is *exactly* what is needed. Indeed, it is nigh impossible to fully change a system from within – to paint the very spot one is standing on. After all, the health industry did not make huge advances in performance all by itself, and neither will government.

In the past four decades, American hospitals have garnered principles of safety from the aviation industry, gathered tips about quality from automobile manufacturers, and gleaned insights into customer service from the hotel trade. These interstellar innovations launched American healthcare into the 21st century. Likewise, the world of Medicine has valuable insights to offer the political multiverse. I am just paying it forward.

The intent of this book, then, is to translate my own observations into lessons for our nation's leaders. To review these lessons, we must go and make our visit – to the bedside of my most memorable cases. A new lesson will the central theme of each chapter – a fresh strand for the golden braid.

We will learn from Natalie, the well-meaning ICU nurse who ignored the ventilator alarm, Juan, the irrepressible AIDS patient who had nine lives, Gerry, the bemused accountant whose brain could not store new memories, and Thomas, the accidental tourist who was raised from the dead.

A dozen other patients will teach us additional lessons in leadership, lessons that will lead us into political hot zones such as income inequality, health care, and climate change. In the final chapter, our lessons will jointly lead us to a proposed cure of the mysterious illness that has left the nation, our patient, in a semi-conscious state – etherized upon the table.

In the pages that follow, I will review America's presenting complaints, her signs and symptoms, and her current physiologic state. I will check her pulse, take her temperature, and elicit the relevant details about her illness. In the best tradition of Evidence-Based Medicine I will bring truth to bear on this patient's condition – to assemble the salient facts, arrive at an accurate diagnosis, and, hopefully, prescribe an effective treatment.

Atonement:
Right the Wrong

Tremble, thou wretch,
That hast within thee undivulged crimes,
Unwhipp'd of justice: hide thee, thou bloody hand...
Rive your concealing continents, and cry
These dreadful summoners grace. I am a man
More sinn'd against than sinning.

From *King Lear*, William Shakespeare, c. 1606

Snickersnack. That was the trick. A Snickers bar chased by a double-strength No-Doze tablet washed down with a large styrofoam cupful of slightly stale coffee from the Roach Coach. At midnight. Right outside the ER.

That's how I did it. How I powered my backup generator. How I staved off desperation, exhaustion, and starvation in one simple cocktail. How I was able to run all night without any sleep and then keep going strong until the next evening – 36 straight hours of dutiful service as an intern on the Bellevue wards. A solid day and a half dashing from patient to patient, drawing blood, checking lab results, controlling blood sugars, inserting IVs, and writing notes. Not to mention embracing my new craft, Internal Medicine.

The key to surviving a 36-hour shift was simple: Pace yourself. Nourish yourself. Keep your head down. Pay attention. Focus. Learn your lessons.

And don't screw up.

Doctors make mistakes. There is probably no statement about the medical profession truer than that. Doctors miss diagnoses and dispense the wrong treatments. They administer the right treatments incorrectly. They overlook the obvious, exercise poor judgment, and just plain screw up.

A compendium of all the mistakes that physicians have made could fill an encyclopedia. After all, they are human, and no human is perfect. When one considers the thousands of critical decisions a physician will make over her lifetime, it is apparent that even the best will miss the mark sooner or later. This is true of every physician who has ever practiced, including me.

In late October of 1983, my first year of training, I was assigned to the Chest Service. This inpatient unit, established in 1903, is a legendary department in my hospital – famous for the treatment of multitudes of tuberculosis cases in the early 1900s, as well as a unique contribution to the technology of Medicine. In 1956, two physicians on the Bellevue Chest Service, André Cournand and Dickinson Richards, won a Nobel Prize for developing the procedure known today as cardiac catheterization.

One of my patients that month was Alec Secceño, a 45 year-old man admitted for symptoms of asthma that we successfully managed with two conventional treatments: an asthma inhaler and an oral steroid called prednisone.[1] Prednisone had the unfortunate side effect of raising Alec's blood sugar level, so we started him on insulin injections to bring it back down. With his blood sugar carefully calibrated by this delicate balance of two medications, Alec improved and went home in four days.

Soon after our patient left the hospital, I discovered a serious mistake in my discharge orders. I had remembered to prescribe the insulin but had forgotten to write a prescription for prednisone. I am not sure why I made this error. It was the second day of a 36-hour shift, so perhaps I was in a fog of sleep deprivation. Perhaps I was in a rush. Perhaps I was just sloppy. But it was a serious oversight. Without prednisone on board to balance the scale, the insulin might drive the blood sugar downward to a dangerously low level.

I tried to call Alec at the phone number listed in his chart, but there was no answer. I could have sent a telegram, but it would not arrive until the next day, and he might suffer serious harm in the meantime. At this point, I knew there was only one thing I could do to protect Alec from my oversight. I would have to make an old-fashioned house call.

At the end of my shift, I went out to First Avenue and hailed a taxi, prednisone prescription in hand. I gave the driver the patient's address on Avenue C, and we headed straight to Alphabet City, an economically depressed neighborhood below 14th Street.[2] As soon as the cab began to move, I leaned against the window and promptly fell asleep.

Fifteen minutes later, my driver stirred me awake, and I sat up and looked around. Compared to bustling First Avenue, this was an alien and hostile world. The streets were dark, storefronts were shuttered, and pedestrians had vanished from the sidewalks. I stared at the imposing facade of a six-story brick building, silhouetted against the night sky.

"Don't go *anywhere*," I implored the driver. "I promise I'll be right back." Again, through the open passenger window as I started up the stoop, I repeated my plea. "Just stay right here – *please*." I pressed firmly on the massive front door, and it grudgingly gave way. More darkness. I was now standing in the first-floor hallway, which was almost pitch black. "People actually live here," I murmured to myself.

As I tentatively stepped forward through the open corridor, I realized I was an open target. As a Bellevue intern, I was wearing my "uniform" – long-sleeved pressed shirt, neatly-knotted narrow tie, and hospital-issued white cotton pants complete with an old-style pager the size of a small brick hanging on my belt. Between my unorthodox outfit and the stethoscope still looped around my neck, it couldn't be more obvious that I did *not* belong here.

Likewise, it was equally clear that this eerily nondescript building, this shadowy, obscure, anonymous edifice deep in the heart of Alphabet City, could swallow me whole, and no one would be the wiser. I was resisting the impulse to turn on my heels and race back to the cab when I noticed a speckled band of light issuing from a doorway at the far end of the hallway. I edged forward to investigate.

As I knocked on the door, it swung open. Four burly Hispanic men were hunched over a card table, playing poker under a bare light bulb. It was a scene right out of a movie set. They did not seem startled by my intrusion but silently eyed me up and down. The one who spoke first was completely bald, wearing baggy jeans and a white t-shirt, and was leaning forward with a cigarette suspended between two fingers of the hand holding his cards. He seemed more annoyed than suspicious. "What do *you* want?" he growled.

I extended my stethoscope, which I hoped he would somehow recognize as a sign of peace. "I am Dr. Link from Bellevue Hospital, and

I am looking for one of my patients, Alec Secceño. I have some really important information for him."

The speaker looked down at my stethoscope and then up at me. After a brief pause, he shook his head and curtly replied, "Sorry, nobody like that lives here." He waited for me to go.

"Well, I really need to tell him something important," I sputtered. *Surely, this was the correct address*. He just continued to stare at me blankly, so I turned around to leave, utterly defeated.

"Wait a minute!" he sharply interrupted. I turned back around to face him, one hand still on the door. He was looking steadily at his companions as he continued in a deliberate voice, "If a guy by that name shows up, what should I tell him?"

I thought for a second as I composed myself, "Tell him that I made a mistake with his prescriptions. Tell him he should *not* take the insulin. That was a mistake. He should come back to the clinic right away, and we will give him further instructions." I paused to let that sink in. "And tell him I'm sorry for the mistake." He nodded understanding and waved me out.

As I walked back down the hall, I folded the prescription and put it back in my pocket. It would have been much too complicated to leave it behind with a detailed explanation. Better just to stop the insulin. And apologize. As I slid back into the cab, I relaxed. "Mission accomplished," I thought to myself. At least I hoped so. Unfortunately, I never heard from Alec again.

In retrospect, the overlooked prescription was a very easy mistake to make and much more difficult to resolve. A good lesson for me. My stressful adventure seemed to be a form of punishment for the oversight. Thankfully, it gave me a chance to right my wrong. My personal opportunity for atonement.

Of course, as a physician-in-training, I had many opportunities to commit errors large and small, some more serious than others. In the spring of 1985, I was assigned to work in the Bellevue Emergency Department (ED). During this rotation, I toiled on the front line. One evening, during the very last shift of my ED experience, I assessed a patient with a cough and fever.

Matthew Tener was a disheveled young man with tattered jeans, a stained flannel shirt, and a faded red baseball cap. One might think he lived in the street. He admitted to heavy drinking, but he was not homeless; he had an apartment and a girlfriend. So he was "plugged in." Before long, his chest x-ray revealed the source of his fever, so I broke the news myself.

"The x-ray shows pneumonia. That means you have a serious infection in your lungs – which explains why you've been coughing."

Matt frowned. "How bad is it?"

"Not too bad. We can treat you with antibiotics. You don't even need to stay in the hospital."

He seemed unconvinced. "You *sure* about that?"

"Absolutely. But you *have* to fill this prescription at the pharmacy. It's for the antibiotics you need to take twice a day. Can you do that?"

"Doubtful." He lowered his voice. "I don't have any cash on me."

"That's no problem," I brightly reassured him. "We have a pharmacy right here. You can pick up the medication on your way out...at no charge." I felt like I was selling him a used car. "How does that sound?"

"All right, then," he replied unenthusiastically. He tugged on his cap and slumped down in his chair.

Since the inpatient units were full, I was reluctant to admit Matt to the hospital. He listened to my instructions and left the ED with the prescription and a follow up appointment to see me in clinic. Nice and tidy. A few hours later, however, at the end of my shift, I had a change of heart.

How could I be sure that he would fill the prescription and take the antibiotics as directed? How did I know that he wouldn't be off drinking somewhere instead of following the plan? Or lying in a gutter, too sick to take his antibiotics. It was easy to imagine these and other ghastly scenarios, so I decided that I should have admitted Matt to the hospital after all. How could I rectify this situation now that he had left? How could I right my wrong?

On my way out, I went to the information desk and requested a telegram to be sent to Matt's address advising him to come back to the ED. The next morning, I reported to my new assignment at the Veterans Administration (VA) Hospital, Bellevue's neighbor to the south.[3] Late in the day, I was paged to a Bellevue number. I was sitting at a nursing station as I returned the call. It was the Director of the Bellevue ED, and he was not happy.[4]

"Did you send this young man, Matthew Tener, *home* yesterday?"

"Yes, I did, but..."

He cut me off abruptly. "A homeless alcoholic?...With *pneumonia*?"

"Actually, he wasn't really..."

Dr. Goldfrank's booming voice completely filled my earpiece. "What were you *thinking*? How did you suppose he was going to get his medication? How was he going to comply with your treatment?"

I wilted in my seat as I struggled to compose a response. "Well, I was thinking that myself," I admitted. "That's why I sent him the telegram, so he would come back to the ED. I *was* worried about him."

"Well you *should* have been worried. He didn't fill your prescription, and now he's back again today, much worse. We are admitting him to the Medicine service for intravenous antibiotics." He paused to let that sink in and then drove his point home. "You should have done the right thing *first*."

I sank further into my chair, head bowed. It was the very outcome I had feared. "I'm really sorry, Dr. Goldfrank. I'm glad he's in the hospital now."

His voice softened. "You know that our patients are not typical. They have special needs. You really need to think before you act."

It was a double whammy. A harmful mistake *and* a stern lecture. As I hung up the phone, I realized this was a conversation I would never forget.

During the next few days, while working at my VA assignment, I fretted about Matt, distracted by mounting curiosity about his outcome. At the end of the week, I went back to Bellevue to check on his progress. Since we did not have a computerized tracking system, I would have to find him the hard way. First, I went to the ED to review the admission log book. I searched for the date of admission, and Matt was right there, his name handwritten in the log. He had been admitted to the 16 East unit.

I then went up to 16 East, but he was nowhere to be found. So I leafed through the log of *that* unit and found him as an entry on the day of admission, as I expected. I thumbed forward through the log and found his name again two days later as a discharge. Not exactly a discharge. A *transfer*. He was transferred to 16 South.

But 16 South was the Intensive Care Unit! What on earth was he doing there? I was feeling uneasy as I walked around the corner to the ICU. Again, he was nowhere to be seen. Now I began to panic. Once again, I turned to the log book. There he was all right, received from 16 East on the day in question. I frantically flipped forward through the pages. Four days later, the log simply said "Matthew Tener – EXP." What was EXP? Experimental?

The nurse gently filled me in. Matt had passed away on the previous day, she told me. His pneumonia had worsened, his illness advanced, and he died of sepsis. EXP was the abbreviation for "expired." In a remarkable and tragic coincidence, his girlfriend had been a Bellevue inpatient at the same time. She died just two days before Matt from complications of AIDS. He never found out about her death.

This was just awful. Barely a week ago, Matt was a living, breathing, soft-spoken young man with a red baseball cap and a treatable illness. He barely resisted when I made the terrible mistake of sending him home. Everyone knew that the best guarantee of survival from a serious infection was to start antibiotics immediately. In his case, the 24-hour delay was most likely the reason for his untimely demise. It was all on me.

How did I handle this realization? How did this earnest, aspiring, freshly-minted doctor respond? Not well, I would say. Not well at all. I was very quick to rationalize. It wasn't my fault that Matt had an alcohol problem, not my fault that he didn't fill his prescription. How could I know that he would be noncompliant? In any case, he probably wasn't completely honest with me. I wouldn't be surprised if he had AIDS as well. Caught from his girlfriend, no doubt. He probably didn't have much time left anyway.

I quickly leapfrogged to the bizarre conclusion that my actions had no effect on the outcome. Strangely, I decided that even if they did, I had at least spared him the pain of losing his girlfriend to AIDS. That was a blessing he could thank me for. Oh, and one more thing: I was just a resident in training. Obviously, I was not very well supervised in the ED. That was not my fault either. Fate had sinned against me.

What an amazing defense I put up in my own mind! But it was undeniably a mistake. *My* mistake. And it took a while for this to sink in. Months, in fact. While I carried on in my daily responsibilities, I brooded about this case. The pent-up guilt weighed me down. I hoped no one would find out. What did this say about me in my second year of training? Was I truly ready to be a doctor? Should patients *ever* trust me?

Having met many physicians who have made errors that harmed patients, I now realize that my experience is commonplace. The day that I went from log book to log book suffering a growing sense of dread with each new revelation is quite familiar to any physician who has seen a case go down the rabbit hole, unraveling hour by hour. One piece of bad news eclipses another as the nightmare grows, as the patient slips and slides down a steepening slope to the point of no return.[5]

Initial shock, denial, and rationalization are typical responses of any ambitious, intelligent, young professional whose self-image may be shattered by such an error. Which begs the question: Since mistakes are inevitable and potentially devastating, how does the profession cope? How do we minimize error and respond to its consequences? How do physicians work through the personal trauma of a serious mistake and prevent a recurrence?

Actually, there *is* a venue for this process, a tradition that goes back nearly a century. The centerpiece of physicians' responses to their errors is the Morbidity and Mortality Review, better known as M&M, which I used to lead as Chief of Medicine. This activity is a monthly conference in which physicians, usually all of a single department, gather together to review their mistakes that have resulted in patient harm (morbidity) or death (mortality).

Cases are typically presented by the physician who took care of the patient. In an academic department, the presenter is often a trainee – an intern or resident – and the audience includes members of the department at all levels of experience. The modern M&M is primarily educational, a way for physicians to learn from each other's mistakes. It was not always so.

In years gone by, the M&M conference was more like a trial, even an inquisition. The presenter, perhaps a first-year trainee, would stand timidly at the podium – atremble at the whipping post – reciting the wretched tale of a patient ending invariably in some sort of disastrous consequence: a stroke, the loss of a limb, or even death. The audience included senior physicians who would make the intern squirm uncomfortably with pointed questions.

The salacious details were divulged and then inspected from every angle. The downward spiral of the patient, as small missteps snowballed into a massive tragedy, made for irresistible fodder for the viewing audience – much like rubbernecking at the grisly scene of an accident.

Sometimes, the patriarchal department chair would make a final, devastating quip such as "If you wanted to kill the patient, why didn't you just pull out a gun and save us all the trouble?" Justice served. The physicians on the case were held accountable through public humiliation in front of their peers.

Obviously, it was highly undesirable to have one's case selected for M&M. Even if the bad outcome was a natural consequence of the patient's disease and through no fault of the physicians, just having their management of a case dissected under the harsh glare of the M&M spotlight was an extremely unpleasant experience.

And there always seemed to be some aspect of care that proved to be questionable through the 20/20 vision of the "retrospectoscope." There was always grist for the mill. For young learners riven with guilt, then, the natural response was to try to conceal mistakes, minimize the appearance of error, and hide bad outcomes under an invisibility cloak, praying that the conference planners would fail to select their case. Errors were taken underground.

Fortunately, over the past three decades, M&M conferences have evolved toward a different objective – education. In the modern version, cases are selected based on their learning potential. "Is there a good teaching point in this case?" In this new paradigm, presenters are treated with respect, even sympathy, and the discussion focuses on lessons learned. Above all, the goal is to avoid a tempting descent into the blame game.

By bringing errors to light in a safe environment, we confront and correct them and minimize the chance that they will be repeated. By sharing these mistakes with a large audience, we multiply their learning value many times over. The public sharing, then, is an exercise in *atonement* – admitting a mistake and turning it into a lesson for others. A selfless act.

I no longer lead the M&M discussions, but I do participate in patient care as an attending physician on the inpatient service. During a recent stint, one of my team's patients was selected for the M&M conference. Her case history is a perfect illustration of the complexities of inpatient care and the value of a retrospective review of a case after an unhappy ending.

Candice Staner was 74 years old and had many medical problems. She had longstanding high blood pressure and severe atherosclerosis (coronary heart disease). She also had weak kidneys and poor liver function. Just one week earlier, she had been admitted to another hospital to manage her heart failure. Heart, liver, kidneys. It seemed that no vital organ was spared from the ravages of her illness.

To make matters worse, while at the first hospital, Candice had developed a blood clot in a large vein in her left arm due to the presence of an intravenous (IV) line. Meanwhile, her liver and kidney function had worsened from the stress of her heart failure, so she was transferred to the care of my team at Bellevue to manage her complicated situation.

In summary, she was an elderly woman with total body malfunction, an incestuous collaboration between all her failing organs to do her in – a patient where anything that *can* go wrong *will* go wrong, as we were soon to discover.

Upon Candice's transfer to Bellevue, one of the important questions to address was whether to give her warfarin, an anticoagulant (blood thinner), to treat the blood clot in her arm. Or not. I could go either way on this because both options had a serious downside.

Don't anticoagulate and you risk that the clot might grow, break free, and flow downstream to the lungs – a life-threatening pulmonary embolism.[6] This was a reason to treat. Anticoagulate and you risk the most dangerous consequence of the blood thinning effect – severe bleeding – perhaps in a vital organ, like the brain. In this fragile patient, *any* bleeding would be life-threatening. This was a reason *not* to treat.

Yet I knew there was a consensus of national experts that a blood clot in the upper extremities *should* be treated by an anticoagulant after removing the IV line. So I decided to treat the patient. It would have been difficult to ignore the advice of national experts.

Unfortunately, after the very first dose of warfarin, the follow-up blood test showed we had already overdone it. The blood was now *too* thin. One measly dose had overshot the mark, and Candice was now at high risk of bleeding, just as we had feared. We stopped the warfarin.

The next morning my resident and I became alarmed by one of the routine lab results, so we went together to assess our patient in her room. She was resting quietly in her hospital bed, gray hair gathered tightly in a bun, arms resting at her side, blanket tucked neatly under her chin. So perfectly serene. Yet… so fragile. So near the precipice. She smiled as we entered.

"Good morning, Ms. Staner. How are you feeling?"

"Good morning to both of you! I'm feeling fine, thank you."

"We came by to tell you that today's test showed your blood count is quite low, and we're not sure why. Can we ask you a few questions?"

"Of course!" She did not seem the least bit concerned by our news.

"Have you been out of bed today?"

"Not since last night."

"Have you been feeling dizzy?"

"Not at all."

"Passed any blood with your bowel movements?"

"Not that I know of."

"Okay, good. But we need to examine you and repeat the blood test."

We examined our patient and found all to be in order including her pulse and blood pressure. There was no sign of bleeding anywhere, so we repeated the test – and got the same result. Somehow, she had lost several pints of blood, and we still didn't know where it went. Back to the bedside.

While standing at the foot of her bed, we suddenly recognized a familiar odor. Melena is the medical term for blood that has leaked into the intestines and then passed all the way through the gastrointestinal (GI) tract to be eliminated, partially digested, as a thick, black, tarry, liquid diarrhea with a characteristic pungent stench – which we were noticing just now.

We pulled back her blanket, and there it was, seeping through the bedsheets – enough melena to entirely explain the dramatic fall in her blood count. Candice was having a massive GI bleed right before our eyes. Without a doubt, this was the predictable consequence of the blood thinner we had prescribed, the treatment that had overshot the mark.

This story did not end well for our patient. She was stabilized with blood transfusions, transferred to the ICU, and fully recovered from the GI bleed. However, she then developed an infection that claimed her life.

Although our anticoagulant did not directly cause Candice's infection, it most definitely triggered the GI bleed that sent her on her downhill course. So my resident wrote up this case as our M&M submission. Not surprisingly, it was selected as one of the cases for discussion at the next conference. In fact, it turned out to be the main event.

M&M has always been the most popular conference in the Department of Medicine. There is just something about bad outcomes that attracts everyone's curiosity. So, on the day of our presentation, we arrived to find the large room packed with 80 members of our department – students, interns, residents, attending physicians, specialty consultants, and senior leaders.

My resident presented our case. The step-by-step, blow-by-blow account of our patient was laid bare before a discerning audience of our peers. What ensued was an intense discussion, and a number of participants made useful suggestions about our management.

For example, a GI specialist offered advice about how we handled the situation *after* we discovered the low blood count. Looking directly at me, he started with this question. "Why did you wait for the confirmatory test result before taking any action?" He continued without waiting for my answer.

"Based on what you knew at the time, this was almost certainly going to be a GI bleed. You could have started treatment right away." He turned to face the audience. "In a situation like this, every moment of delay puts the patient at risk." An approving murmur rippled through the room. I had to admit this was a good teaching point.

To my surprise, no one offered a comment about our decision to anticoagulate the patient, so I made the point myself near the end of the discussion. In my opinion, the *root* cause of this adverse event was making the choice to put the patient on a blood thinner in the first place. Had we not done so, I believed our patient would still be alive. It was a decision we had not taken lightly, but, in retrospect, it caused great harm.

If I were to face a similar situation in the future, I would be hesitant to prescribe the medication. The guideline to treat blood clots in the arm with anticoagulants was based on studies of healthier patients, so we should have thought twice before applying that "recipe" to a patient like ours who was clearly at higher risk. I felt this was a lesson for everyone.

Being able to make these points in front of a supportive audience was hugely therapeutic. We discussed the events, reviewed the facts, and shared our opinions. We were honest, transparent, and respectful. By the end of the hour, we had unpacked all the details, debated each point, and followed every thread. Hence, I did not brood about this case for months on end as I did about Matt. I got to a healthy place early on.

Now, what does M&M conference have to do with leadership of our country? What lessons drawn from this clinical exercise, deeply ingrained in the culture of Medicine, could possibly bear fruit for elected officials in the chambers of our nation's capital? Is there any relevance?

Let's start with the obvious. Leaders make mistakes. Just as doctors do, they make mistakes of all sizes: small slip-ups, large flubs, and colossal blunders. Without a doubt, leaders with any substantial responsibility are bound to make plenty of mistakes.

The important questions are: Do they admit, accept, and learn from their mistakes? Or do they deny, repress, and forget them? Just as important, do they learn from the mistakes of *others,* or do they ignore, suppress, and repeat them? Let's review a few historical examples.

Richard Nixon, our 37th president, is infamous for resigning from office in 1974 in the wake of Watergate, the blunder of a lifetime. Yet two decades earlier, in 1952, he was accused of improprieties related to a secret campaign fund that gave the appearance that donors were gaining political favors.

Nixon's career survived only by virtue of his brilliant "Checkers" speech, nationally televised to 60 million viewers. It was a well-composed defense of his actions, but at no point did he admit ethical or legal wrongdoing.

Nor did he learn from his mistakes. Two decades later, the Watergate scandal exposed Nixon's ongoing penchant for clandestine activities: undisclosed lists of political enemies, covert "dirty tricks," and secret tapes, which ironically produced the smoking gun that brought down his presidency.

Here is another example that spanned three presidencies, and one that we will discuss at length in a subsequent chapter. One result of President Ronald Reagan's introduction of Supply-Side Economics, the lowering of tax rates for the wealthy to stimulate the economy, was a massive increase in the federal budget deficit, which was never acknowledged by Republican leaders.

Two decades later, George W. Bush repeated the act with the same result: a healthy Clinton surplus became a mammoth Bush deficit, setting the stage for the economic bubble that burst in 2008. Even worse, Donald Trump, our 45th president, once again signed off on a *third* round of tax cuts for the wealthy. Once again, we borrowed money we didn't have and gave it to people who didn't need it. Once again, the federal deficit exploded – to over $1 trillion per year![7] Why are we unable to learn from our mistakes!?

Finally, let's review a more recent example of the lack of accountability. At an advisory board meeting in March, 2019, Trump mistakenly referred to Tim Cook, CEO of Apple Corporation, as Tim *Apple.* It was a trivial, inconsequential error. Totally understandable. Humorous, even. But Trump could not laugh it off and move on. He could not even admit it had happened.

Two days later, at a meeting with campaign donors, Trump falsely claimed that he actually had said "Tim Cook Apple" *really fast.*[8] Slow-motion replay clearly showed this was a lie – the transparent fib of a three-year old caught with his hand in the cookie jar. If Trump could not admit even to a silly slip of the tongue, how would he ever self-reflect on mistakes that really mattered?

Thus, it seems that national leaders are vulnerable to the same cycle of repeating errors that doctors are. Yet their decisions are much more impactful, affecting the health and well-being of tens of millions of Americans. Why can't they admit even to their slightest mistakes? How will they ever learn the valuable lessons of their experiences? Where is *their* M&M review?

Indeed, where in the political arena can an elected official openly share his experience with an important decision, lay bare the cognitive process behind that decision, and prepare an open forum for the thoughtful, objective feedback of sympathetic members of both parties? I must be dreaming!

The principal means for reviewing decisions and their outcomes is the congressional investigation committee – the antithesis of the modern M&M. In fact, these highly charged, withering, partisan interrogations are designed to achieve maximum discomfort, embarrassment, and reputational injury to any government official so unlucky as to sit before them. As we shall see in the next chapter, this is the old-style M&M on steroids.

Let's close by reviewing the most potent tool of atonement: apology. A genuine apology has the mystical power to restore trust after a horrendous mistake. Indeed, it is often the case that nothing less than a sincere apology can right the wrong and restore the balance. Moreover, it is in the exact moment of the apology that healing begins. But this is not an easy art to master.

There are three essential features to an effective apology. First, it must be specific. I must acknowledge what I did to you. Second, it must be contrite. My words must be genuinely sincere. Third, it must be unconditional. No ifs, ands, or buts.

Whenever an apology includes a conditional clause, it becomes a limp piece of lettuce. "I'm sorry if I offended anyone." If? You are not even sure you did anything wrong? Anyone? You don't even have the sense of decency to name the one offended? A bad apology is utterly toxic.

On the other hand, as most physicians well know, a sincere apology is a magical potion, our most powerful tool to reset the balance and restore trust. Yet elected officials are notoriously poor at delivering apologies, a disturbing symptom of their inability to cope with mistakes. Allow me to demonstrate. The following are three examples of apologies given by American leaders. Please select the one that matches my description of an effective apology.

> Despite this, I regret the concerns this has raised regarding the use of taxpayer dollars. All of my political career I've fought for the taxpayers. It is clear to me that in this case, I was not sensitive enough to my concern for the taxpayer.[9]

> I am sorry that they, you know, are finding themselves in this situation, based on assurances they got from me.[10]

> Indeed, I did have a relationship with Miss Lewinsky that was not appropriate. In fact, it was wrong... But I told the grand jury today and I say to you now that at no time did I ask anyone to lie, to hide or destroy evidence, or to take any other unlawful action... In addition, I had real and serious concerns about an independent counsel investigation that began with private business dealings 20 years ago, dealings I might add about which an independent federal agency found no evidence of any wrongdoing by me or my wife over two years ago.[11]

If you selected none of the above, you are correct. The first was a self-serving statement by former Health and Human Services Secretary, Tom Price, in response to an outcry about his use of government jets for personal travel. Note that he is not actually apologizing for his actions. He regrets how they were *perceived.* Merely a glancing blow. Terrible!

The second was a tepid apology to some Americans who lost their health care coverage after the Affordable Care Act was implemented. It was given by President Barak Obama, who selected the wrong pronoun. Hint: Do not start an apology with "I am sorry that *they*..." Much better to start with "I am sorry that *I*..." Obama did many exceptional things during his presidency. This was not one of them.

The third apology was an early version of Bill Clinton's public account of his affair with Monica Lewinsky. The sheer length is a dead giveaway that this tortuous confession is unduly laden with legalistic clauses that fatally dilute its potency. Clinton was understandably defensive, but it did not help his case to pull the punch on his apology. Why is this so difficult for national leaders?

Fortunately, Clinton did finally get it right with this final version, which he offered on the eve of impeachment hearings. In fact, he nailed it. I doubt it would have affected congressional behavior, but it would certainly have meant a great deal to the American people if expressed in this form early on.

> What I want the American people to know, what I want the Congress to know, is that I am profoundly sorry for all I have done wrong in words and

> deeds. I never should have misled the country, the Congress, my friends, or my family. Quite simply, I gave in to my shame.[12]

One might argue that it is naive to expect national officeholders to openly admit mistakes and apologize for their actions. Certainly, it was difficult to imagine Trump doing anything of the kind. Indeed, our news media and our electorate will unmercifully pummel the courageous leader who steps out on this limb to seek atonement. Or will they?

My answer is that it once seemed just as unlikely that the culture of *my* profession would ever permit this long overdue advancement. Hospitals obsessed about their public persona. Physicians fretted about their career standing. Attorneys agitated about their legal risk. Professional reputations and academic stature always seemed to demand an image of perfection.

Yet, step by step, our modern health care system has inched toward an ethos of honesty and transparency, even if that means ceding cherished traditions such as the aura of invincibility, the infallibility of authority, and the veil of secrecy. In the final analysis, transparency requires honesty. Honesty compels disclosure. Disclosure means always having to say you are sorry.

Remarkably, some hospitals such as ours have instituted policies of immediate disclosure and sincere apology to their *patients* whenever serious errors are committed, even if those patients otherwise have no inkling that a mistake has occurred, and despite the obvious risk of a lawsuit. It is an *ethical* imperative. Likewise, we need courageous political leaders to step up in the same way to show the interests of their constituents come before their own.

What would be the consequence for such a leader? Would she lose respect? Popularity? Votes? I think not. Contrary to popular opinion, admission of error is an intimate act that transcends boundaries, brings people together, and, paradoxically, fosters credibility. Confession conveys integrity. Atonement elicits empathy. Apology inspires trust.

As leaders in my world eventually discovered, transparency around errors surprisingly *improves* relationships with patients and staff – and *enhances* performance. As I have learned myself, honest confession of a mistake and sincere apology for its consequences can leave a relationship even stronger than it was before the transgression took place.

Alas, the professional climate of national governance is still stuck in first gear, the starting time and place of American hospitals more than a generation ago. The time when primitive egos steadfastly maintained a false façade of make-believe perfection. The place where everyone's primary goal was to deny fallibility, hide mistakes, and take errors underground.

This is an extremely unhealthy leadership culture – a significant contributor to our nation's malady. The inability to admit mistakes erodes trust in government. The reluctance to share lessons learned squanders an opportunity for enlightenment. The conspicuous lack of atonement at the upper echelons of government makes it impossible to right the wrong.

There is a joke I used to enjoy sharing with my young children. I told them that I was wrong only once in my life. It was the time that I thought I had made a mistake when I really hadn't. The joke always made my children laugh because even at a very young age they were fully aware of my imperfections.

And that is why atonement is the first chapter of this book – the first strand of our braid. No matter who we are, we will make mistakes. Learning from our mistakes, then, is central to our personal development – to becoming the best person we can be. It is fundamental to good doctoring and essential to great leadership. In the next chapter we will discuss what to do when *others* make mistakes.

Forgiveness:
Favor the Just

Tis best sometimes your censure to restrain,
And charitably let the dull be vain:
Your silence there is better than your spite,
For who can rail so long as they can write...
Good-nature and good sense must ever join;
To err is human, to forgive, divine.

From *An Essay on Criticism*, Alexander Pope, 1711

"Why does it rain?"

"Because the air is full of moisture and must sometimes release it to the earth below."

"Why is the air so full of moisture?"

"Because water in the oceans, lakes, and rivers evaporates into the atmosphere."

"Why does the water evaporate?"

"Because heat in the water energizes molecules to escape into the air."

"Why is there heat in the water?"

"Because the sun warms the earth."

"Why does the sun warm the earth?"

"Because it is fiery hot."

The Five Whys.

A number of years ago, a disturbing event was reported to our Quality Management Department. A patient in the Intensive Care Unit (ICU) was being treated for respiratory failure with mechanical ventilation. This meant that a stiff plastic tube had been inserted through his mouth into his windpipe so that he could be connected to a ventilator. Attached to this tube was a long flexible hose through which the ventilator piped oxygen-rich air deep into the patient's lungs. As such, he was completely dependent upon the ventilator for each life-sustaining breath.

According to the report I received, the ventilator had malfunctioned, which set off an alarm designed to alert the nurse who could correct the problem or at least call for the help of an expert to address it. All ventilators were equipped with alarms for this very purpose. The alarms would create an annoying sound that emanated from the patient's room and set off a flashing light at the central nursing station. When the alarm sounded, a nurse would immediately attend to the patient.

In this particular case, Natalie Ghintino, the patient's nurse, did not respond to the alarm. She ignored it. She did not attend to the patient but just continued working with another patient. At the central nursing station, no one responded either. In fact, someone there actually silenced the alarm so that it would not continue to annoy the staff. A short time later, the alarm went off again.

This time, Natalie went into the room and discovered there was a mechanical obstruction that interrupted the flow of air to her patient's lungs. He was deeply sedated and therefore not conscious of the problem or able to summon help. Within a scarce minute, the patient went into cardiac arrest from which he could not be revived. It was a fatal error.

In our hospital, this event was the equivalent of a five-alarm fire. Almost immediately, the news raced up and down the corridors of hospital administration. Physician and nursing leaders were summoned into an emergency meeting. A detailed review would commence without delay, but the explanation was already apparent.

A hospital employee had committed an egregious error. It was a willful breach of protocol – a clear dereliction of duty. By failing to answer the alarm, Natalie had violated a principle tenet of her profession, to do her duty to keep her patient safe.

We were all in agreement. The nurse must be punished. This would most likely lead to counseling and suspension, if not outright termination. Too bad for her, but she should have known better than to break the rules. We would now have to make an example of her for all the *other* employees.

But first we had to conduct a detailed review, which was our usual practice. There was a systematic approach to this work – a standard process of gathering facts, assembling a timeline, drawing conclusions, and planning corrective action to guarantee that this event could never happen again.

The goal of this review was to dig deep into the evidence, understand thoroughly the sequence of events that led to the fatal outcome, divine the connections linking those events, and thoroughly answer the "why" question. In other words, get to the heart of the problem. The *root cause*. For this reason, the detailed review was known as the Root Cause Analysis (RCA).

Our hospital had a detailed procedure for performing an RCA. We would quickly assemble a team of hospital staff who would review a summary of the event and then jointly plan a comprehensive investigation – with no jurisdictional boundaries. Members of the team would conduct detailed interviews of all parties involved, taking copious notes.

They would further scour the medical chart, line by line, for additional clues. They might also review written policies, test medical equipment, or talk to patients. Once the facts were established, the team would meet to link the evidence into a causal chain that would explain the adverse event.

Of the many tools that would be employed to arrive at the correct conclusion, none was more important than the Five Whys, a technique for getting to the true root cause. The inquiry simply follows a succession of "why" questions until the primary source is uncovered. This is best illustrated by the classic example of a curious child employing the Five Whys in search of the truth, the dialogue that opened this chapter.

In this string of questions, what is not intuitive soon becomes apparent: without the sun there would be no rain. The beauty of the Five Whys is that they force the line of questioning to go beneath the surface – to dig toward the root. Once the root cause is exposed, the investigative team may design changes in hospital procedures or alterations in work flow to correct the deficiency and prevent a repeat occurrence.

At this point, we would bring in leaders of the relevant departments to help design the Plan of Correction (POC) because they would be responsible for its implementation. The POC is the end-product of the process, and crucial to the outcome. Without a POC, we will never fix the problem. We will just keep marching around in circles without getting anywhere.

When the RCA team first meets, their initial objective is to determine whether the "standard of care" was met – if the treatment of the patient met an objective acceptable level of performance. If the adverse outcome was simply due to the natural course of the patient's underlying illness, the team might conclude that the standard was met even though the case ended badly.

But if there was any deviation from acceptable medical practice, any shortfall in staff response, and certainly if any frank error was committed, the team would conclude that the standard of care was *not* met. For those cases, the team must make a critical determination: was this error due to a system problem or due to the misconduct of a staff member?

By system problem, I mean a deficiency in written policy, standard procedure, staff training, or medical equipment. By misconduct, I mean the deviant behavior of a staff member – a negligent approach that puts the patient at risk. The difference between a system problem and a "people problem" is not so clear as one might think.

If a floor nurse forgets to check a patient's vital signs because she has too many patients, if a well-meaning physician overlooks a tiny detail in a laboratory result, if the respiratory therapist accidently selects the incorrect ventilator setting, the RCA team might well conclude that it is a *system* problem. The work schedule of the nurse needs to be modified, the laboratory result needs to be presented more clearly, or the respiratory technician needs better training.

The important distinction is whether this was the kind of mistake that could be made by any well-meaning staff member, or whether this particular individual was an unusually careless employee who willfully violated a standard protocol – i.e., a bad apple. To be sure, whenever the bad behavior is practiced by *multiple* employees, it is almost *always* a system problem. We just have to find it. The distinction between a system problem and a people problem is crucial to the plan of correction, as we shall see momentarily.

To bring this process completely into perspective, let's consider the snafu that capped the night of the 2017 Academy Awards presentation – the mistaken announcement that *La La Land* had won the Oscar for best picture, only to be reversed moments later by the declaration that *Moonlight* was the true winner. Most certainly, this on-stage blunder failed to meet an acceptable standard of performance.

In the hospital, we would call an error of this magnitude a *Never Event*, the equivalent of operating on the wrong patient or amputating the wrong leg. Never Events are especially bad outcomes that must *never* be allowed to happen. Given their extreme severity, they require a systematic approach with multiple layers of protection to prevent their occurrence.

Sometimes Never Events are simply the product of one person's egregiously bad behavior. More often, however, they are the result of a coincidental series of unfortunate events. In the Academy Award snafu, for example, several factors lined up, like the holes in Swiss cheese, to produce this calamitous outcome. An RCA would likely have concluded this was a *system problem*.

First, a crucial contributor to the error was the existence of duplicate copies of every award envelope. This paved the way for one envelope (in this case, the Best Actress award) to be substituted for another, virtually identical, envelope (the Best Picture Award), much like two medications with similar names or appearances being mistaken for each other.

Second, the envelopes were not well marked. A new vendor for design of the envelopes had reportedly changed the colors, contrast, and font size of the envelope labels, making them more attractive but also more difficult to read in the muted lighting behind the stage curtains, permitting the PricewaterhouseCoopers (PwC) representative to select the wrong envelope.

Third, the cards themselves were not designed for clarity, so the duplicate card could not be easily identified as such. While the uninformative label, "OSCARS," enjoyed marquee billing at the top, and the movie title and actor credit were prominently displayed in the center, the all-important *category* of the award, "Best Actress," was barely visible in a tiny font at the bottom. As is usually the case, it is easy to see the design flaw through the perfect lens of the retrospectoscope.

Finally, although Warren Beatty was momentarily thrown off by the appearance of Emma Stone's name on the award, he was not sufficiently alarmed to question what he was seeing, probably because he had complete trust in the "system." In a hospital, much work is done to make staff feel empowered to raise their hand and "stop the assembly line," to interrupt a procedure in progress, if they have even an *inkling* that something is not right.

Of course, the PwC representative who actually selected the wrong card was a central player in this scenario. He clearly made the crucial error, possibly because he was distracted, as reports later surfaced that he had been tweeting just prior to the moment of truth. Nonetheless, it was not an intentional error, and there was probably no one more remorseful about the outcome than he was.

In the RCA following this event, we would carefully review the protocol. Was this representative well-trained in a standardized approach to his work? If so, and if he broke a clear protocol, he would be held accountable. But I would not be surprised if he was left to his own devices, more or less.

In response, the Plan of Correction would include a redesign of the cards as well as the implementation of what we call "standard work," a new set of detailed instructions for those doing this function in the future, such as:

1. Keep envelopes in a pre-specified order.

2. Before each award, have a second person double-check the envelope.

3. As each award is presented, dispose of the duplicate card.

4. Be familiar with all the winner's names. If you hear an announcement made in error, enter the stage immediately and read from a script designed exactly for this purpose. Don't let your mistake fester in front of 33 million viewers.

5. Relinquish your cell phone before commencing with this crucially important backstage role!

These items mimic the overlapping interventions we use to prevent errors in the hospital. For example, whenever administering medications, we always expect the nurse to check two patient identifiers AND use a bar code scanner to avoid misidentification of patients. For high-risk situations, we actually require two nurses to work in tandem, each checking the work of the other, to prevent an error.

To avoid making a substitution error akin to the Academy Awards fiasco, hospitals employ a clever device. "Look-Alike-Sound-Alike" medications are labeled by large bold lettering with selective capitalizations to emphasize differences in spelling. For example, Clomiphene, a fertility drug, looks a lot like Clomipramine, an antidepressant. To avert a dispensing error, their names appear on the labels as ClomiPHENE and ClomiPRAMINE.

Finally, we encourage other staff not to interrupt the nurse during the vital function of medication dispensing. This crucial "no-distraction" policy, analogous to #5 above, was not our own brilliant idea. The principle was inspired by the airline industry, which, to be fair, adopted the systematic approach to safety decades before American hospitals.

In 1974, Eastern Airlines Flight 202 landed short of the runway in dense fog, an accident that resulted in 72 fatalities. After the cockpit recording revealed pilots were engaged in casual banter during the landing sequence, the Federal Aviation Administration passed the "Sterile Cockpit Rule," which prohibits members of the flight crew from participating in non-essential activities during critical phases of the flight. Once again, it is the systematic approach to human error that so powerfully prevents a recurrence.

In the case of the missed alarm, we assembled an investigative team that included an ICU physician, two nurses, and a biomedical technician (an expert on how the alarms actually worked). This team interviewed Natalie, several other ICU nurses, the physician who was in charge of the patient, and the respiratory therapist who was monitoring the ventilator settings. They went to the ICU and observed the alarm system in use. They set off an alarm to better understand how it worked.

On first glance, this was definitely a rare case of employee misconduct. The policy on alarms was clearly written. As the nurse assigned to the patient, Natalie was responsible for responding immediately to every alarm. She admitted that she did not respond as she had been trained. She was remorseful, but she did not contradict any facts of the case. In essence, Natalie gave us a full confession. Case closed. We could lock her up and throw away the key.

Then we talked to her colleagues.

Natalie's fellow nurses in the ICU were eager to talk about the alarms. It was a fairly new system and quite problematic. The alarms went off *constantly* – mostly for minor aberrations. The heart rate was slightly high. The patient shifted position. The patient hiccupped. The endless parade of alarms led to a predictable response in the nurses. They stopped interrupting their work to respond to this barrage of false alarms. They began to ignore the alarms altogether.

They had "alarm fatigue" – a well-known phenomenon that could lead to bad outcomes like this. They also learned that they could turn the alarms off at the central station so that they would not even need to go into the patient's cubicle. In fact, they started turning off the alarms for each other – a conspiracy of silence. These were intelligent, competent, well-meaning professionals who collectively found a way to solve an annoying problem that got in the way of their important work.

Now this *was* a dilemma. If we were going to suspend Natalie for bad conduct, we really ought to suspend all of her fellow nurses for the exact same behavior. She was no worse than the rest; she just had the bad luck of an alarm that went off for an important reason.

And now that we had talked to the others, who confessed to the same infraction, this nurse did not seem to be a bad apple after all. Putting ourselves in *her* position, she certainly did not seem to be unusually careless or willfully malicious. Thus, we arrived at a new and unexpected conclusion.

This was a *system* problem.

We recognized this twist in the case at a meeting of executive hospital leaders. When it was suggested that this was a system problem, however, there was an immediate and critical backlash. An egregious error was committed. A patient died. Calling this a system problem somehow seemed to exonerate the perpetrator. How would it look if we gave in to a charitable impulse and let Natalie off the hook? Where was the accountability?

Further discussion led to the devastating truth. There was accountability, all right. But not at the level of the employee. Not with Natalie. Not with her fellow nurses. Not at the rank of the front-line staff, who had zero input into the design of policies and procedures that led to the error. The responsibility for this failed system rested at a *higher* level. *Ours.*

The nurse supervisor had failed to escalate what was an apparent problem for her staff. Upper echelons of leadership had failed to set up an effective system, failed to monitor staff performance, and failed to promote a culture of transparency – of open communication with the staff so that such a problem could be identified before it led to patient harm. Thus, the greatest degree of accountability rested with *us* – the executive leadership team.

That was a sobering thought. *We* were responsible for this mess. *We* were going to have to clean it up. So we immediately went to work devising a plan of correction. Our biomedical team reset the alarms so that they would only sound off for a serious problem. They reprogrammed the system so that the alarms could not be turned off at the central nurse station, only at the patient's bedside. We retrained the nurses, not only in the Medical Intensive Care Unit, but in all the other ICUs on the critical care floor.

And then we set up a system for monitoring the alarm response. Every month, a report was generated that summarized the average amount of time it took for an alarm to be answered. This report became part of our quality control program. To this day, more than a decade later, we have not had another example of alarm fatigue leading to an adverse event in those units.

This, then, is the value of an RCA. To turn a bad case inside out, to get all the facts out into the open, and to doggedly pursue the truth until we arrive at a diagnosis. Only then can we prescribe the proper treatment. Only then can we solve the problem. Only then can we cure the "disease."

And this case showed the value of thinking in terms of systems. If we had done the obvious – blamed the nurse and punished her for the crime – we would have felt that justice had been served. That would have been highly satisfying, no doubt. But we would have missed the point. We would have neglected to uncover the true root of the problem and would have failed to enact our far-reaching solution. Most important, our extensive investment of energy would have been totally in vain. The event would likely have recurred repeatedly until we finally came to our senses.

By now the reader will recognize the themes that run across our improvement efforts. In each activity there is a fascination, almost an obsession, with errors, missteps, and fallouts. Each process tells the story in agonizing detail, hunts for the weak spot, and goes for the kill. Still, the conclusions are objective, constructive, and non-judgmental.

While M&Ms focus on physician judgment, RCAs address system error, both aiming to take us to a better place. And they have one more thing in common. They are just. They do not blame. They do not punish. I can sum up the philosophy in three concise statements: Seek the truth. Tell the truth. Learn from the truth.

It is devilishly difficult to do this. To step completely outside our biased conceptual framework. To take a clean look inward with an open mind. To situate ourselves in the position of a doctor or nurse way back in time at the indelible moment of truth, looking at the situation through *their* eyes while pretending to forget what we know about the events that followed. Only then can we render a pure judgment about a fateful error without lacing it with the prejudicial knowledge of its eventual consequences.

There is a name for this blame-free environment: the *Just Culture*. The Just Culture defines a leadership approach that presumes employees are trying to do the right thing. In the Just Culture, the staff get the benefit of the doubt. The review of a poor outcome, then, is an open-minded exercise that probes for weakness in *process* that leads the employee astray.

Usually we find it – the stress point. Sometimes it is as simple as a minor oversight. At other times we find that a series of coincidences lined up, as in the *La La Land* debacle, to permit the patient's care to follow the wrong path. In most cases, there is indeed a weakness in the process.

By promoting the Just Culture, then, we are more likely to find that weakness and address the *real* root of a problem. Just as important, our employees will bring errors to our attention, knowing that we are not intent on blaming them for the outcome.

Of course, it is not easy to instill the trust that entices employees to bring their errors to the attention of their supervisors. Indeed, our internal hospital surveys have consistently shown that our frontline staff have always harbored universal fears about the consequences of speaking up.

As hospital leaders, we all review these findings with dismay because our primary goal is transparency, the best defense against adverse outcomes. I know of no better way to illustrate this point than to relate a true example of a medication error related to misidentification of a patient – a Never Event.

Bellevue Hospital has an historically-acclaimed inpatient Psychiatry Service for which the hospital is justifiably famous. Patients who reside here are especially challenging – in numbers *and* severity. For example, while most private hospital Psychiatry Departments are comprised of a single unit of 20 or fewer patients, Bellevue has a dozen units with 250 patients.

Moreover, blessed with stable homes and sustained by loving families, private patients will typically volunteer to be admitted for their manageable psychiatric disorders and usually agree to cooperate with their providers. In contrast, Bellevue's imposing inpatient service is heavily occupied by homeless people, who are picked up by city police for erratic behavior, admitted by court order for public safety, and then treated by hospital staff over their objection. It seems miraculous that these seemingly hopeless cases can so often dramatically improve with just two weeks of intensive treatment.

Some years ago, we had an adverse event on a psychiatric unit. It appeared that a nurse, Stacy Hippocrates, had mixed up two patients with the same last name and administered the dose of a strong psychiatric medication to the wrong one. The recipient of the errant dose had no tolerance for its effect and became severely sedated to the point that he stopped breathing. He had to be resuscitated and transferred to the ICU, where he recovered.

Again, on first glance, this was an adverse outcome due to human error. No doubt Stacy had failed to use two patient-identifiers, our airtight standard for medication administration. If she asked for the patient's full name *and* checked his wristband, it would be virtually impossible to make this mistake.

The two-identifier standard was one of our steadfast principles for patient safety, a rule that must never be broken. Violating this standard was strong evidence for malicious behavior, the rare case where the employee was purely at fault. Once again, a meticulous review of the case presented an entirely different picture.

First, we learned that Stacy was a model employee with an impeccable resumé. She had a Master of Arts degree from Wellesley College and fifteen years of nursing experience under her belt. That did not sound like a bad apple to us. Second, we learned that Stacy did not normally work on this unit. She had been floated in to fill a temporary staffing gap, and so was not personally familiar with the patients. This put her at a disadvantage.

On the psychiatric unit, the patients are not medicated in their rooms; they approach a medication cart when called by the nurse. The affected individual had answered to another patient's name, and Stacy had given him the medications intended for the other patient without realizing it.

In the interview, Stacy confessed to her omission. The affected patient was a large man, freshly admitted and not yet under control for his psychotic symptoms. Stacy, a woman of slight build, was intimidated by his imposing appearance and remembered *not* asking him to show her his ID band.

About a half hour later, when the other patient in this mix-up presented for *his* medication, Stacy realized her mistake. Then she did something quite unusual. Something that is one of the primary objectives of the Just Culture. Something that almost *never* happens in a blameful environment.

She raised her hand.

Upon realizing her mistake, Stacy reported her own error to her supervisor, essentially blowing the whistle on her mistake and exposing herself to severe disciplinary action. More important, she set in motion a series of events that saved the patient's life.

She went to his room and found him deeply sedated. In fact, he was barely breathing. Then she immediately paged the rapid response team (RRT), which attended to the patient, addressed his respiratory insufficiency, and transferred him to the ICU for his safety. By the next morning, the effect of the medication had worn off, the patient was awake, and there were no lasting ill effects. Because Stacy had unselfishly called attention to her mistake, she kept the patient safe.

This is absolutely one of the goals of the Just Culture: to encourage *self*-reporting of events before they bring harm to a patient – by promoting transparency and openness so that the safety of patients always comes first. As for Stacy, she received a counseling session but no disciplinary action. Quite the contrary. She atoned, and we forgave her.

At a public forum, Stacy openly shared what she had done wrong and what she had done right, then she received a commendation for her courage in saving the life of her patient. She was a heroine and a great example for all our staff. What a tribute to the power of the Just Culture!

What is the lesson here for our national leaders? Is there a comparable process of systematic review of adverse outcomes? A root cause analysis of governmental snafus? A deep dive to identify process issues versus individual culpability? Indeed, there is. Unfortunately, the political counterpart to the RCA is the congressional investigation.

We are familiar with committees that have conducted congressional investigations into historical incidents such as the Red Scare, Watergate, the Iran-Contra affair, 9/11, the Iraq war, and Benghazi. Every one of these inquiries focused on placing blame and was subject to political pressures, resulting in controversial findings. Of all these examples, perhaps the most egregious was the investigation instigated by Joseph McCarthy during the Red Scare of the Truman and Eisenhower administrations.

McCarthy was a former Marine who was first elected as U.S. senator from Wisconsin in 1946. The first several years of his tenure were unremarkable, until 1950 when he dramatically captured national attention through a provocative speech he delivered in Wheeling, West Virginia, claiming to possess a secret list of Communists working for the State Department.[1]

In response to these sensational allegations, the Senate charged a subcommittee of the Senate Committee on Foreign Relations to investigate. Democratic senator, Millard Tydings, chaired the committee, which ultimately concluded that McCarthy's charges were a fraud and a hoax. Republicans struck back by charging the Tydings committee of "the most brazen whitewash of treasonable conspiracy in our history."[2]

McCarthy thus persisted in making public accusations, including those of alleged homosexuals working in sensitive positions in the government. Following re-election in 1952, he became chair of the Senate Permanent Subcommittee on Investigations and continued to rail against alleged Communists in government with the assistance of his zealous chief counsel, Roy Cohn.[3] McCarthy was the instigator, and Cohn was his attack dog.

In 1953, the subcommittee conducted highly publicized hearings during which McCarthy would browbeat government personnel with hostile questions, subversive innuendo, and provocative claims of undisclosed evidence. His targets included staff members from the Voice of America, one of whom committed suicide during the investigation, the overseas library program of the International Information Agency, which went so far as to burn newly forbidden books, and the U.S. Army, which discharged one of its majors in response to his refusal to testify before the subcommittee.

Then the Army fought back, accusing McCarthy and Cohn of pressuring the Army to show favoritism toward a former McCarthy aide, David Schine. The hearings were broadcast on live television and cast McCarthy in an unfavorable light, exposing his bullying practices.

At one point, the Army's chief legal representative, Joseph Welch, famously challenged him head on, "Have you no sense of decency, sir, at long last?" As a result, McCarthy's popularity plunged, and he was ultimately censured by his fellow senators. From that point on, he became a pariah, largely ignored until he died of liver disease in 1957 at the age of 48.

McCarthy's unethical abuse of the levers of government, his unsubstantiated allegations against innocent citizens, and the unchecked partisan responses of his colleagues were striking examples of the "Unjust Culture" of politics. I wish I could say this was an isolated case. Alas, subsequent congressional investigations that purported to uncover the truth have been similarly driven by blameful objectives, regardless of party or circumstance.

In recent years, the highly partisan investigation into loss of life at the government compound in Benghazi, Libya squandered an opportunity to identify system problems that could have led to a bipartisan plan of correction. Here is a sampling of "questions" put to former Secretary of State, Hillary Clinton, by Republican members of the House Committee on Benghazi. Compare the tone of the "why" questions below to the spirit of an RCA.

1. *"Why did the State Department compound and facility not even come close to meeting proper security specifications?" [loaded question]*

2. *"Why didn't you fire someone? Why has no one been held accountable? How come not a single person lost a single paycheck connected to the fact we had the first ambassador killed since 1979?" [browbeating the witness with three pretend "why" questions]*

3. *"So, if there's no evidence for a video-inspired protest, then where did the false narrative start? It started with you, Madame Secretary."*

Even as recently as February, 2019, in a hearing before the House Oversight and Reform Committee, the questioning of Michael Cohen, former personal attorney for President Trump, reinforced the unjust culture of politics. I can't begin to imagine an RCA going off the rails this way.

1. *"No one can see this guy as credible...He's a fake witness and his presence here is a travesty." [not a question]*

2. *"You lied to financial institutions in order to secure loans. You have lied to banks and to Congress. It seems there is not much you won't lie about." [browbeating the witness]*

3. *"Liar, liar, pants on fire." [this one speaks for itself]*

Browbeating, grandstanding, and editorializing. Polemics, insults, and innuendo. Why didn't they just pull out a gun and save us all the trouble?

For one final example, let's review the first impeachment of Donald Trump in 2019. A democratically elected president makes a mistake and is taken to the woodshed. A highly charged congressional process founders on the shoals of political partisanship. Where is the Just Culture here? Let's review the facts.

First, there is little doubt that Trump committed an egregious act. He secretly withheld military funds that had been appropriated by Congress to support a European ally that is struggling to repel the encroachment of Russia, our longstanding adversary, and did so merely to stain the reputation of a political opponent. It is not a stretch to find similarities to the action of a nurse who willfully bypassed a safety measure and gave a life-threatening medication to the wrong patient.

I would argue that the Just Culture *should* be applied here. A sitting president should *not* be fired for a single mistake, no matter *how* egregious. He should be given the opportunity to admit his mistake, apologize for it, and convince the rest of us that it will never happen again. In a word: *atone*. Just as Stacy did. After that, we should forgive the transgression and move on.

As everyone knows, that did not happen. Not only did Trump *not* apologize, he made false statements about his actions, denied that they mattered, and did everything possible to impede the investigation by prohibiting his own staff, State Department employees, and federal budget officials from even discussing the case with investigators, much less testifying under oath or submitting documents that could shed light on the incident. In other words, he become a non-cooperator, a saboteur, an *obstructionist.*

What happens in the Just Culture when an employee dissembles, hides facts, or otherwise impedes the RCA? That's *easy.* We fire him. Immediately. Summarily. Without regret. Because the Just Culture *does* hold people accountable for their actions, and the unforgiveable offense is to stand in the way of the truth. In fact, I can recall multiple examples in which we fired an employee for obstruction. The Just Culture is a two-edged sword, after all.

So, in the case of Donald Trump, our first impulse should have been to seek his explanation, uncover the truth, and give him the opportunity to set things right – which he did not. Once he failed to do that, we should have lowered the boom without hesitation – which *we* did not. The unfortunate outcome is that the path toward the truth was thwarted and the Just Culture took another hit. Same old, same old.

It is amazing to me that our political culture has barely budged in six decades. Most unfortunately, compared to the highly refined, transparent, and objective process of performance improvement in American hospitals, the political counterpart is a farce, an endless parade of finger pointing, political posturing, and gamesmanship that is highly destructive to the integrity of national leadership and the pursuit of high performance in government.

The net effect on our nation, as patient, is an array of distressing signs and symptoms: anger, shame, and mistrust. And these manifestations bring out our worst: defensiveness, denial, and dishonesty. Not to mention seething resentment, which boils over into a vengeful outburst at every pendulum shift in the power structure. Not exactly a culture that favors the just.

It should be apparent by now that we have taken a plunge into the art of leadership, but why did I open with atonement and forgiveness, of all things? These attributes have a religious connotation that one typically associates with *humility*, not with governance.

My response is that these traits are crucial to success as a person *and* a leader. Moreover, humility is the key to *many* attributes of great leadership, including trust, compassion, and coalescence. By way of example, Abraham Lincoln, our most revered president, was arguably the humblest of them all.

And Lincoln is not my only example. In *Good to Great*, his insightful book about corporate leadership, Jim Collins researched attributes of chief executive officers (CEOs) who led successful companies and compared them to those who failed.[4] Interestingly, failing leaders were more likely to be "alpha males" – high-octane, outward-facing, and ego-driven – while the *successful* leaders were more likely to be low-key, self-effacing, and ego-checked. In a word – humble. Why? Because egotistical leaders serve *themselves* ahead of the company, and humble leaders put the organization first.

Humility, then, is not just imperative for pastors, teachers, and social workers, it is essential for physicians, executives, and national leaders. Humility opens our minds to the truth. Humility opens our hearts to kindness. Humility checks our ego. Humility is the first rung of the leadership ladder.

Trust:
Build the Base

Trust starts with truth and ends with truth.

Santosh Kalwar, Nepali poet

The best way to find out if you can trust somebody is to trust them.

Ernest Hemingway, American author

"Good morning, Dr. Link."

"Hi, Melanie. How's everything?"

"All good." She notices the stethoscope dangling around my neck. "Are you on service this month?"

"Yep. 16N2 team. Two more weeks."

"That's nice. Then you must be looking for your new patient."

"Yes, I am. That would be Tomen. Did he make it to the unit yet?"

"Oh yes. Bed 12. He came up a couple hours ago." Melanie looked up from the medication cart and paused for a second. "Good luck with Mr. Tomen," she added with a knowing smile.

Now what did she mean by that?

At 7:30 am I was just getting to see the fresh cases – patients who had been admitted overnight to the hospital and would now be under the care of my housestaff team. As the attending physician, their supervisor, I was ultimately responsible for all our cases, and meeting a new patient was a ritual somewhat like unwrapping a present. I began by reviewing Nate Tomen's chart, which was sitting in a rack at the nurse station.

Nate had arrived in the ED shortly after midnight because of chest pain. Based on his symptoms and test results, it seemed most likely that he had a partial obstruction in one of his coronary arteries. A narrow point in the vessel impeded the blood flow to his heart muscle and had already caused damage to the muscle tissue – a mild heart attack. This event was not a serious outcome on its own, but it was a warning that Nate was at high risk for something much worse.

If the narrowed blood vessel became fully obstructed, he could sustain a massive, life-threatening heart attack. So it already seemed clear that our patient would require a cardiac catheterization – a procedure in which a narrow catheter is inserted into an artery in the arm or leg and threaded up through the vessel back into the heart to clear the obstruction. This is the modern version of the Nobel Prize-winning technique invented by physicians on our Chest Service more than fifty years earlier.

Although this approach could rarely cause a serious complication, it was the most effective way to prevent the worst-case scenario and offered the patient his best chance at long-term survival. In this situation the case was strong for doing the "cath" – a no-brainer, as we would sometimes say in our conversations with patients.

As I carefully reviewed the patient's problem list, however, one diagnosis caught my eye: "chronic undifferentiated schizophrenia." I quietly groaned to myself as I continued to read the chart. This was an unfortunate twist.

As most people know, schizophrenia is a severe mental illness that may first express itself in early adulthood with its initial symptoms – social withdrawal, odd utterances, and eccentric behaviors. In the worst expression of disease, however, patients will lose all touch with reality and express florid psychotic symptoms, such as hearing voices that are not real (hallucinations) or holding beliefs that are not true (delusions). Hallucinations and delusions are the hallmark of schizophrenia.

To a large degree, symptoms may be controlled by medication, but compliance can be a huge challenge. As every New Yorker is aware, the streets of Manhattan teem with non-compliant patients with schizophrenia – society's "misfits" who have rejected all attempts at treatment.

I entered the cubicle and stopped short. Nate was an arresting sight. He was a large African American man with wild hair. By large, I mean big and tall – not obese. But *huge*. He must have weighed 300 pounds. By wild, I mean his hair was frizzy and unkempt, spilling out in every direction.

He was lying flat on his back without a pillow, arms folded across his chest, the way he might be in a coffin and just as perfectly still – with open eyes and an enigmatic smile. That struck me as extremely odd and caused me to hesitate in my approach. I really didn't want to disturb this giant in repose.

I was wary about Nate because of my previous experience with schizophrenic patients. With one of the largest Psychiatry Departments in the nation, a busy Emergency Department in one of the world's most populous cities, and a charge to treat every patient that crossed our threshold, Bellevue Hospital had justifiably become the preferred drop-off point of every emotionally disturbed person picked up on Manhattan streets.

Therefore, astonishingly, schizophrenia is the most common diagnosis reported in our hospital. It is even more common than pneumonia, heart failure, and childbirth – the pantry staples of most community hospitals. Because of that, our physicians have extensive experience with all varieties of this challenging diagnosis, and I was fully aware that Nate would be a difficult test for me. That is what Melanie meant when she wished me luck.

I inched my way to the bedside and braced for the worst as I offered my standard greeting. "Hi, Mr. Tomen. I am Dr. Link. I will be the doctor in charge of your case, and I came by to say hello."

He turned toward me and widened his smile as he reached for my hand. "Hi Dr. Link," he responded warmly. "Nice to meet you."

Whoa! I was definitely not expecting *this*. Nate did not appear to be suspicious *or* paranoid. And he was not the least bit menacing or intimidating. In one brief, calm, gentle greeting, he shattered every stereotype already forming in my mind. I had imagined him to be chronically homeless and acutely psychotic, but I could not have been more wrong.

Following my greeting, I found Nate to be as pleasant and reasonable as any other patient on my service. He sat up, and we chatted amicably. I learned that he was not a street person as I had assumed. He belonged to a residential community for patients with chronic mental illness. His care was closely supervised, and he was provided with medications that were effectively treating his psychiatric symptoms. His was a *success* story.

At least psychiatrically. But medically he was still in grave danger. I described the nature of his condition and the risks he faced. I informed him that we would be consulting Cardiology, and they would likely recommend a catheterization to manage his condition. With this revelation, Nate abruptly frowned. "No way. I'm not up for that," he responded.

"Why not?"

He shook his head emphatically. "No sir. I'm doing just fine. I don't need anything like that."

I knew instantly that this would present a dilemma. In my experience, no rational person ever turned down a cardiac cath in this circumstance. If we could not convince Nate to undergo this necessary treatment, we would need to be sure that his underlying mental illness was not perversely affecting his judgment. He had to demonstrate a full understanding of his situation, including the risk entailed in choosing not to be treated.

Unfortunately, he did not do that. In fact, he would not admit he was at any risk at all. He maintained that since his symptoms had subsided, his cardiac problem had completely resolved. By denying a true understanding of his condition, Nate failed to demonstrate the capacity to make an informed decision. We would have to make it for him.[1]

But the cardiologists wanted no part of this. The attending was especially adamant. "There is no way that I am going to sedate this patient, tie him down, and cath him against his will. That would be a travesty. I don't care how little he understands. He knows what he wants." That was quite definitive.

And I had to agree. Although Nate could not express an accurate understanding of his situation, he was certainly explicit about his wishes. There was no doubt about his true preference, and that counted for a lot. If I were in his situation I would want *my* wishes respected. But his life was in danger. So we remained at an impasse.

At this point, there was only one perfect solution, only one win-win strategy to preserve autonomy *and* achieve a successful outcome. We had to secure our patient's consent. To do that, we had to earn his trust. In Nate's case, this meant building rapport to overcome his instinctive mistrust of hospitals and doctors. And that is exactly what happened. We earned his trust.

I must give full credit to the cardiologists, who returned several times to the bedside to review the options. They were fully transparent about the nature of the procedure and its risks and benefits. They listened carefully to Nate and answered all his questions. They did not confront him head-on. They did not press the issue. And they waited patiently for him to come around, which he did.

At the end of the second hospital day, Nate gave his consent for the catheterization, which demonstrated a partial obstruction in one of the main coronary arteries, as expected. The artery was successfully reopened by the procedure, restoring blood flow to the cardiac muscle tissue and markedly diminishing the risk of a massive heart attack. In the end, everybody won.

What would have happened if we had not secured consent? Quite simply, we would have been stuck. Without the patient's permission, or the legal equivalent, it would not be acceptable to take matters into our own hands. Although we could have and *should* have pursued the legal route to obtain a court order from a judge, no one could bear the thought of forcing this patient to have a procedure he clearly did not want. So the key to the case was securing trust. As it always is.

Regardless of a patient's inclinations, no doctor-patient relationship can succeed without trust. Prescribe a medication. Order a test. Suggest a treatment. None of that will happen unless the patient trusts the doctor. And not just any trust. Not a shallow, superficial, skin-deep trust, but rather a deep, meaningful, life-affirming trust.

Hence, a physician cannot get to first base, cannot pass Go, cannot even begin to exchange words without earning a patient's confidence. Nate's case was an extreme example of a universal truth: trust is the basis of *all* relationships. That is true for brief, momentary interactions and even more so for longstanding, continuous relationships lasting many years.

In contrast to Nate Tomen was my memorable AIDS patient, Juan Verdad. During my years of training, Juan regularly attended my outpatient clinic and was an unusual case in many ways, the most striking of which was that he was alive. As I will share in detail later, the Acquired Immune Deficiency Syndrome (AIDS) dominated my training experience. At that time, in the early 1980s, there was no effective treatment. It was a terminal disease like cancer that has spread throughout the body. It was a rare AIDS patient who survived the initial hospitalization and then went on to keep even one clinic appointment. But Juan apparently had not read the textbook. He seemingly had nine lives.

Diagnosed two years earlier, he had the classic appearance of a person with advanced AIDS – pencil thin with hollow temples, thinning hair, and flaking skin. But in other ways he was completely different – upright, walking, and talking. It seemed that every time Juan was admitted to the hospital with a new infection, he cheated death. He overcame the infection, survived the incident, and went home to tell the tale. Repeatedly.

And he was something of a celebrity, as he never failed to remind me. At each visit he would chatter proudly about his interview for a local news show – as an informal spokesperson for all AIDS patients in New York City. His good nature, his shining optimism, and his irrepressible personality were inspiring. I always looked forward to these visits.

Nonetheless, Juan lived on the edge. Having no home of his own, he slept on couches, bummed cigarettes, and dabbled in drugs. I have no idea how he obtained food, clothing, or transportation without any visible means of support. In this respect, his life was a gravity-defying feat. He was a chestnut sparrow – always flitting about, lighter than air, brightly chirping without a care in the world.

But even Juan had his limits. During one memorable clinic session, he brought up an uncomfortable subject. "Doc, I've had enough," is how he opened the conversation. He was fidgeting on the edge of his seat, bobbing up and down, more kinetic than usual.

I was moved by his candor as he related his weariness with the repeated hospitalizations and endless courses of treatment. He was ready to stop, and he wanted my help. The next time he was admitted to the hospital, he wished to be simply left alone. No diagnosis. No treatment.

"Just let me go, Doc," was his simple plea.

"Seriously, Juan?" I queried. "What if it is just another pneumonia? We can treat that with antibiotics, like before, and send you home again."

"That's what I'm *saying*," he replied. "I don't *want* to go home. Next time, I want you to leave me alone. I'm so tired of all this." He became perfectly still for a moment as he implored with an earnestness that I had never seen in him before. "*Please*, Doc. I'm counting on you."

He was passionate in his appeal, so I agreed to respect his unconventional request. In those days we did not have official forms to document a "Do Not Resuscitate (DNR) order," but I did carefully include this expression of his wishes in my clinic note.[2]

Juan's plea showed great insight. He faced the truth. He confronted his diagnosis and gave voice to his wishes. I could also see that he had great trust in me to reveal his deepest feelings and to place his life (and death) entirely in my hands. Normally it is the physician who initiates this difficult discussion, but Juan was the bold one.

Thus, my pact with Juan was sealed. I grasped the seriousness of his request, and I was determined to meet it. I solemnly responded that I would do everything in my power to carry out his wishes. At that instant, however, I could not foresee the unexpected encounter that would bring me to his bedside at the moment of truth – a moment in which I would have to break convention in order to keep my promise.

These are only two among thousands of cases I have experienced in which trust was the fundamental force behind all progress. Whether my patient had a chronic illness, a medical emergency, or a psychological debility, the essential first step to a solution was to earn her trust – to establish an understanding that I was safe, honest, and credible.

Establishing trust, then, is a core element of the art of Medicine. It is so fundamental to success I wonder why it is not emphasized more explicitly in education and training. No doubt some physicians are more naturally gifted than others in the interpersonal skills that engender trust, but no physician-patient relationship can succeed without it.

So let me take a moment to describe the interpersonal behaviors that beget trust, the lecture I would give to medical students if this topic were placed in their curriculum, and the advice I would give to America's leaders if anyone would listen.

First, be honest. Be consistently honest. Be impeccably honest. *Tell the truth.* One single lie, however insignificant, may dissolve a lifelong relationship. Second, be sincere. Say what you mean. Believe what you say. Show that you care. Most patients can sense insincerity when they feel it, even if you cannot tell how they know it. Third, be reliable – as dependable as the sunrise. Fulfill every commitment. Follow through on every pledge. Keep every promise. Once again, I am reminded of the value of the *systematic* approach.

I am also struck by how closely these attributes – honesty, sincerity, and reliability – track to what we call *integrity*. Maybe integrity is all you really need to build trust. That seems like such an obvious thing to say and such an easy thing to do. So why do we, physicians, sometimes fail to live up to that?

I do not have the answer to that question. But a *single* fallout can doom a relationship beyond repair. Perhaps the importance of trust can best be illustrated when it fails. The next two examples demonstrate the consequences of a breach of trust – lessons that I carry to this day.

As an intern, I took care of a patient who was perhaps the greatest challenge of all my years of training. Philip DeSare was 42 years old and an arresting sight. He was short and stout with prematurely gray hair and one stump where his left arm used to be and another stump where his right leg should have been. Despite his limitations, he was remarkably spry.

Phil had a dreadful medical condition; his blood clotted too easily. This problem had plagued him most of his adult life and had led to the loss of two limbs from arterial clots that obstructed flow through his blood vessels.[3] He was transferred to Bellevue from an outside hospital in hopes that we could manage his condition more effectively.

You might think Phil would be severely depressed by his terrible misfortune. That he would be angry, resentful, and uncooperative. I would certainly understand if he was all of those things. But he was not any of them. He was sweet, kind, and pleasant. One of the nicest patients I have ever known. He coped well with his disability, cooperated with our procedures, and seemed generally interested in *my* welfare as few patients ever are. So we formed an especially tight bond – partners in trust. Our interactions were the favorite moments of my day.

"Hi Doc. What can I do for you this morning?"

"Good morning, Mr. DeSare. Time to change your IV again. It's been three days." I am so self-conscious about my intrusion, I hastily apologize.

"Don't worry, Doc. No problem at all," he cheerfully replies.

"We have to keep the IV going until the pills start working," I explain as I drop my supplies in a heap onto his bedside table.

He wriggles up to a seating position and continues to chat. "I noticed you were here pretty late last night. Don't you ever get any sleep?"

"Not enough," I confess. "Sleep is not much of a priority around here."

"I understand. Well, I'm sure you're going to be an awesome doctor when all this is over. You already are." He extends his right arm and leans back, eyes closed. I place the IV on the second try. He must be so tired of this, but he does not complain. He doesn't even stop smiling. Here is a man with endless reserves of good will.

And that was a good thing because Phil's medical problems were especially complex and challenging. We simply could not determine what lay behind his extraordinary tendency to clot his blood. Even worse, we could not seem to overcome Phil's natural resistance to blood thinners.

We had started him on warfarin, the standard oral anticoagulant, but it was having no impact whatsoever. Every day we checked but his blood refused to thin. We advanced the dose to six times above normal, and yet his blood continued to be resistant to the effect of the drug.

I was extremely vexed. And so was my supervising resident as we went down one blind alley after another, vainly in search of the truth about our patient's mysterious ailment. We seemed to be getting nowhere.

Midway through my one-month assignment, my resident moved on to another rotation and was replaced by a new resident, who was equally enchanted by my enigmatic case – my *fascinoma*. After rounding on our patient a second time, however, my new resident stopped me in the hallway.

"Funny thing. I think I *know* this guy," he began. "I feel like I have met him before. Has he ever been a patient at Bellevue previously?" I shook my head. Phil had a "fresh" medical record number, indicating that he had never before crossed our threshold. "Well, I can't shake the feeling that I know this guy," he replied. "And I swear to you, I am going to figure it out."

The next morning, my resident greeted me with a triumphant grin. He had an article in his hand from a leading journal. "I was right! I *do* know this guy!" he exclaimed. "I know him *socially*," he continued. "He is related to my wife's uncle. I met him at a family gathering. And..." he waved the article as he continued. "He's a fake!" I drew back in surprise. "He has Munchausen Syndrome! One of the most famous cases on the eastern seaboard. He is written up in this article. Read it!"

So I did. Sure enough, my patient was a well-described case of a bizarre psychiatric condition named for Baron Munchausen, a fictional character based on a real-life German nobleman who was distinguished by his propensity to tell outrageous tall tales. In this condition, the patient is attracted to medical attention like a moth to a flame, and feigns illness in order to receive treatment, even to the point of self-harm.

Phil's elaborate medical history of the coagulation disorder was a complete fantasy. His blood did *not* clot abnormally; that was a ruse to get treated intensively by the medical staff. His missing extremities were *not* a result of blood clots; they were complications of the countless invasive medical procedures that he had fooled the medical profession into providing. His masquerade had actually led to severe harm and permanent disability.

This would explain why Phil's tests had failed to uncover a diagnosis. There wasn't any. This would explain why the warfarin was ineffective. He was undoubtedly cheeking the tablets, hiding the medication inside his mouth to fool the nurses into believing that he had ingested it. This would explain his unnaturally pleasant demeanor and positive outlook. He was actually happy that his case was so difficult. It kept up the ruse.

I was had.

You might think I would have been fascinated by this turn of events. Excited to realize I was caring for a famous patient, virtually a celebrity. Again amazed by my Bellevue experience, which always seemed to deliver learning experiences beyond my imagination. But I was none of those things. I was not fascinated, excited, or amazed. I was crushed. I was disappointed. I felt betrayed.

Phil was my favorite patient. We were buddies. We had a deep bond of friendship. And it was all a lie. In seven days on my team, Phil had mustered not a kernel of truth. I knew that Munchausen's was a psychiatric condition, a self-destructive sickness, a compulsive behavior over which the patient might not actually have control. And it was the patient, of course, who suffered the consequences.

But I was also aware that by cheeking his medications, Phil was a knowing participant in his elaborate deception. His purposeful behavior signaled his intent to dupe me, his trusted confidant, his sincere advocate, his earnest benefactor.

So that was it. I was done with him. We were through. I tersely informed Phil that, upon reviewing his tests, we concluded that his blood clotting was normal, and he was not in danger of recurrent complications.

All good news. He was free to go. I did not confront him. I was advised that you could not reason with a Munchausen patient. The situation was hopeless.

I am not sure why I experienced such an intensely negative reaction to learning the truth about Phil. It could be as simple as resenting the con. Of having fallen for it. But I think it went much deeper than that. The trust between physician and patient is fundamental to our profession – the essence of all our relationships and the foundation of our success.

In this breach of trust, I learned a valuable lesson about what it feels like to be on the *receiving* end of a deception: as a child tricked by his older brother, as a worker cheated by her employer, or as a citizen deceived by a national leader. It is all the same and it feels pretty awful.

There was one final loose end to tie up. Phil had been transferred to Bellevue from another hospital. Surely, they must have known about his true diagnosis. If they had just properly alerted us, we would have been spared a lot of grief. I decided that I would call them to complain, so I reviewed his transfer documents at the nursing station.

The first line of the summary identified the patient, with his diagnosis in capital letters: "The patient is a 42 year old male with MUNCHAUSEN'S DISORDER." Somehow this information had been completely overlooked by the accepting physician and never passed on to me and my resident.

Wry note to self: always read the transfer documents.

So I learned a valuable lesson about the importance of trust from this most interesting patient. Of course, I felt vindicated by the purity of my intentions in our brief but intense relationship. Perhaps I was even a touch sanctimonious in my response. For I also have the capacity to betray trust, and there are, unfortunately, multiple examples in my career where I have let a patient or colleague down, always to my profound regret.

But the most illuminating example of my own breach of trust originated with an event that took place well before my residency training. Even before medical school – in my junior year of college. At first this might not seem to be a lesson learned from my medical practice; however, in a remarkable turn of events, this story arc eventually found its way to a Bellevue bedside encounter many years later. But let me start at the beginning...

In 1975, I matriculated to Butler University, a small liberal arts school on an attractive campus in north Indianapolis. Butler was best known for its basketball team, a David among Goliaths. In 1967, lowly Butler played for the NCAA basketball championship, losing to powerhouse UCLA in the national finals, a feat it would duplicate twice more nearly fifty years later.

Butler's social life was dominated by fraternities and sororities, to which most residential students belonged. There were nearly 20 of these houses on campus that offered attractive accommodations and an active party scene. Although I started out as a dormitory resident, I could see that the social life of campus was centered around the Greek houses. In my sophomore year, I decided to join a fraternity myself.

Most Americans are familiar with Greek life through popular, if cartoonish, cinematic depictions. The process of joining a fraternity occurs during Rush Week, when candidates systematically learn about their options and make connections with the members of the individual houses through tours and social engagements (rush parties). When house members make a social connection with a newcomer, they sponsor his application, shepherding acceptance among the other members.

After a candidate formally declares his interest in joining (pledging), the fraternity's entire membership votes on the pledge in a secret meeting. One of the traditions of this election is the blackball rule. Although voting is primarily by majority vote, a single member can veto (blackball) any potential candidate by stating his objection.[4] In this manner, the selection of a new member must essentially be unanimous.

I went through Rush Week with a clear idea of my preference. I was personally sponsored by two members and was able to socially connect well enough with their housemates, or at least convince them of my normalcy, that my candidacy was fully accepted. In the secret vote I was invited to join. Thankfully no one blackballed me.

I was now a member of the incoming pledge class, seventeen of us in all – mostly freshmen – who would spend the next semester as second-class citizens in the fraternity house. We were junior members, barred from the chapter room where house meetings took place and constantly reminded of our inferior status by continual signs of disrespect, large and small, but mostly good-natured.

In the second semester, my pledge class advanced to the cusp of full membership. But first we had to endure two final weeks of pre-initiation torment, including "hell week" – long days and nights of meaningless tasks, such as repeatedly waxing the bathroom floor, scraping the rust off iron railings with a toothbrush, and sweeping the lawn – a punishing gauntlet of hurdles designed to foster group loyalty and bond us as a pledge class.

It worked like a charm. By the time of our initiation ceremony, I felt intensely bonded to my peers. I could not imagine a greater bunch of guys with which to experience my remaining college years.

In the fall of my junior year, I was now a full-fledged member – on the *inside*. During the activities of Rush Week, I was hosting tours and meeting candidates myself, and I realized that I had an important responsibility in the selection of the new pledge class. Early in the week, I was especially interested in an applicant who really stood out from the others.

Will Thomason was a native New Yorker – a young Black man from Harlem – and he danced. *Seriously* danced. In fact, he came to Butler on a dance scholarship, but his real goal was to attend medical school. He was pre-med – like me. So that was pretty exotic. A pre-med dance major from Harlem. Here was an earnest young man with ambitious goals and an engaging personality. He had me at hello.

And I was not alone. Several of my fraternity buddies were similarly captivated by Will. So we courted him. We struck up friendships, took him on a tour, introduced him to our housemates, and sang his praises. Fortunately, he was an easy sell – personable and accomplished. We secured enough positive feedback to know that his acceptance was guaranteed. He would pledge to our fraternity and join the incoming class.

The final step was the vote. All fifty members of the fraternity were present at this crucial meeting of the brotherhood. We packed ourselves into our great room, a large gathering place just inside the entrance doors, which were locked shut for the privacy of this solemn occasion.

My housemates were seated on upholstered couches, folding chairs, and end tables, anywhere they could find a space. I was lying on the carpeted floor as we reviewed the candidates. One after another passed muster and were voted in. A routine exercise. By the time an applicant made it to this stage, it was pretty much a done deal. Then we came to Will.

My friends and I made our recommendation. We presented his case, told his story, and delivered our pitch. Other members joined in and yet others nodded in agreement. Then we put it to a vote. Will easily passed by a solid majority. He was in.

Then a member of my pledge class raised his hand. "Not so fast," he started. "We have never had a *Black* member before and I don't think this is a good time to start. I vote no." The speaker was invoking the blackball rule – a very rare event. This caught everyone completely by surprise.

"What the hell?" someone blurted out. Others joined in. The meeting was now in an uproar as a cacophony of dissenting voices filled the room. This was blatant racism. This was completely unacceptable. This was *1977*. It was simply inconceivable that we could bar a member based on his race.

Then a *second* blackball was cast. "I agree we should not accept this Black guy. How is he going to live here? He's just not going to fit in."

"Why not?" someone asked, practically shouting.

"Well for one thing, no one is going to trust him." This was followed by one of the most bizarre rationalizations for prejudice that I have ever heard. "And what if something gets stolen around here? Everyone is going to think *he* did it. That's not going to be fair to *him*."

And another chimed in. "Yeah, and it is going to be so awkward. What happens during hell week? How are we supposed to pick on a *Black* guy? That will seem *racist*." That was it. Three blackballs. All from my own pledge class. My buddies. Guys who I would risk my life for.

Of course, the basis of the argument was completely irrational. The decision was ethically unacceptable and probably expressly prohibited by campus rules.[5] Strangest of all, Will was favored almost unanimously by the full group. Even the dissenters were otherwise fine people who I respected. To this day, I cannot reconcile the disconnect.

But a rule was a rule. The principle of consensus was a long-established tradition that had served us well and maintained a spirit of collaboration among our house family. This tradition had to be respected. After a long and spirited debate, the three dissenters held fast, and that was the end of it.

All that remained was to inform Will that he had not passed the vote. This was to be handled delicately by the fraternity president. He would be careful not to suggest that race had anything to do with it. The party line was that as a full-time dance major and a pre-med student, it was obvious that Will would have an enormous challenge meeting his academic load.

The time demands of fraternity life were simply not compatible with his academic success. Never mind that several of us also had demanding loads of pre-med and pre-law coursework. We were just being realistic with Will, protecting him, really, from the harmful consequences of joining our fraternity.

I observed this conversation through a window. At an evening event, our president took Will outside and shared the scripted lines while they stood together in the moonlit backyard. I could see Will listening intently, and then he abruptly turned and walked away. I did not speak to him again.

I was disturbed. I was resentful of my friends and troubled by the outcome. I had a persistent uneasiness about my participation in the whole affair, as if I were marked by a stain. It took some time for the wounds to heal, but they did. Our chapter house became whole again and life went on.

The pledge class had a successful year, went through hell week, bonded as all pledge classes do, and were initiated as new members in an emotional ceremony. Meanwhile, I heard that Will was leaving college at the end of the year. Apparently, that double burden of dance and pre-med *was* too much for this New York transplant. At least that was what I chose to believe.

At the mid-year elections, I ran for president of the fraternity and won. My campaign was built on a promise of healing. I promised to bridge the growing divide that threatened the unity of our fraternity – the rift between the pot smokers and the abstainers – by negotiating an acceptable compromise. One of the truly "momentous" issues of campus history. There was nothing in my message about racism, prejudice, or our glaring *system* deficiency: the blackball rule.

But I knew in my mind that I had betrayed Will. I had lured him in, promised an outcome, and then failed to deliver. Even worse, I passively accepted an indefensible act. He had trusted me, and I had let him down. There was an important lesson to learn here, but I was not ready to learn it. That would have to wait fifteen years until I had sufficiently matured to fully account for my actions.

I put the affair of Will Thomason behind me, an inconvenient blemish on an otherwise successful college career. Little did I know that I would have a second chance at redemption with Will, literally at the bedside in a Bellevue Hospital encounter, through an astonishing coincidence that would shake my world and leave me forever changed.

So what are the lessons in trust for national leaders? What relevant conclusions may we export from the bedside to the political arena? The core point is that trust is just as essential to a leader as it is to a physician. Democratic leaders govern entirely through relationships and trust is the basis of every one of them. Therefore, heads of state must earn the trust of their colleagues, their counterparts, and their constituents, in exactly the same ways that physicians must win the trust of their patients.

For starters, unless our leaders can trust their *colleagues* – their partners in executive, legislative, and judicial branches of government – they cannot coalesce forces to bring about positive change. They cannot advance any sort of mutual agenda, and they most definitely cannot move the needle on the contentious issues facing our nation.

The perennial standoff between the White House, Congress, and the Supreme Court fundamentally derives from mistrust and corrosively impedes national progress, which depends on alignment of disparate forces. Hence, a successful president must develop trust *across* political branches and party lines.

The same is true in international relationships, which have the same characteristics as interpersonal ones. They can be defined by honesty, respect, and trust, or by bullying, lying, and intimidation. After all, countries are made up of people, and people can be expected to respond collectively as they do individually. It follows, then, that our national leaders must establish faith with foreign heads of state, their counterparts, if they wish to summon the collaborative impulses that are necessary to achieve peaceful co-existence.

Historically, America has had mixed success, mostly positive, in international affairs. Indeed, our greatest accomplishments (two World Wars, the Marshall Plan, the Peace Corps, nuclear treaties, global trade, and human rights) have been fostered by trusting relationships, reciprocal exchanges, and mutual alliances.

On the other hand, some of our worst domestic and foreign undertakings (the Slave Trade, Japanese internment camps, McCarthyism, Bay of Pigs, Watergate, and Iran-Contra) were engendered by self-interest, duplicity, and mistrust. Moreover, whenever our national leaders propped up autocrats at the expense of their citizenry, we betrayed the trust of the people and squandered the good will of an entire generation. Some of those betrayals have haunted us ever since.

Thus, it appears that trust is just as important in foreign affairs as it is in personal ones. As obvious as that seems, it is a lesson that often fails to gain traction at the highest levels of government. Witness Donald Trump's first presidential trip abroad, when he notably chose *not* to publicly reaffirm our commitment to mutual defense of NATO allies – the bedrock of a 68 year-old bond with our oldest and best friends in the world. Imagine the impact of this highly publicized omission upon *all* our international relationships. Are we a nation that deserves *anyone's* trust?

Finally, leaders must find a way to earn the trust of their constituents – the voters. After all, the principal role of a leader is to take people to a new and better place. To define that new place through clarity of vision. To strategize how to get there through a systematic approach. And to bring the people along. The final step requires persuasion, motivation... and trust. Without the trust of the people, the leader isn't taking them anywhere.

Diagnosis:
Face the Facts

A long time ago in a faraway land, the king of the realm hires two weavers to design a magnificent new suit. The dishonest tailors promise to fashion an extravagant garment with a unique feature: the fabric is invisible to anyone who is a fool. On the fateful day, they pretend to dress the king. Neither the king nor his ministers can perceive any clothing, but no one wants to admit he is a fool.

Soon afterward, the king marches stark naked in a procession before his subjects. The townsfolk turn out for the parade, and all pretend to admire the fine suit. Finally, a boy in the crowd, too young to know better, cries out, "The emperor is wearing no clothes!" Immediately others in the crowd pick up the chant until the king is driven out of town in disgrace.

Adapted from *The Emperor's New Clothes*,
Hans Christian Andersen, 1837

"Hi, Gerry. I'm Dr. Link. I will be the doctor in charge of your case, and I just came by to meet you."

"Hi, Dr. Link."

"Is this your first time at Bellevue Hospital?"

"I suppose it is. Yes."

"Well, I guess you know by now that we admitted you to the inpatient unit because we think you might have meningitis."

"My God. That sounds serious."

"It's not as bad as it sounds, but we do need to keep you here for now."

"I'm not sure I understand. Where am I, anyway?"

"Like I said, you are here in the hospital – Bellevue Hospital."

"I'm sorry, but nobody said anything about a hospital. And who are you? Have we met?"

One of the great joys of Medicine is to make a difficult diagnosis: to sift through the facts, eliminate the alternate possibilities, and then nail down the simple answer that explains everything. It can be very much like opening a gift wrapped in many layers – one box inside another box inside yet another, and so on. When one finally gets to the heart of the matter, it can be a truly spectacular "Eureka" moment.

One of my favorite cases of my internship year was a diagnostic dilemma such as this. A young man of 28 years, Gerald Menard, was brought to our Emergency Department (ED) by ambulance. He had been picked up from the street because of an altered mental status.

To an ED physician, the phrase "altered mental status" could mean any of a number of things: agitation, confusion, psychiatric disturbance, or even a comatose state. And there were many possible reasons for this presentation: drug use, alcohol withdrawal, sepsis, or even a stroke. In this case, the patient had a peculiar neurological symptom, which I will describe shortly.

Gerry underwent urgent testing in the ED. On first glance, blood test results were unremarkable and computed tomography (CT scan) of the brain was normal. However, a lumbar puncture (spinal tap) showed the presence of white blood cells in the cerebrospinal fluid (CSF).

A lumbar puncture is exactly what it sounds like. With the patient curled up on his side like a fetus, a hollow needle is inserted into the lumbar spine (the midline of the lower back) through the skin, between two vertebral bones, so that it "punctures" the fluid-filled space surrounding the spinal cord. The goal is to draw out some of the CSF from the spinal canal for analysis. It is surprisingly easy to do this. More important, this is the same crystal-clear fluid that circulates around the brain. To do a lumbar puncture is like taking a sample of fluid from the brain itself. Only much safer.

Gerry's CSF was not normal. There were white blood cells present that suggested there was an inflammatory process going on inside his central nervous system. Not a large number of cells, but just enough to declare that something was definitely not right. Without a doubt, there was a diagnosis lurking behind Gerry's presentation, and we would have to find it. At this point, it seemed most likely that he had aseptic meningitis, a viral infection of the membranes surrounding his brain and spinal cord.

This diagnosis sounds pretty bad, but actually it is not. It certainly is not anything like its evil twin, *bacterial* meningitis, which can take a patient's life within a few hours. Aseptic (i.e., *non* septic) meningitis is typically caused by a virus that produces meningitis symptoms such as fever, stiff neck, and headache, but which will usually resolve within a few days without any treatment being necessary. Nonetheless, we didn't have a definite diagnosis, so at midnight Gerry was admitted to the hospital, assigned to my team.

By now, even as an intern, my job was clear. I would meet the patient, take his full history, examine him, review all his lab tests, and then write an admission note that captured all the information. The crucial final part of the note was the assessment and plan, in which I would discuss the diagnosis and treatment.

In this section, I would think out loud – review the facts, consider diagnostic possibilities, and then make my case for the one or two contenders that I felt were most likely. The diagnosis would, of course, determine the treatment plan, which I would review with my supervising resident.

There was a systematic approach to this work that always started by casting the widest possible net. To this end, I would gather all the evidence at hand, then I would consider all the possible explanations for the findings. This complete list of "suspects" is known as the differential diagnosis. I would then review all these possibilities one by one, prioritizing some and eliminating others, through a method of clinical reasoning analogous to identifying the assailant in the game of Clue.

If I were lucky, the process would lead to a single, clean diagnosis in the Great Reveal: Colonel Mustard did it with a Lead Pipe in the Conservatory. If not, I would be left with multiple possibilities to sort out with further testing. Sometimes we would have to begin treatment without a definitive answer. In that case, it might be necessary to treat two or more diseases at once until the truth could be sorted out further down the line.

What was crucially important was to gather *all* the facts: to compulsively collect as much information as possible from the patient's history and physical exam, and to review lab tests, x-rays, electrocardiograms, and any other conceivable results gathered from the patient. No stone could be left unturned. Without an accurate diagnosis, it would be impossible to identify the curative treatment.

I came down to the ground floor to meet my new admission. Based on the story, I expected to see one of our typical ED patients, a chronic alcoholic denizen of the Bowery. In that case, the patient would be disheveled, shaky, and agitated – in the delirious haze of severe alcohol withdrawal. Practically in a single glance, I would be able to make a diagnosis.

But Gerry was surprisingly normal appearing. He was clean-shaven, polite, and articulate, sporting horn-rimmed glasses, short brown hair, and a faintly bemused expression. He could have been anyone's tax accountant. He was certainly not shaky, agitated, or confused. I introduced myself and then began asking questions. He was calm and lucid as he went through all the details of his life and his medical history, which were basically nondescript.

Gerry had grown up in Connecticut, recently moved to New York City, and was living alone in an apartment on the West Side. He had no idea why he was brought to the hospital as he had no recollection of the trip to the ED. There was really not much to go on. In fact, I was beginning to believe the case was completely bogus, except for the CSF findings, which were definitely *not* normal.

I left the room to grab his chart and then returned scarcely a minute later to continue our conversation. Gerry gazed at me from his hospital bed with a blank expression. He then stared at the stethoscope hanging around my neck, puzzled. "Who are *you?"* he asked.

I was startled. "Excuse me?"

"Have we met before?" he continued.

"Don't you remember that I was talking to you just a minute ago?" I was completely thrown off my stride. "I am Dr. Link, and we were talking about your medical condition."

He seemed completely baffled. "Where *am* I?"

In a few seconds it became clear that he did not recognize me and had no recollection of our previous encounter. I looked at him suspiciously before realizing he was completely earnest. I filled him in once again – who I was, where we were, and why he was here. He followed me carefully and showed complete understanding. At the end of my spiel, he asked me again. "So what *is* this place?" He had completely forgotten what I had just told him. What he seemed to have absorbed had vanished without a trace.

Then I did a formal memory test. "I am going to give you the names of three objects. I want you to remember what they are. Okay? In a few minutes, I'm going to ask you to recall the names of these objects. Ready?"

"Fire away."

"Picture in your mind a red balloon, a teacup, and an umbrella. Got it?"

"Got it."

"Now repeat after me. Red Balloon...Teacup...Umbrella." Gerry correctly repeated the name of each object, one at a time after my cues. I asked him once again to picture them in his mind and to remember them.

Sixty seconds later I asked him to recall the objects. Not only did he fail to recall them, he couldn't even remember that we were doing a test – or that I was a physician. Despite a phenomenal recollection of his life story and an impressive array of facts, Gerry could not remember anything fresh from one minute to the next. He was incapable of storing *new* memories.

If you have ever seen the film, *Memento*, you will recognize the bizarre condition my patient had. Gerry's distant recall was normal, but he could not store *new* information, just like Leonard, the ex-insurance investigator searching for his wife's killer in the film. It was as though the movie of his life could be played forward until about noon on the previous day, and then it was just a blank. No new frames, no fresh scenes could be added to what was already there. He could not store new facts, make new friends, or accumulate new knowledge. He was unable to *learn*.

This is an utterly debilitating condition that I have seen in only one other patient in my career – a victim of near drowning who suffered severe brain damage. In Gerry's case, it still wasn't clear what was behind all this. Could this be some unusual manifestation of a brain infection? Was there another insidious disorder lurking behind these signs and symptoms? Some exotic diagnosis? The physical examination was not much help.

Except for a mild fever, Gerry had no other physical signs of illness. Apart from the short-term memory loss, the remainder of the neurological exam was completely normal. But we were concerned. We knew something was definitely wrong, and we did not want to overlook an important diagnosis. Although this was not a classic presentation of bacterial meningitis, we decided to treat him with antibiotics anyway – just in case. As we like to say in our profession, the patient doesn't always read the textbook.

Through the remainder of the night, I attended to my other patients. In the morning, I returned to Gerry's bedside. Of course, he did not remember me, but he was just as pleasant as ever, seemingly oblivious to the gravity of the situation. It was no use trying to inform him otherwise. Even if I brought him to his senses, I could leave the room and return a minute later, and it would all be forgotten, slate wiped clean.

Then I repeated the physical assessment. His neurological exam was unchanged – nothing new there. But on the cardiac exam, I noticed something quite unusual, an extra heart sound alongside the rhythmic and regular lub-dub, lub-dub. Right after each "dub" was a faint whisper, like a soft exhaled breath. I recognized this as a type of heart murmur that was caused by insufficiency of the aortic valve, the gate that stands between the left ventricle and the aorta.

The left ventricle is the heart's main pumping chamber and the aorta is the outflow track to the circulatory system. With each heartbeat, the aortic valve swings open and closed, like saloon doors, to permit one-way flow of blood from the ventricle into the aorta, between the lub and the dub. The second heart sound, the "dub," is caused by the doors slamming shut after the blood has been ejected into the aorta. This prevents any backward flow between heartbeats.[1]

However, in this case the valve was leaking. After it closed, some of the blood that had been ejected into the aorta was slipping backward into the heart because the saloon doors did not shut as tightly as they should. This backflow was producing the faint whispery sound that I heard after the dub.

Well that was certainly unexpected. Why had I not noticed that the previous night? *I should really be more careful when I examine patients*, I told myself. I brought my resident to the bedside, and he concurred with the finding. It was subtle but definitely present. Now that was quite strange. An abnormality of the heart in a patient with a memory problem. Was that a coincidence? A red herring? Or was it a crucial clue, not to be ignored?

I was annoyed by this inconvenient "loose end," as neither my resident nor I could put the facts together into a nice and tidy diagnosis. But it was important to consider and track every crucial piece of evidence, so we ordered an echocardiogram, which was an image of the heart taken with sound waves.

The echocardiogram revealed a surprise diagnosis. In addition to the backflow of blood, which could clearly be seen, the aortic valve had a growth on it, a "vegetation" about a half-inch in diameter. The growth was attached to the free edge of the saloon door and flopped up and down as the valve opened and closed. This was a sure sign of endocarditis, a bacterial infection of the heart valve. To make matters worse, the bacteria had burrowed into the adjacent tissue, forming an abscess within the heart muscle itself.

The most likely cause of this infection was a dental procedure that the patient had undergone two months earlier. During that event, agitation of the patient's gums probably allowed bacteria from the mouth to enter the bloodstream, travel to the heart, and lodge themselves on the surface of the valve. Over the ensuing two months, the bacterial growth evolved into the vegetation seen on the echocardiogram.

This was a perfect explanation of the cardiac findings. What about the memory loss? Was that a coincidence? The Neurology consultant felt the vegetation that was flopping around on the valve was releasing tiny bacterial fragments that travelled straight up to the brain and lodged there, causing local infection and obstruction of blood vessels. On a repeat look at the CT scan, there were subtle abnormalities that supported this conclusion.

Although we had finally determined the "root cause" of Gerry's symptoms, he was still at risk for an unhappy ending. Given the severity of the infection, we knew that it could not be cured with antibiotics, so we summoned the cardiovascular surgeons to the bedside. They took Gerry to the operating room and opened his chest, cleaned out the abscess, and replaced the aortic valve. The surgery was a success, Gerry quickly recovered, and he was discharged from the hospital several weeks later.

So our mystery case finally had an answer. Despite all early signs pointing to a neurological disorder, there was a subtle clue, an apparently unrelated and absurdly trivial detail that alerted us to the correct diagnosis and helped us save Gerry's life. Imagine if we had ignored that fact!

Every physician is familiar with the value of information from a single clue like this, which is sometimes the crucial hint that makes all the difference – the key to the kingdom. To that end, no fact should ever be overlooked, no evidence should ever be ignored, and no truth should ever be denied.

Yet physicians do ignore facts – all the time. After all, they are only human, and it is easy to overlook things. In the hospital setting, however, a fact that is ignored – leading to the wrong diagnosis and treatment, and then causing harm to the patient – will eventually have its day in the sun.

The ignored fact will rise like a phoenix, spread its wings, and display its colorful feathers for all to see. It will once and for all become the center of attention, the focus of analysis, and the heart of discussion of many brilliant, medical minds. Where else will this take place but at the monthly M&M Report, the final resting place of all vital, consequential, overlooked facts.

Yes, indeed, the failure to notice, accept, or otherwise acknowledge an important fact is the surest way to the podium at the M&M conference. And the most common way for a fact to be overlooked is for a physician to stubbornly stick to a hypothesis when contradictory evidence emerges. This particular cognitive error is so common, we have a name for it: anchoring.

The physician who anchors has become so attached to a presumptive diagnosis that he simply cannot accept a fact to the contrary. If possible, he will twist the truth around to make the new fact fit the original hypothesis, when instead he should be revising his theory to fit the new evidence.

The best way I know to describe this is to share a joke I used to tell at M&M conferences. This is my favorite joke of all-time, not because it is funny, which it is not, but because it is wise.[2]

> Two sons take their elderly father to the doctor's office. "What brings you here today?" he asks.
>
> "We need your help," says the older son. "Dad thinks he is a corpse."
>
> "A what?" asks the doctor in disbelief.
>
> "A corpse. Dad believes he is a dead body. No matter what we say, we cannot convince him otherwise."
>
> Now the doctor is intrigued. He steps up to the father and asks a few questions. Sure enough, the father is convinced he is a corpse. The doctor tries his best to change the father's mind but to no avail. When he is just about to give up, the doctor has an inspiration. "Let me ask you this," he says to the father. "Do corpses bleed?"
>
> "Of course not," answers the father emphatically. "*Everyone* knows that corpses can't bleed!"

> Whereupon, the doctor grasps the father's thumb and pricks it with a needle. A bright spot of blood appears and the father registers complete surprise. He looks at the doctor, and then, to his sons' great relief, a wave of understanding comes over his countenance, as if the clouds have parted, and the sun is now shining through. The father turns to the doctor and loudly exclaims, "I didn't know corpses could bleed!"

Like the father in the story, physicians sometimes reinterpret facts to support a diagnosis that they should really let go of. Let's review a typical medical example by comparing two conditions: heart failure and pneumonia. Both can trigger cough and shortness of breath, but heart failure usually causes fluid to back up equally in both lungs, while pneumonia is accompanied by a fever and usually affects only one lung.

Imagine a patient appears in the ED with cough and shortness of breath, and the admitting physician jumps to the conclusion that pneumonia is the diagnosis. Perhaps she becomes so enchanted by this idea that her mind is closed to the alternate possibility.

When the chest X-ray shows abnormalities in *both* lungs, the physician might conclude that this is an especially bad infection that started on one side and spread to the other. When the temperature check reveals no fever, she might rationalize that the patient is too ill to mount a fever.

In this way, the physician anchors to the original incorrect diagnosis by explaining away the new facts rather than letting them point the way to the correct diagnosis: heart failure. In the M&M conference, she will be gently invited to explain why she treated heart failure with antibiotics.

Why do we find it so hard to let go of our fixed, firm beliefs? Why does the truth have such a difficult time earning a seat at the table? These are important questions for anyone, but especially for national leaders, for whom making the correct assessment is so crucial to deciding on a course of action that may affect millions of citizens.

Yet the political arena is exactly the place where decision-makers have the greatest trouble accepting facts, where people in power cast aside irrefutable evidence with casual abandon, and where authorities seem downright allergic to the naked truth. Indeed, I am dumbfounded by the perpetual disregard the political elite have for confirmed facts.

Of all the examples where truth takes it on the chin, however, none is more perplexing than climate change, where prominent national leaders have staked out positions on opposite sides. This hardly seems possible given the volumes of scientific data that have been gathered over the past century, so let's start by reviewing the facts.

As every grade school student knows, climate change is the long-term impact on the earth's temperature and climate that is induced by increasing atmospheric levels of greenhouse gases, such as carbon dioxide and methane, that absorb and emit radiation. As early as the 19th century, scientists became aware of the warming effect of these invisible vapors and further observed that industrial activities were increasing their production through the burning of fossil fuels, such as oil, coal, and natural gas.

Today, more than 33 billion tons of CO_2 gas are released into the atmosphere each year, which advance the CO_2 concentration by about 2 parts per million annually. That CO_2 is a greenhouse gas is well-established. That atmospheric CO_2 levels are steadily rising has been confirmed by direct measurement.[3]

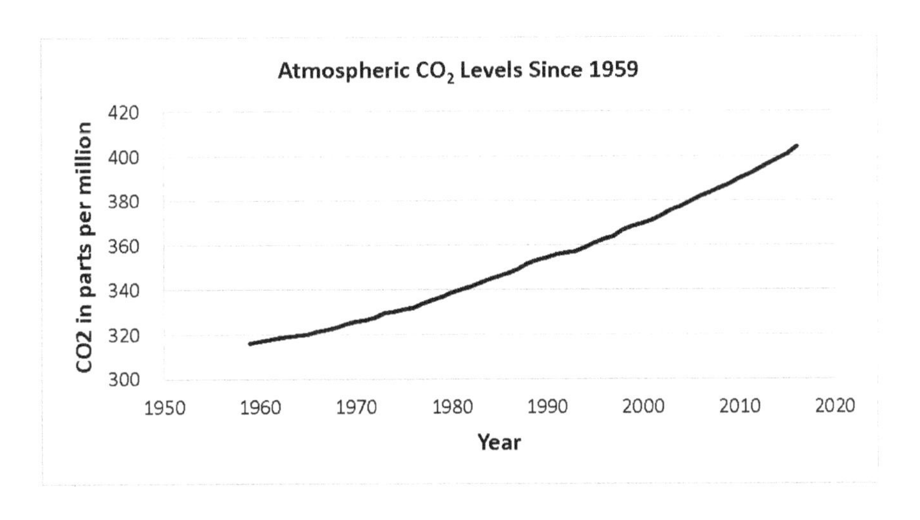

Sampling air bubbles trapped in polar ice, scientists have determined that, over the past 400,000 years, the carbon dioxide level had always varied between 180 and 300 parts per million but *never* exceeded 300. Since 1950, however, the CO_2 level has been over 300 ppm *every* year, rising steadily to the current level, which is now over 400 ppm. Based on the rising levels of greenhouse gases, scientists predicted early in the 20th century that global temperatures would rise as a result. By the mid-1990s their voices had swelled to a chorus. Let's review whether those predictions came true.

The best evidence for the warming of the earth comes from global land and sea temperature measurements that are regularly reported by the National Oceanic and Atmospheric Administration (NOAA), a U.S. government agency charged with assembling and reporting facts about climate change. According to NOAA, the world's average temperature (currently about 59 degrees Fahrenheit) has increased steadily over the past century. Not only was 2016 a record-breaking year, the past five years have been the hottest five years in recorded history. The following graph depicts the rise in the average global temperature over the past 100 years, since 1918.[4]

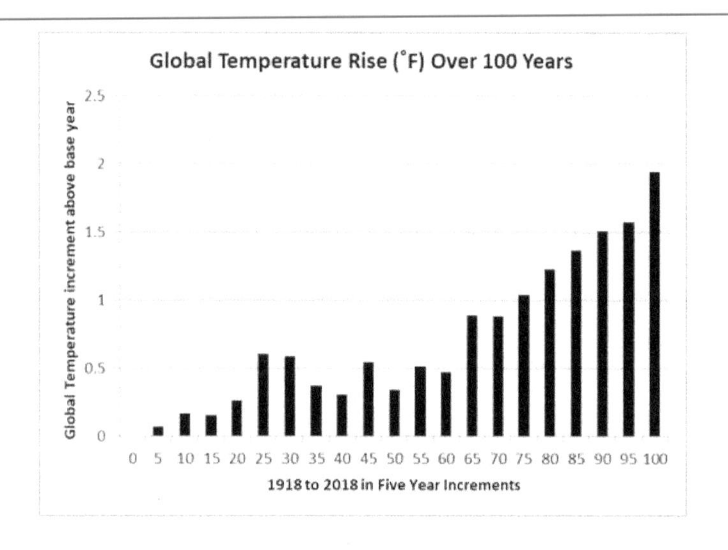

It is apparent in this graph that average global temperatures have increased by nearly 2 degrees Fahrenheit over these past 100 years. More important, the rise in those temperatures appears to be accelerating. While it took 75 years to gain the first degree, it took only 25 years to gain the second.

Thus, it appears that our earth is running a fever. So here are three important facts that cannot be denied:

- The earth is getting warmer at an astonishing rate. The record-setting pace over the past century is unprecedented – it would normally take 5,000 – 10,000 years to achieve an increase of this magnitude.

- The pace of the warming trend is *accelerating*. Among the first 18 years of the 21st century were the 17 warmest years of modern history. (1998, as the 7th warmest year of all time, is the missing member of this group).
- This increase was predicted with remarkable accuracy by scientists in the past century, using measurements of carbon dioxide production by fossil fuel consumption. Global warming is no longer a prediction. It actually came true.

The evidence speaks for itself, but what do scientists say? The Intergovernmental Panel on Climate Change (IPCC) is an internationally accepted authority on the topic. In its 2014 Synthesis Report, the IPCC stated:

> Warming of the climate system is unequivocal, and since the 1950s, many of the observed changes are unprecedented over decades to millennia. The atmosphere and ocean have warmed, the amounts of snow and ice have diminished, and the sea level has risen.

The work of the IPCC has been endorsed by countless scientific societies around the world, including the prestigious U.S. National Academy of Sciences, which was founded in 1863 by an Act of Congress, believe it or not, specifically *to provide scientific advice to the government!* In 2014, the Royal Society and the U.S. National Academy of Sciences issued a joint statement:

> Climate change is one of the defining issues of our time. It is now more certain than ever, based on many lines of evidence, that humans are changing Earth's climate.

At this point, it is clear that climate change is as established a fact as any in the field of science. We are just as sure of global warming as we are of the roundness of the earth or the existence of gravity, and there is no major scientific academy that disputes the evidence. You would have to place your head deep in the sand to miss this truth.

Unfortunately, based on the clear trend in atmospheric CO_2 levels and the equally clear rising trend in the average global temperature, we are now heading into uncharted territory, to levels of warmth never before experienced by modern humans. The implications for sea levels, crop yields, polar navigation, weather patterns, biological diversity, and human existence are truly beyond our imagination.

It is time to review how our national leaders have responded. How have they incorporated this "new truth" into their assessment and plan? Let's start by looking at the positions that have been staked out by leaders of the major political parties.

Bill Clinton – Democrat

"Climate change is more remote than terror but a more profound threat to the future of the children and the grandchildren and the great-grandchildren I hope all of you have...It's the only thing we face today that has the power to remove the preconditions of civilized society." – Bill Clinton, former Democratic U.S. president, speaking to the graduating class at University of Texas Lyndon B. Johnson School of Public Affairs, May 21, 2006

Barack Obama- Democrat

"The science is compelling...The baseline fact of climate change is not something we can afford to deny. And if you profess leadership in this country at this moment in our history, then you've got to recognize this is going to be one of the most significant long-term challenges, if not the most significant long-term challenge, that this country faces and that the planet faces" – Barack Obama, Democratic U.S. president, as reported by Thomas L. Friedman, New York Times columnist, June 7, 2014

Ted Cruz – Republican

"Climate change is not science. It's religion." – Ted Cruz, Republican U.S. senator, as told to Glenn Beck on October 29, 2015

Paul Ryan – Republican

"Climate change occurs no matter what. The question is, can and should the federal government do something about it? And I would argue the federal government, with all its tax and regulatory schemes, can't. " – Paul Ryan, Republican Chair of the House Budget Committee, as quoted by Peter Hamby, CNN National Political Reporter, July 30, 2014

Marco Rubio – Republican

"I do not believe that human activity is causing these dramatic changes to our climate the way these scientists are portraying it." – Marco Rubio, Republican U.S. senator, as stated on ABC's *This Week* on May 11, 2014

Donald Trump – Republican
"The concept of global warming was created by and for the Chinese in order to make U.S. manufacturing non-competitive." – Donald Trump, private citizen, in a tweet on November 6, 2012

"It's really cold outside, they are calling it a major freeze, weeks ahead of normal. Man, we could use a big fat dose of global warming!" – Donald Trump, private citizen, in a sarcastic tweet on October 19, 2015.

Sometimes a platform is worth a thousand words. The following are excerpts from the Democratic and Republican party platforms of the 2016 national party conventions.

Democratic Platform – 2016
Climate change is an urgent threat and a defining challenge of our time. Fifteen of the 16 hottest years on record have occurred this century. While Donald Trump has called climate change a "hoax," 2016 is on track to break global temperature records once more.

Republican Platform – 2016
The Environmental Protection Agency has rewritten laws to advance the Democrats' climate change agenda. Climate change is far from this nation's most pressing national security issue. This is the triumph of extremism over common sense, and Congress must stop it. We reject the agendas of both the Kyoto Protocol and the Paris Agreement.

How unfortunate. One political party embraces the truth and the other vigorously denies it. Over time, unscrupulous Republican leaders have fashioned their responses in a disgraceful progression – from a denial that global warming will happen, to an acceptance that it is happening but a denial that it is due to human activity, to an acceptance that it is due to human activity but a denial that it matters.

This is a brain-teaser, a real head-scratcher. The Republican party is full of intelligent, well-educated, duly-elected leaders. Why would they ignore the truth? It is an interesting question that we will address later.

Thus, Republican climate change deniers are notable for their inertia. They are consistently one step behind the truth, like the man who believed he was a corpse, like doctors who anchor to the wrong diagnosis. Unfortunately, the stakes are much higher. A physician who ignores the truth can lose a patient; an influential world leader who ignores the truth can kill a planet.

In closing, it is worth mentioning the freshest example of the devastating consequences of a refusal to face facts: the woeful response of the Trump administration to the COVID-19 pandemic, which we will discuss at length later on. Hampered by magical thinking that the U.S. was somehow resistant to the "foreign" viral invader, a view that was reinforced by lack of epidemiological information through an inadequate testing program, President Trump remained ensnared in his self-spun fantasy of American invincibility to a worldwide threat.

While data flooded in from abroad to contradict Trump's paradigm, his persistent rejection of the truth, reinforced by reflexive praise from Republican leaders, was the root cause of an irresponsibly tepid governmental response. In this case, the avoidance of facts was materially responsible for the preventable loss of American lives.

What are we to make of a national party that cannot face reality, that cannot accept ever-increasing evidence that is crowding in from all directions, that cannot acknowledge the consensus of the international scientific community? Will anyone in the party step up, like the boy in the crowd, and expose the pretense? As a physician, I can think of no greater evidence of lack of fitness to lead than this: persistent and stubborn denial of the truth.

In this chapter, we have moved on to the science of leadership, using our lesson about facing facts as a launching pad to review a controversial national topic: climate change. We will do this again and again as we visit additional divisive themes such as income inequality, universal health care, abortion, and gun control. These will be formidable challenges for the strands in our braid. But if our lessons in leadership fail to address hotbed issues, what good are they?

It should further be noted in this shift to science that we have crossed over to the *left* side of the brain – an exercise in neural topography. While the right side of the brain is the seat of intuition, creativity, and subliminal expression, the left side remains the center for logic, math, and overt language. Art and Science. Yin and Yang. Two parts to the whole.

Discrete as they are, we frequently call upon these core functions as one to address challenging problems in a complementary way. After all, a complicated mystery patient, like Gerry Menard, and a controversial political issue, like climate change, each can tickle the mind and tug at the heart at the same time. We are most effective when we use *both* sides of our brain.

The next chapter follows directly from this one, as surely as treatment follows diagnosis. Indeed, a systematic approach always starts with the facts. So before moving on, please re-read *this* chapter to solidify the lesson. Then click your heels three times and repeat this mantra. "The correct treatment depends on the correct diagnosis." Say it again, this time with *feeling. "The correct treatment depends on the correct diagnosis."*

Then say it in a different way: "The correct decision depends on an accurate assessment of *all* the facts." Or "Be sure you're right, then go ahead." I cannot overemphasize how important it is to accept the truth. It doesn't really matter whether you are a physician or a world leader or a poor soul just trying to make it through life. If you can't face the facts, you don't have a chance.

Treatment:
Execute the Plan

Be sure you're right, then go ahead.

Davy Crockett (1786-1836)

This quote could be any physician's motto – in two parts. Be sure you're right: Make the correct diagnosis. Then go ahead: Treat the patient. Both parts have a nuance. First, don't act until you have made an apt assessment. How many times have we broken this rule? Have leapt without looking?

The second part is just as critical. Once you are sure you are right, act. How many times have we broken that rule? Have dithered while the house burnt down? Diagnosis and treatment. Inseparable twins. An essential dyad, like art and science. A systematic approach to any problem.

Sometimes after a successful but exhausting search for the truth, I sit back, stare at the diagnosis, and say "*Now* what?" Like the dog that finally catches up with the car, I am not always sure what to do with this elusive prey that I have captured through evidence, logic, and reason. For patients, thankfully, there is a well-established treatment for almost every diagnosis.

When there is a clear solution, as there was for Gerry, my patient with the heart valve infection, it is best to go straight to it. When the path forward is not so clear, as in the case of Candice, my patient with the blood clot, it is better to tread cautiously with eyes wide open, remaining fully prepared to change course if circumstances require it.

But for the leader of an organization, there is rarely a clear signpost pointing the way forward, even when a problem is accurately diagnosed and perfectly described. Quite frankly, the diagnosis may be only the beginning of a long journey in problem-solving. All that is known at this juncture is the starting point. Defining the destination and getting from point A to point B is exactly the task at hand: generating and executing the plan. The *how* of this objective is the topic of this chapter.

At this point, I should offer a disclaimer. Virtually every story I have told, and every example I have shared so far is a case gone awry. Inappropriate treatment, wayward staff, and medical mishaps seem to abound. Reading these accounts, one might think that there is an epidemic of medical errors running rampant through our hospital. You may rest assured this is not typical of patient care in our hospital or any other.

Bellevue Hospital has about 30,000 inpatient admissions and a half million outpatient visits per year. Against this number are a sprinkling of serious adverse events, which I can count on one hand, that dominate our attention and become our obsession. These, of course, are the interesting cases to talk or write about. Our fixation on these errors keeps us humble and makes us better. Thus, the persistent drive to root out errors is an attribute of a high performing organization and not a sign of inferior care.

On the contrary, our hospital works hard to constantly improve patient outcomes and prevent undesirable events. This perpetual attention to error has slowly but surely improved our performance and increased the survival rate for virtually every medical disorder we treat. In this chapter, it will be my pleasure to share some remarkable accomplishments of our hospital: the hows and whys of top performance.

In telling these stories, I hope to demonstrate that the net result of our systematic approach has been a slow and steady improvement in outcomes across all medical and surgical conditions. But none more so than for our treatment of severe sepsis.

One of the most common reasons for a patient to be admitted to the hospital is infection, especially by bacteria: germs that invade the lungs, kidneys, intestines, brain, bladder, and skin. When the infection produces serious signs of illness, such as fever, rapid heart rate, or elevated white blood cell count, we use the term *sepsis*.

When sepsis is so advanced as to affect the function of vital organs – brain, lungs, kidneys – we use the term *severe sepsis*. In this advanced stage of infection, the body's defenses have been breached, the fortress walls have crumbled, and the barbarians are pouring into the courtyard. The condition is now life-threatening. Indeed, the traditional mortality rate for severe sepsis is 30 to 50%.

It is interesting to note that in the advanced stages of sepsis, the body acts against *itself,* as immune cells release chemical substances that injure the very organs they are meant to protect. In this way, the failing host's systems turn on each other much like the political factions in our ailing nation. This self-destructive state is the harbinger of death to a septic patient and a marker for impending demise in almost any organization, large or small.

In response, the medical community has adopted international guidelines for management of severe sepsis. The recipe for "Surviving Sepsis" relies on the rapid execution of a "bundle" of interventions that are based on scientific theory (good), professional experience (better), and the objective results of medical research (best).[1]

Principles of the recommended bundle of care are regularly reviewed, updated, and re-published every few years. Currently, this bundle includes early identification of sepsis and immediate administration of fluids and antibiotics. In this bundle, the perceptive reader will recognize our familiar dyad of diagnosis and treatment, as well as our repeating theme of the systematic approach. Left brain stuff.

To promote consistent use of the bundle, we have worked hard to implement these guidelines for every patient who might *possibly* have severe sepsis. That is certainly a tall order when one considers all the different places where sepsis might be encountered – the Emergency Department, the inpatient wards, the ICU, the operating room, and even the psychiatric units.

To make matters worse, severe sepsis is often disguised as something else. Pneumonia might resemble heart failure. A kidney infection might masquerade as a kidney stone. An abdominal abscess might feign a stomach flu. It takes a sharp eye to identify severe sepsis at its earliest point and a strong process to implement the sepsis bundle consistently in every case.

To address that challenge, we assembled a swat team of professionals: physicians, nurses, and quality control experts.[2] We wrote protocols and work assignments for all the staff who might be involved in the care of such a patient – including the triage nurse who greets patients upon arrival to the ED, the laboratory technician who draws their blood, and the physician who commences treatment. We streamlined processes for lab testing, antibiotic delivery, and fluid administration, and we trained staff on the new protocols.

But, most important, the swat team met biweekly for several years to review every single case of severe sepsis, poring over the electronic medical record, carefully constructing a time-line, and identifying opportunities for improvement in our timely application of the sepsis bundle. In essence, every potential sepsis case was reviewed by a mini-RCA.

Here is a conversation that might have taken place in that biweekly meeting, a gathering of physician and nurse leaders, quality support staff, and administrators, all seated around a large table in a conference room adjacent to the Emergency Department.

"Let's review the case of medical record number 0927165. Can somebody put this up on the board, please?" A screen shot of the medical record appears on a large display mounted on the wall. "There we go. Who wants to lead this one?" One of the Emergency Department physicians raises his hand.

"This is Eugene Shaffertis, a 61 year-old male who came into the ED at 1:45pm last Tuesday with a cough. He did not have a fever at the triage desk, so the sepsis alert was not triggered at that time."

"Okay, that makes sense. Did he have a fever later on?"

"Yes, he did. Take a look at the vital signs taken at 4:08pm. Line 36. There is a temp recorded there of 101.4. That is his earliest sign of sepsis."

"Right. I see that. That would be Time Zero. Now that should have activated the flowsheet, right? Did we use the flowsheet?"

"Apparently not. We could not locate a flowsheet. But the nurse alerted the physician who activated the sepsis bundle. You can see the order for fluids and antibiotics at 4:22pm. And the nurse note shows the fluid bolus being started at 4:30."

"That is awesome! Great job everyone!" The antibiotic order was a timely response to the first sign of sepsis. One of our better efforts. Around the table, heads nod as a murmur of appreciation ripples across the room.

"So when was the bolus completed? Did we finish on time?"

"I wish we knew. Unfortunately, we can't tell when it was completed."

"Why not?"

"No flowsheet."

The discussion then turns to the flowsheet – a paper form to document the time points of our treatment. Without the flowsheet, not all the time points are captured, so we cannot prove we completed the treatments on time. The staff are so focused on treating the patient, they neglect to record the success of their efforts. For that reason, this case becomes a fallout.

The ensuing discussion of this case then becomes an exercise in how to make sure a flowsheet is started in *every* case of suspected sepsis. It is a mind-numbing detail but crucial to our success. Through this systematic review and monitoring of progress, Bellevue has done its part to promote the international sepsis guidelines in hopes of saving lives.

And the effort has paid off. Bellevue's mortality rate for severe sepsis in the 2018 report of New York State was an astounding 14%, way below the state average of 25%.[3] Of the 87 hospitals who treated more than 200 severe sepsis cases, Bellevue's rate was the absolute lowest. In view of the 450 severe sepsis cases we treat, we are saving about 50 extra lives per year compared to the performance of the average hospital in our state.

Note that the key to this performance is repeatedly to confront our gaps, week by week. The stories I share about adverse outcomes, then, must be matched against the many lives saved through careful attention to performance improvement. In fact, I will argue that our *systematic* response to adverse outcomes is exactly the key to saving those lives.

That has always been our charge, of course. Save the life. No matter who, no matter what, no matter how. Never hold back. That is our mission, after all. What is absent from the expressed objective, however, is to *coddle* the patient – to cater to our "client's" personal needs for a comfortable bed, a delicious meal, and some tender loving care. That is not how we have traditionally envisioned our mission as a safety-net hospital, not as a place where a patient would be showered with attention. Our attitude would best be expressed by the motto: "We are here to save your butt, not to kiss it."

And it showed. In the early returns of surveys completed by discharged patients, which were instituted by The Centers for Medicare & Medicaid Services (CMS) more than a decade ago, our patients, grateful or not, were unhappy with their experience. Whatever our performance in the medical realm, it was not translating into a satisfied customer.

On the general question, "How would you rate this hospital on a scale of 1-10?" only 57% of our patients gave us a top rating. The 57% was known as our top box score, the primary marker of our performance. That put us at the 35th percentile against all hospitals in New York State, which meant that nearly two-thirds of New York hospitals pleased their patients more than we did.[4] Not exactly what you would expect of a world-famous hospital with a 280-year legacy to protect.

These results definitely shook our world. We had always assumed that our patients felt grateful, if not fully indebted, for the outstanding care they received. But the surveys clearly showed otherwise. So, in the early part of 2013, we took this up as our number one goal – to improve the experience of our patients to a degree that would be reflected in our survey scores.

But how? How would we get to the root of this problem? How would we make it better? We had already learned that improving patient survey results was devilishly difficult. We knew that hospitals rarely improved their scores by more than a couple of points, and those that did usually lost their gains in the following year. For some reason, American hospitals were pretty much locked into their current performance level in patient experience.

Thus, we had to settle on a plan of action. Having no other viable alternative, we turned to a systematic approach we had successfully used to upgrade other aspects of hospital performance. A process that we had trained our leaders and our staff to employ in order to "move the needle," to bring about measurable, sustainable change. A method known as *Lean*.

Lean is a quality improvement approach that originated in the Japanese automotive industry in the 1970s. Utilizing this method, which eliminates redundancies, minimizes inventory, and emphasizes a harmonious flow of processes, Japanese car manufacturers advanced to the head of the class. They built higher quality cars with fewer manufacturing defects and grabbed market share from the traditional companies in the western world.

Over subsequent decades, the Lean approach spread across the Pacific to take root in Detroit auto companies, and then expanded to other industries. Since 2000, the Lean philosophy has seeped into the service sector, including American hospitals, where flow and efficiency are just as important as in manufacturing. In 2009, Lean came to Bellevue.

Our version of Lean always starts with some measure of performance in a major service. The first step is to define the starting point, known as the "current state," and then to specify the goal line, known as the "target state." In other words, "Where are you now?" and "Where would you like to be?" In subsequent steps we must measure the gap between our current state and the target state, and then come up with a solution to close the gap.

For example, when a patient is admitted to the hospital from the Emergency Department (ED), we would hope to assign her an inpatient bed and move her into it as quickly as possible. The amount of time this takes is called the dwell time. Not much happens during the dwell time except waiting, so it is considered a form of waste that impairs the patient's experience.

Let's say that we measure the dwell time and find it to be 4 hours on average. That is our current state. Not so good. Who would want to spend 4 hours waiting around in the ED? Let's now say that we have decided this really should be only 1 hour on average. That would be our target state. The gap, then, is 3 hours. Simple math. We need to lop off 3 hours from the dwell time.

What follows next is the "gap analysis," a highly structured review of the process from A to Z, to develop an understanding of what obstacles are standing in the way of the goal. Why *does* it take so long to move a patient to her room? At this point, it is usually necessary to draw a detailed process map, a step-by-step account of what normally happens along the way.

In this case, the map would identify a number of successive steps: the request for a bed to be assigned by the Department of Admissions, the search for a potential open bed by their staff, the discharge of the previous occupant from the potential bed, the cleaning of that bed by housekeeping, the notification of the ED that the bed is ready, the "hand-off" from the ED nurse to the ward nurse, and the actual transport of the patient to her room.

An A-to-Z map like this is always more complex than it seems at first. At each step of the way, we will ask ourselves whether the process is efficient or whether it introduces a delay through some form of wasteful inactivity. The reader may recognize this as the assessment phase – getting to a *diagnosis*.

What follows next is the *"solution approach,"* primarily expressed in terms of speculative "if-then" statements. For example: "If housekeeping staff were to be permanently stationed on each inpatient unit, then a room could be cleaned without delay following the discharge of a patient."

Or would it? These potential solutions must be tested by rapid experiments. Hence, for one day, we might assign a housekeeper to a unit to see if the idea really works. The speculation must be confirmed by a test, by proof of concept. Here, I channel the words of Franklin D. Roosevelt (FDR), perhaps our first scientific president.[5] "It is common sense to take a method and try it: if it fails, *admit it frankly* and try another. But above all, keep trying."

As complicated as this seems, all of the above steps can be done in a single week-long exercise called a Rapid Improvement Event (RIE). In an RIE, a team of front-line staff members are assigned to meet all day every day to define the target state, perform the gap analysis, come up with the solution approach, and carry out the experiments, all over a few consecutive days.

If the diagnosis is correct, and the "treatment" is administered as prescribed, the results can be highly gratifying. One of our most striking accomplishments using Lean was to reduce the average waiting time to pick up medications in the outpatient pharmacy from 3 hours to a mere 15 minutes. That result, achieved in a single week, made believers out of all of us.

In fact, Bellevue has conducted hundreds of RIEs and other projects using Lean principles and has achieved many similar successes in improving flow. So when we were confronted by patient experience scores practically demanding an intervention, we naturally turned again to Lean.

Once again, our first step was to establish our current state. That was easy enough. That was our top box score of 57%. Next, we had to establish a five-year target state, one that would be a stretch but not hopelessly beyond our grasp. After considerable debate, we settled on a top box score of 70%. This was nearly an impossible reach but would move us into the top third of hospitals in New York State, so we couldn't resist the challenge. Then we turned to the gap analysis, and this is where it really got interesting.

As is typical for a Lean exercise, we mapped out the process a patient might experience. Then we looked at each step and asked ourselves two questions. "What does the patient need for personal comfort at this step and what are we doing to meet that need?" This was not about flow, efficiency, or waste – the usual targets of Lean. We would not be using stopwatches to assess our performance. This was about *feelings*. More art than science. We would measure our progress through patient surveys. Right brain stuff.

One example of a process we examined was the admission of a patient to the hospital from the ED, this time through the eyes of the patient. What *did* the patient need during her dwell time? Upon reflection, we decided she mostly needed *information*, especially the answers to several questions: Why am I being admitted? What is wrong with me? What is going to happen next?

When we tried to determine who was currently providing those answers, we drew a blank. It did not appear to be any specific person's official job to answer these questions, and there was no standard process in place to make sure all the issues were consistently addressed.

The second necessity of this patient was to have her comfort tended to while waiting for transfer: a comfortable stretcher, a blanket, privacy, personal attention, pain relief, food, and drink. What were we doing to meet those needs? Again, we drew a blank.

Once the ED staff had decided to admit a patient, they handed her off to the inpatient team and turned their attention, understandably, to more pressing needs, such as the next sick patient coming through the front door. The inpatient team, on the other hand, typically waited until the patient was physically moved upstairs before getting involved. The patient, apparently, was in no-man's land during her dwell time

It seemed we had uncovered two major gaps in our patients' experience. No one was giving them the information they needed, and no one was tending to their comfort while they waited to be moved to their destination. This was surprising and disheartening. Apparently, we were so focused on the medical condition, we forgot about the patient.

And it just got worse from there. Once the patient arrived on the floor, there was no proper welcome by the staff and no orientation. No explanation of the visiting hours. No attempt by staff to reach family members. And so on. Everyone had a *medical* job to do, but no one had a responsibility to meet the patient's *personal* needs.

This deficit in personal attention characterized not only the admitting process but every other hospital experience: food service, medication administration, diagnostic tests, medical procedures, and discharge to home. Over and over we kept discovering that all of our processes centered on delivering excellent medical care and ignored the patient's experience. No wonder our patients were unhappy. No one was tending to their happiness!

Our Lean process did a great job diagnosing the problem. The next step was to come up with the solution approach – our "treatment." So we revisited each deficit in the process and came up with an idea about how to improve it. Typically, we would identify a staff member who would be responsible and then gave that individual new tasks to address the gap. We called these tasks "standard work." We came to realize that standard work was the key to systematic implementation of the new work flow, just as in a five-star hotel that trains staff to consistently meet the needs of its guests.

For example, we gave the ED physician the standard work of informing the patient he was being admitted and why. We gave the ED nurse the standard work of tending to her admitted patient while he remained in the ED. And we gave the ward nurse the standard work of how to welcome a new patient. We even wrote a script, word for word, for the initial conversation.

We tackled process after process, identified gaps, created standard work with scripts, and then trained the staff. We did this upon admission, upon discharge, when being transported, when being x-rayed, when having blood drawn, and for the handling of personal property, delivery of snacks, rounding by the nurses, activation of the television, and many more. But none of our projects were more revealing than the one on television use.

In the deep dive of this RIE, we learned that our hospital contracted with a private vendor to provide television service, but the process was haphazard in the eyes of the patient. Patients who were admitted in the evening had to wait until morning to turn on their television, patients who were moved from one room to another lost the service they had paid for, and a large number of patients simply had no money at all to pay for a television, so they lay in bed all day staring at the ceiling – completely bored.

We had never thought about this before. Some of our patients don't even have five dollars to their name. We solved the problem by eliminating the vendor and the payment. Free TV for everyone!

So, what was the impact? How did all the RIEs affect the surveys? The answer is really quite remarkable. Beginning in the first year of our work, the patient surveys began to return with an uptick in scores – small improvements, but steady and incremental. Over the full five years, the small increments snowballed into enormous advances. Let's take a look at the evidence.

In the following graph, the height of the bar is the top box score, the percent of patients who rated us as a top hospital, starting in 2012 at 57.3%. By the end of 2017, this had improved to 68.5%, just a hair below our 70% goal, a whopping 11% improvement over the starting point.

The continuous line displays our percentile ranking in New York State, which improved from the 35th percentile to the 64th percentile during this five-year period. This means we leapfrogged 30% of the hospitals in the state. Not quite to goal, but a huge improvement, nonetheless.[6]

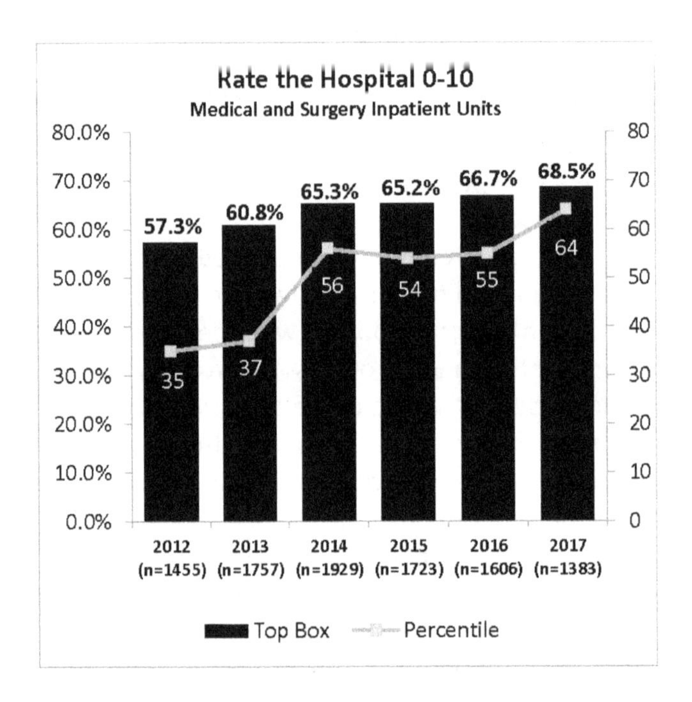

What was the key to our success? It was the very logical three-step approach that we borrowed from Lean and had used successfully for severe sepsis and pharmacy waits: Establish a target state. Analyze the gap. Institute a solution approach. The process is so straightforward, so sensible, so plainly logical, it is hard to imagine doing it any other way.

And it did not happen all at once. The gains were agonizingly slow and deliberate – an accumulation of incremental tiny steps that slowly but surely climbed the mountain. I am reminded by the phrase coined by Woody Hayes, legendary football coach for the Ohio State Buckeyes, to describe his team's offense: "Three yards and a cloud of dust." Repeat as many times necessary to reach the end zone.

Do we see this systematic approach driving the levers of government? Do national leaders set targets, measure gaps, and implement a plan for improvement? Not that I can see. Not in the House. Not in the Senate. Not in the Oval Office. At this high level, I do not sense that our nation is being led by any sort of rational process like Lean. Let's review an example.

Practically as soon as the Affordable Care Act passed into law, the Republican opposition began plotting its demise. Over and over again, more than fifty times in three years, the Republican majority in the House passed bills that would repeal, amend, or replace Obamacare. Replace with what? What was the new target state? What was the new destination for our health care system?

Actually, there wasn't any. At no time did Republicans agree on a new plan for addressing the plight of the uninsured. Some felt that coverage should be neither mandatory nor subsidized by the government. Others felt there should be bare-bones coverage requiring a greater contribution from the patient. Yet others felt the government had no role in health care at all.

We will take a closer look at the specifics of Obamacare in a later chapter, but one thing is clear in reviewing the Republican response. *They could not agree on a target state.* They knew what they did *not* want, Obamacare, but they did not know what they *did* want.

Without a target state, without a *mission*, there was no compass setting to aim at, no goal line to strive for, no destination to march toward. Without a target state, there was not even a gap to measure, much less analyze or eliminate. It is not surprising that the effort to repeal Obamacare failed. How do you set your GPS navigator when you can't even plug in an address?

When we extend our focus beyond health care, toward the usual hot-bed issues, there is absolutely no consensus on a target state, and therefore no hope of addressing the gap. Do we want 50 million uninsured Americans or 20 million? Lower taxes on the rich or broad-based prosperity? Corporate deregulation or environmental protection? Dare I mention climate change?

Can you imagine if we were to address climate change with a systematic approach? Agree on a target state? Analyze the gap? Identify a solution approach? Then, march forward, step by step, continuously measuring our progress, constantly adjusting our approach, and always sharing our status transparently with the electorate? There is no problem we could not solve.

But until we come to consensus on a target state, there is no point in discussing how to close the gap, much less in planning how to implement a solution approach. To make matters worse, political opponents don't even agree upon the facts that describe our *current* state (again, see previous chapter on climate change). We can't even agree on who we *are*!

The situation appears bleak, but there is a glimmer of hope. As unlikely as it may seem, I do believe it is possible to agree on a compass setting for our nation, one that most Americans can agree on. Hence, in the final chapters of this book, I will suggest a target state and a solution approach for our nation. In this respect, I will emulate at the national level the method for improving performance that hospitals have successfully employed on their own.

It is worth noting that the systematic approach we have seen in these examples is a scientific principle that originated with the earliest traditions of the medical profession. The same strict, steadfast, methodical routine applied to every ailing patient is ingrained in all aspiring physicians through four years of medical school and at least three subsequent years of training.

Medical history, physical exam, test results, diagnosis, and treatment – the well-tempered quintet – always in that order, each step with its own multi-part sequence. Gather information before making conclusions. Make conclusions before taking action. First diagnose, then treat. We have repeated this instruction set thousands of times. By the end of our training, we can do it in our sleep. Why? What is the point of this obsessive conformity?

First, it works. The systematic approach, which is our second major theme, represents the accumulated wisdom of centuries of Medicine – a universal best method that has improved slowly through continual refinement. It makes sense that everyone should adopt the consensus standard rather than try to invent their own. We will see the wisdom of this when we apply the systematic approach to our nation's chronic illness in the final chapters.

Second, the systematic approach yields reproducible results, which give our work consistency. It is deliberate, not impulsive. Premeditated, not reactive. Predictable, not capricious. In patient care, physician training, and medical education, we are all speaking the same language. As a result, the systematic approach has supported the advancement of Medicine as a *profession* – with identifiable, verifiable, and repeatable standards.

Finally, as demonstrated here, health care organizations have adopted the systematic approach for their own purposes – to promote quality and safety. Principles of safe care have evolved into well-defined rules of organizational management, which have been developed, refined, and disseminated throughout our nation's hospitals and account for the high standards of performance that drive the health care industry forward.

In the preceding two chapters, we reviewed the simple sequence of decision-making practiced by physicians since the age of Hippocrates: Diagnosis and Treatment. Assessment and Plan. The One-Two Step. These two lessons, if practiced consistently together, will ensure a cohesive and systematic approach to decision-making that is essential to effective leadership and necessary for organizational success.

But not sufficient. Necessary, but not sufficient.

In addition to these two historic elements, we must introduce a novel implement of the modern era, a layer of complexity that is a byproduct of the information age, a new standard of decision-making that delves deeply into the rich interior of our collective experience. In my field, this approach is known as Evidence-Based Medicine, and it has revolutionized the practice of physicians over the past three decades.

Our charge, then, is to master the principles of evidence-based *leadership.* In the next chapter we will start in a familiar place – the bedside. We will later transition to the political domain, where we will practice the principle in order to imbed the lesson. Finally, as proof of concept, in the closing chapters we will discover that the solution approach to America's mysterious malady rests entirely on relevant, measurable, and verifiable evidence.

Evidence:
Respect the Truth

Conch shell lies face down
in wet sand. Hard,
like clenched fist,
its flaccid contents
rotted or consumed...

Siphonal canal once meant
for the flow of pearly salt
from ocean swells,
ends now as lifeless petal,
barely bloomed.

From *Heart Attack*, Mara Feingold—Link, 2015[1]

"So how's everything going?"

"Great"

"Any problems you would like to discuss?"

"Nope"

"Really? Nothing? No issues with your medications?"

"Nope"

"Did you take them this morning?"

"Nope"

Stanley Loritan wasn't a conversationalist, but at least he was honest.

"Really? Why not this morning?"

"I wanted you to see what my blood pressure really is."

"I do want to see what your blood pressure really is. But I already know it's high when you don't take your meds. I want to see what it is when you do take your meds. Like I explained the last time." (and the time before that!)

"Sorry"

Why did he always do this? Skip his meds on the day of the visit. Surely, he was not *trying* to vex me. Not *hoping* to deny me the satisfaction of seeing the impact of my treatment. Like so many of my patients, Stan assumed I wanted a "pure" blood pressure reading – a result that was not tainted by the medication. I know he was just trying to please me, so I am ashamed to make this confession: sometimes I felt I would rather he take his meds on the day of the visit than all the days in between.

"How about the other days? Have you been taking your meds on all the other days?"

"Nope"

In 1983, during my first year of training, I attended the Primary Care Clinic on the second floor of Bellevue's main hospital building. Here I managed the equivalent of a private practice in order to master the skills of outpatient Medicine.

My patients had chronic conditions typically treated by practitioners of my specialty: high blood pressure, diabetes, asthma, emphysema, and heart disease.[2] They were ethnically diverse and often financially disadvantaged. Bellevue attracted them because we were willing to charge a price based on their income. If they could not pay the fee, we would see them anyway. That was our mission, after all: treat everyone without exception.

These patients would travel across the city by bus or subway, take the elevator to the second floor, and stand in a long line to register at the front desk of our clinic. Then they would sit in our packed waiting room, often with purses or shopping bags full of medication bottles, sometimes in winter coats with hats and scarves, and occasionally with grandchildren in strollers at their side – anticipating their visit with me, their doctor.

I was supervised by an attending physician who was on the faculty of NYU School of Medicine, Bellevue's next-door neighbor to the north. All our attendings retained faculty appointments at the medical school, which had, and still has, a contractual relationship with the hospital to provide physician services. NYU and Bellevue have been married in this way since 1841.[3]

In fact, I could easily imagine NYU, private medical school, as my father, and Bellevue, public urban hospital, as my mother. Fortunately, it has always been a healthy marriage, and we remain a happy family, but I knew then and still know now that if my parents ever divorced, my mother would get full custody. For me, it was always about Bellevue.

One of my longstanding patients was Stanley Loritan, an elderly gentleman with severely high blood pressure (BP). He lived in Manhattan's Lower East Side with no close friends or relatives, and no income to speak of. He was a short, stocky man of 70 years and always wore the same plaid suit and a fedora, which he would place on my desk as we chatted during our visits.

"So why haven't you been taking your medications? Did you have trouble filling your prescription?"

"Nope."

"You have all the meds at home?"

"Yep."

"So why not?"

"I just keep forgetting...Sorry."

Whenever Stan spoke, he would tilt his head back, look up at the ceiling, and tightly close his eyes, which were magnified by thick-lensed dark-rimmed glasses. Although I was treating him with several medications at once, his BP remained stubbornly elevated because of his poor adherence to treatment. For whatever reason, he just simply could not, or would not, remember to take his medications.

At every clinic visit it was the same story: first he would claim everything was just fine, then I would discover that his BP was sky high, say 180/110, and finally he would fess up. And then he would apologize, with his face turned up to the ceiling and eyes tightly shut, as if he was squeezing out the truth one word at a time.

Poor adherence to treatment was hardly unusual in my practice, which included patients from all possible points of origin: immigrants, international visitors, even people from the street. And patients with enormous behavioral health challenges: depression, alcoholism, and drug use.

But non-adherence to BP meds was especially important. Of all the relationships in Medicine, the link between blood pressure and stroke is one of the strongest. It is defined by a very simple metric. For every 6-point reduction in the diastolic BP, the risk of stroke goes down by 30%.

The diastolic BP is the bottom number, the 110 in Stan's reading. Cut it to 104, and the risk of stroke goes down by 30%. Drop it to normal, and you have decreased the risk by 75%. Leave it alone, and the risk stays sky high. Franklin Delano Roosevelt's BP was 240/130 during the months prior to his fatal cerebral hemorrhage. Lack of effective treatment killed our president – the biological equivalent of a political assassination.

Stan was exasperating beyond measure. He was an English-speaking, native New Yorker with a stable home and no special obstacles in the way of his adherence to treatment. I could not believe he could so calmly admit to his noncompliance and continue to ignore my advice.

Thus, each clinic session ended with my stern lecture on the risk of a stroke from uncontrolled blood pressure. Stan always listened intently and ended the session with a sincere apology and a promise to do better. But he never kept his promise.

During one memorable visit, Stan's BP reached the Rooseveltian threshold of 240/130, a level so dangerously high that I decided to admit him to the hospital. Fortunately, I was currently serving a stint on 16 North, one of Bellevue's inpatient units, so I was able to place him under my own care, which would give me a chance to observe him firsthand on the hospital ward.

During the second evening following his admission, one of the nurses summoned me to Stan's room because he was experiencing pain across his chest. Chest pain was a common symptom among Bellevue inpatients, so I was prepared to perform my standard three-part assessment: review of his symptoms, physical examination, and electrocardiogram (EKG). Fortunately, this routine complaint usually did not turn out to be anything serious – often just acid reflux, musculoskeletal pain, or anxiety.

However, when I entered Stan's room, I could immediately sense that this was not the usual chest pain call. He was lying face-up in bed, agitated and restless. There were tiny beads of sweat on his forehead, and he visibly struggled to breathe while writhing in his sheets. He was so distracted by his discomfort that I had trouble gaining his attention.

I asked him a few questions, briefly examined him, and then quickly wheeled in the EKG machine from the nursing station. While Stan continued to squirm, I unbuttoned his damp shirt and hurriedly applied the leads with elastic bands and suction cups: one on each bare wrist and ankle, and six across his chest.

The leads were attached to the main unit with long insulated wires, ten in all, arrayed across his torso and extremities like long, slender tentacles embracing a victim. When I turned on the machine, a thin band of paper rolled across the top, over the side, and onto the floor – like ticker tape at the stock exchange. I gathered the tape from the floor and examined the result.

Running across the strip was the familiar tracing of the heart's electrical activity with one obvious deviation from normal. In several leads, the "ST segment" was markedly shifted upward. This was a classic finding that is practically the first EKG abnormality ever taught to medical students, so recognizable that I could identify it immediately.

Stan was having an acute myocardial infarction, a classic heart attack, and he was having it right in front of me. I instantly knew this was a life-threatening emergency. Hence, without hesitation, I did what four years of medical school education and nine months of hospital training had taught me to do in this exact situation: I called my supervising resident for help.

As every medical student learns early on, the heart is a muscular pump about the size of a clenched fist. With each heartbeat, it propels blood into the aorta, the main arterial trunk, which then distributes the blood throughout the body via the vessels of the circulatory system. The steady flow of this vital elixir – blood cells and plasma proteins suspended in salt water – supplies oxygen and nutrients to all our cells, tissues, and organs.

What is not so obvious is that the heart must siphon off blood back to *itself,* an export tax of sorts, to nourish the pump. Toward that end, two small vessels branch off the aorta just outside the heart. They circle back to the outer surface of the heart, giving rise to even smaller branches that penetrate and feed the heart muscle itself. These are the coronary arteries.

When a coronary artery becomes narrowed due to atherosclerosis, the portion of heart muscle normally fed by that vessel suffers from decreased blood flow and oxygen delivery, a condition known as ischemia. This may cause the patient to feel chest pain, also known as angina, during exercise.

In the worst-case scenario, the narrowing of the artery can progress to a full-blown obstruction, which can happen suddenly if a blood clot forms in the narrowest section. That would be like a farm field being deprived of water from an obstruction in the lead irrigation pipe. Almost immediately, the plantings would begin to suffer. Within days, the crops would wither and die unless the water flow could be promptly restored.

Similarly, when the coronary obstruction becomes complete, the heart muscle is totally deprived of oxygen and begins to complain loudly in the form of severe crushing chest pain that sometimes radiates down the left arm. The patient might report this as the worst pain he has ever experienced. If he is lucky, it won't be the *last* pain he ever experiences.

The pain may persist for hours until that portion of muscle tissue dies, turning into a lifeless, flaccid scar that may permanently impact heart function, depending on its size. At that point, the pain subsides. We call this event a myocardial infarction (MI), and this is what was happening to Stan as I stood at the bedside.

The modern approach to the treatment of an MI is to try to reverse the process – to immediately reopen the obstructed blood vessel and restore blood flow. At minimum, we will give the patient aspirin, which is a type of blood thinner, to inhibit further clot formation. We will supplement this treatment with additional medications to lower the stress on the heart and improve the patient's chance of survival.

Even better, we will infuse t-PA, a so-called "clotbuster" drug, to immediately *dissolve* the clot before its impact on the heart muscle reaches the point of no return. This would be the medical equivalent of pouring liquid Drano into the obstructed irrigation pipe – to restore flow before the plants even begin to wilt.

If possible, and best of all, we will rush the patient into a cardiac catheterization laboratory where specialists will insert a hollow wire (catheter) through the skin into a blood vessel of the arm or leg, then thread the catheter back up through that vessel into the aorta, and then gently guide it into the obstructed coronary artery where it can disrupt the clot and expand the vessel with a tiny balloon, the medical equivalent of a Roto-Rooter.

After restoring blood flow and oxygen to the starving heart muscle, the specialist will leave a tiny mesh metal tube (stent) in place to keep the artery open. This amazing procedure is known as a percutaneous coronary intervention (PCI). If the vessel can be opened within 90 minutes after the patient arrives in the ED (the "door-to-balloon" time), the patient has an excellent chance of surviving the event with minimal impact. This is the modern approach to an acute MI.

At Stan's bedside in 1983, I did not administer aspirin. I did not chase it with medications to reduce stress on the heart. I did not prescribe T-PA, nor did I rush the patient to the cath lab for the occluded blood vessel to be opened with a PCI. I did none of the above.

Instead, I followed my supervisor's instructions and administered the four treatments that were the standard of care for treatment of a heart attack way back in 1983. I gave him morphine to relieve his pain, oxygen to fortify his blood cells, nitroglycerin to dilate his coronary vessels, and the only treatment that could conceivably improve his chance of survival: lidocaine.

Lidocaine is a drug that stabilizes the heart rhythm to prevent one of the most dreaded complications of a myocardial infarction: ventricular fibrillation ("v. fib"). In this event, the electrical system of the heart suddenly goes haywire as the steady electrical impulses of the heartbeat give way to a chaotic cloud of electrical activity leaving the heart muscle a quivering mass.

The result is immediate and complete loss of heart function and sudden death of the patient unless the proper impulse can be restored with an electric shock administered by the external paddles from a defibrillator.

I gave lidocaine to Stan because I had learned that it could stabilize the heart rhythm and might possibly prevent this catastrophic outcome. I also gave lidocaine because I knew that failing to administer this highly accepted treatment would leave me with some serious explaining to do on morning rounds. If there was one thing I had learned as an intern, it was not to question the party line.

Why did I not provide the other treatments that I have described above? Suffice it to say that those treatments were not known to be effective in 1983. Even aspirin, which had been used for more than a hundred years as a treatment for fever and arthritic pain, was not yet known to have a useful role in coronary artery disease.

So Stan received none of the above modern treatments. Nonetheless, he had a reasonably successful outcome. We moved him to the coronary care unit and continued our treatments while his infarction completed its course and his chest pain resolved. We discharged him from the hospital about two weeks later in good condition.

Cardiac tests before discharge showed that Stan's heart was not pumping as strongly as before, because the portion of heart muscle that was affected by the obstruction had turned into a scar, as expected. Nonetheless, he got along well enough. He remained my clinic patient until he succumbed to a stroke at age 78.

I cannot say our response to Stan's health event would have won any awards. Fortunately, our treatment of heart attacks has come a long way since 1983, leading to spectacular improvements in survival. The advances in outcomes are largely due to a movement that started in the early 1980s, gained momentum over the next two decades, and now sets the standard for decision-making across the health care continuum. That movement is known as "Evidence-Based Medicine."

The goal of an evidence-based approach is to rest treatment strategies on hard facts that are gathered carefully through a rigorous process of investigation - so that medical decisions can rest on a solid foundation of confirmed information – i.e., the truth.

Although medical care has always been informed by science, the previous standard for evidence was not so rigorous as it is today, and published research did not always adhere to the highest standards. Moreover, most physicians drew their knowledge from textbooks, which were written by experts, of course, but relied excessively upon personal knowledge and opinion, even speculation.

More to the point, differences of opinion at the bedside were settled by the academic hierarchy. Senior physicians ruled over juniors who outranked the residents. Usually, the most experienced professor had the final word.

Sometimes, however, the difference of opinion was settled by personality. Whoever spoke the most definitively and confidently (or the most loudly and obnoxiously) carried the day. Worst of all was the "Trumpian" alpha male who blustered made-up facts with absolute conviction and lured unsuspecting colleagues into his pretend world of truth.

Evidence-Based Medicine replaced this "might-makes-right" approach with a *new* paradigm, a world in which facts rule over opinions, and evidence drives out speculation. Above all, it is a world where objective reasoning dominates dogma. In this world there is no room for "fake news."

In the remaining part of this chapter, I will review in some detail how evidence-based principles advanced the medical profession, continuing with the case of Stan Loritan. I will follow this, in Chapter 10, with an example of how these principles might be applied in national governance. Indeed, I will attempt to emulate the paradigm of evidence-based decision making throughout the remainder of this book.

The first giant step forward in advancing treatment of acute MI was a landmark study published in 1988. ISIS-2, the Second International Study of Infarct Survival, was conducted in several European countries over a 5-year period.[4] The two important facts established by this study altered our treatment of heart attacks forever.

ISIS-2 was a randomized trial, the most rigorous method for assessing a treatment. In brief, the study subjects were adults who showed up in emergency rooms with signs and symptoms suggestive of a heart attack. If the treating physician concluded they were having a myocardial infarction based on the presenting EKG, they were invited to participate in the study. These simple criteria for entry made the results of the study applicable to virtually any patient with a presumed infarction.

The study was designed to measure the impact of two medications that could potentially clear an acute coronary obstruction: aspirin, which prevents blood clot formation, and streptokinase, the original "clot-buster" drug that can dissolve the clot *after* it forms.

The 17,200 subjects who were enrolled in the study were each randomly and secretly assigned to one of four groups. Group 1 was given an aspirin tablet *and* a streptokinase injection. Group 2 received only an aspirin tablet. Group 3 was given only a streptokinase injection. Group 4 received neither treatment. By the clever use of placebo (dummy) tablets and injections, the researchers were able to disguise the treatments, so that subjects could not tell which group they were assigned to. Nor could their physicians.

Thus, by random assignment, every subject received aspirin, streptokinase, both, or neither. The purpose of making the assignments randomly (by the equivalent of a coin flip) was to make sure there was no bias in those assignments – so the four groups would be alike in every way. Elimination of bias was the fundamental goal of this study design.

Hence, any difference in outcomes could be attributed solely to the treatment that was administered. To decide which treatment was better, the researchers compared mortality rates among the four assigned groups. This method of research, known as a randomized controlled trial (RCT), remains the gold standard for gathering evidence in medicine.

Notably, the study focused only on mortality – the ultimate outcome. No effort was wasted looking at minor, transient, or secondary effects of treatment, such as cardiac symptoms, heart function, or patient experience. If the treatment failed to save lives, the researchers weren't interested.

And the results were crystal clear. Among the completely untreated subjects, 13.2% died. Of those who received aspirin only, 10.7% died. Of those who received streptokinase only, 10.4% died. Of those who received both in tandem, 8.0% died. So aspirin and streptokinase were roughly equally effective as single agents, and even more so in combination.

Or to put it another way: if 100 patients with a suspected MI were to receive *both* treatments together, 5 lives would be saved, because only 8 patients would die instead of 13. In relative terms, there would be nearly 40% fewer deaths overall. That would be a stupendous advance in the treatment of MIs. Since the treatments were inexpensive and safe, this was a no-brainer.

As a blinded, randomized trial, the results of the study were unassailable. And the significance cannot be overstated. From the moment this study was published, aspirin and streptokinase became the new standard of care for treatment of MI among cardiologists around the world.

Over subsequent decades, new trials identified other treatments such as beta-blockers and ACE-inhibitors, which could save even more lives when given in combination with aspirin and clot-busters. And streptokinase was overtaken by t-PA, an even more powerful clot-buster – proven in an RCT.

Subsequent advances, such as rapid transfer from the ED triage nurse directly to the cardiac cath lab for a PCI ("from door to balloon") have dropped this mortality rate to its astonishingly low current level of 4%, just by chipping away at mortality 1% at a time.[5] Nowadays, if you can make it to the hospital alive, your chances of surviving a heart attack are approaching 100%. What a tribute to the evidence-based approach!

So whatever happened to lidocaine? Remember, this was the one treatment in 1983 that everyone agreed could *definitely* improve Stan's chance of survival. However, when the true effect of lidocaine was finally assessed through randomized trials of MI treatments during the 1980s, it was determined *not* to improve outcomes. In fact, it appeared to be harmful.[6] Ironically, the only "truth" I knew in 1983 turned out not to be true after all!

The evidence-based approach has given us an effective remedy for "truthiness," as Stephen Colbert would say. It is also a useful antidote to speculation, even when that speculation is seemingly based on scientific knowledge. Just as important, a solid foundation of evidence gives new meaning as to who has "standing."

As I noted earlier, in days of old, the final word was always given by the senior person at the bedside. The patriarch. The alpha male. As the universally respected oracle, his word was taken as gospel. The rise of the evidence-based approach changed all this.

In the modern world, might does not make right. Credibility comes not from one's standing in the hierarchy, but rather from standing on the secure foundation of medical evidence. The gray-haired senior physician might have a great deal of personal experience using streptokinase, but if there is unassailable evidence favoring the use of t-PA, that truth drives hospital policy.

Therefore, the pharmacy director, hospital administrator, or even the lowly intern, has "standing" to assert that t-PA should be used if that claim is based on well-designed randomized trials. Evidence trumps experience and drives the decision about treatment.

You can imagine how difficult this transition was for the medical profession, formerly a hide-bound tradition-based old-boys network, an exclusive club where credibility understandably came from seniority, academic rank, and personal accomplishment.

Indeed, there was initially some resistance to the new world order exactly where you would expect to find it – in the upper echelons of the specialties – where traditions were the most entrenched, and where the most senior physicians ruled the roost. For that reason, the evidence-based revolution was started primarily by non-specialists – a grass roots movement by medical generalists, who were pioneers, searching for a better way.

But in the end, it was specialists who gave the evidence-based movement its biggest boost. It was the leaders of professional specialty organizations who collectively reviewed the research literature and created the most comprehensive national guidelines, such as the sepsis bundles, for practice within their respective branches of Medicine.

Today, the most dependable guidelines are meticulously researched and backed by hundreds of citations, while still being subjected to consensus among national experts. In this way, we have the best of both worlds – evidence *and* experience. And there is very little room for speculation in these highly influential recommendations.

Whenever a guideline is based on consensus opinion because of the lack of applicable studies, this is clearly stated and fully transparent to the reader. In this way, the dissemination of information and advice has become *systematized.* In this paradigm, fortunately, there is no place for "fake news." In the current culture of medical practice, everything rests on an objective truth. Can you imagine our political world meeting this standard?

I am also pleased to report that experience still matters. Certainly, I would much rather be treated by a senior cardiologist than a new graduate. But I would even *more* prefer to have a senior cardiologist who keeps abreast of the latest scientific knowledge emanating from clinical trials than one who bases all her treatment decisions purely on her own personal experience.

And when that cardiologist makes a bold assertion about the best treatment for my condition, it is absolutely appropriate for me to put her on the spot. How does she know that is so? On what evidentiary basis has she made this assertion? Where is the beef?

The question of standing applies to me as well, as *author*, especially when I step more deeply into the political realm – as I will in upcoming chapters. What right have I to comment on national topics from my safety-net hospital soapbox, from my *physician's* perspective? Where is *my* beef?

That is a fair question. My answer is that you, the reader, should hold me accountable for every assertion I make, as if I were a physician treating your life-threatening condition. You should expect me to base my claims on facts and to name my sources.

So, I intend to do exactly that – to meet that reasonable expectation. When I make claims about non-scientific topics, I intend to stand upon a solid foundation of evidence, and not upon my accumulated feelings, opinions, and personal experiences. That would be true even if I were a veteran politician. By all means, please hold me to that evidence-based standard.

We have completed our review of the three-step systematic approach to decision-making: setting a target state (mission), analyzing the gap (diagnosis), and developing a solution approach to close that gap (treatment) – all informed by the available evidence. This is all logical and good. But is it complete? Is it all we need before we move on to our solution approach?

Most definitely not. There is much more to great leadership than a systematic approach to decision-making. Effective governance depends upon relationships between leaders and their constituents, just as effective doctoring rests upon rapport between physicians and their patients.

In our next section, we will return to attributes of governance that promote relationships. These are the soft and subtle skills that complement the science by introducing the human factor. The nuance. The intangible. In other words, the *art* of leadership. We will start with one that is dear to the heart of every member of the health profession: *compassion.*

Compassion:
Ease the Suffering

Almost none of the ill survived past the fourth day. In all the city, there was nothing to do but to carry the dead to a burial...And many died with no one looking after them. And many died of hunger... Abandoned by people, without food, but accompanied by fever, they weakened...Many died unseen. So they remained in their beds until they stank.

> Marchione di Coppo Stefani (1336-1385)
> on the Black Plague, in *Cronaca fiorentia,*
> *Rerum italicarum Scriptores, Vol. 30.,*
> *ed. Niccolo Rodolico. Citta di Castello: 1903-13.*

"We always start morning rounds at 7:30 in the 16 East Doctor's Station. Just make sure you've seen all your patients beforehand."

"Okay, thanks." I looked down at the handwritten names of my new charges. "So this is it? Just ten patients? Doesn't seem so bad to me."

"Don't worry. They'll keep you hopping from sunup to sundown."

"Okay. I'll take your word for it. And what are the asterisks for?"

"Oh, yeah, those. Those are your five patients with AIDS."

I looked up, puzzled. "AIDS? Should I know what that means?"

Brian silently looked me over, incredulous at my ignorance. "Really? You haven't heard of AIDS?" His eyes widened as he read my blank expression. "Sweet Jesus! St. Louis must be farther away than I thought!"

I bristled. "Well, isn't that why I'm here, after all? To learn at the Mecca?" My sarcasm was only half in jest. In fact, I came to Bellevue for exactly this reason. For the zebras: the mysterious, rare, and exotic cases that would challenge my clinical skills and stretch my imagination.

"You poor thing! You really have no idea, do you?" Brian's sympathetic expression turned into a mischievous grin. "Oh, you're at the mecca all right," he continued. His grin widened as he leaned forward and hissed in a low voice for dramatic effect. "The mecca of AIDS."

I earned my medical degree from Washington University School of Medicine in St. Louis in 1983. In my fourth and final year of medical school, I applied for a three-year residency position for training in my specialty – Internal Medicine. As a medical student, I had acquired most of my clinical experience at the major private hospitals of the university. But I had also spent some time at St. Louis City Hospital, a sprawling, aging complex deeply imbedded in the urban landscape. It was a deteriorating structure that would eventually close, but for me it was a place full of wonder.

The patients were poverty-stricken. Their medical problems were complex. Their social histories were captivating. And I felt I could make a difference. Because the hospital was so understaffed and resources so limited, the contributions of medical students had a noticeable impact on patient care. This was a huge contrast to a private hospital, in which medical students largely felt invisible. Based on this clinical experience, I knew that I wanted to do my post-graduate training in an urban public hospital.

To my delight, I matched at NYU-Bellevue for my residency training.[1] New York University was a highly regarded medical school with a 140 year-long relationship with Bellevue Hospital, the flagship of New York City's public hospital system. Here, I would have a chance to learn from NYU professors in the setting of Bellevue's outpatient clinics and inpatient wards.

No doubt I would dive deep into the clinical and social challenges of New York's indigent patients, who hailed from the far reaches of the earth, whose life stories would endlessly fascinate me, and whose medical conditions would present great challenges and unique opportunities for learning. Little did I know I was about to step into the epicenter of one of the great and terrible health epidemics of the 20th century.

From my sequestered life as a medical student in the Midwest in the spring of 1983, I had no inkling of the advent of Acquired Immune Deficiency Syndrome (AIDS) in New York City. But for two years now, a mysterious illness had been stalking gay men, resulting in highly unusual presentations of rare conditions such as pneumocystis pneumonia (PCP), a lung infection normally seen only in patients with advanced cancer, and Kaposi's sarcoma (KS), a skin cancer characterized by purplish lesions all over the body.

Both of these diseases were extremely rare under normal conditions, but since 1981 they were afflicting gay men with increasing frequency.

They were also the harbinger of death. Patients with these conditions would typically go on to suffer from a chronic wasting illness that ended in the demise of the patient within one year or less.

Imagine my surprise when I arrived at Bellevue and reported for my first clinical assignment on the inpatient service. My supervising resident handed me the list of my patients, and I noted that several were marked with an asterisk. These were patients who were dying from AIDS.

Amazingly, prior to that moment, I had never even heard of AIDS. My resident was stupefied by my ignorance. He laid out the unadorned truth. These men are all dying, he said. They are wasting away – just melting into their beds. They will be our patients until they expire, he predicted.

Sure enough, when I went to the bedside, I found these patients to be mere skeletons – thin, emaciated, with parched lips, vacant eyes, and hollow temples – the familiar visage of an end-stage cancer patient just before death. Their sparse hair was falling out, and their dry skin was flaking away. They responded feebly to questions with barely the strength to drink from a straw. Their faint, fetid breath would not bring fog to a mirror.

These were hollow men, pale ghosts of their former selves. And they were half my patients. The other half were patients with diseases of the heart, lungs, and liver – the usual fare for an Internal Medicine resident. For the remainder of my training, this would be the ratio: half and half.

At that time, AIDS had a name, but no one knew how the immune deficiency was acquired or why it specifically singled out gay men or intravenous (IV) drug users.[2] There was a theory going around that individuals who used intravenous drugs and men who had sex with men were exposing their bodies to a bombardment of foreign substances (antigens) that were somehow breaking down their immune systems. Unless you practiced those behaviors, you could not get AIDS.

This was wishful thinking, however. Much more likely was that AIDS was caused by a novel infectious agent, transmitted by either sexual contact (gay men) or by blood exposure (IV drug users). This was not a popular theory among my colleagues in the training program, however. If AIDS were caused by a transmissible disease, then it would be contagious. A contagious disease could be spread theoretically to anyone, including us.

During that first month of my internship year, one of my patients was Vigo Ferness, a 40 year-old man with AIDS, which he had contracted through his use of intravenous heroin injections. He was not so emaciated as the others, but he had a fever from some unknown source. Because of abnormalities in blood tests of his liver, Vigo underwent a biopsy to determine if an infection was lurking there.

The biopsy was done by inserting a large needle into the upper area of his abdomen, through the skin and directly into his liver, to remove a tiny piece of tissue. We hoped that the laboratory would be able to identify an infection in this sample. With a proper diagnosis, we would be able to administer the correct treatment. As one can imagine, the most serious possible complication of this exercise was internal (i.e., invisible) bleeding, so it was important to perform blood tests afterward to make sure the blood count remained stable.

The day of the procedure, I happened to be on-call, which meant that I would stay overnight to watch over all my patients plus the patients of two of my colleagues. By alternating this role every three nights in rotation, the three of us would provide 24-hour coverage for each other's patients.

During these nights on call there was no rest for the weary. We not only watched over our own patients and our partners' patients, we also accepted new admissions through the Emergency Department and covered the Intensive Care Units. Typically, we would get no more than an hour or two of sleep, and then we would work all day the next day until the evening. These 36-hour shifts were typical of residency training in those days.

Thus, on the evening following Vigo's procedure, it was my job to draw his blood and check the results. At around 10 pm, I drew the blood sample and took it to the lab. Two hours later, the result was disconcerting. His blood count was lower than it had been prior to the procedure. Could this be a sign of internal hemorrhage? I had to check it again.

At midnight, I went to draw another sample. I had been on the job for 20 hours, and was barely halfway through my shift. I had no trouble obtaining the sample, but while recapping the needle I had used to draw the blood, I felt a sharp prick on my thumb and saw a bright red drop of blood appear. I had punctured myself with the needle that was contaminated with Vigo's blood. His *AIDS* blood.

The surge of adrenalin I experienced in the aftermath of the needlestick imprinted this event in my memory for all time, a scenario that I mentally played out repeatedly for the next five years.[3] Although it was my only AIDS blood exposure ever, it happened on my second night on call in the first month of my training. Although I did not know for sure that AIDS could be transmitted through contact with blood, I certainly understood that this was potentially a grave risk, possibly even a death sentence.

For the next five years, every physical sign, every subjective fever, every unexplained symptom I experienced revived a deep-rooted anxiety that this was the first sign of AIDS that I had contracted from Vigo. Frankly, I became something of a hypochondriac – believing that it was just a matter of time until my AIDS diagnosis was confirmed. Indeed, the main reason I chose not to seek a subspecialty fellowship after completing my residency was this uncertainty about my future. An investment in further training made no sense if my life expectancy was going to be a few short years.

During the winter months of my final year of residency, it all came to a head. I was on assignment at the Veterans Administration (VA) Hospital next door on Bellevue's southern flank, again responsible for the patients on an inpatient unit. While attending an educational conference, I looked down at my hands and noticed a faint, cheesy film in the creases of my palms.

I was able to scrape it off with my fingernail, but I knew exactly what it was. It was obviously thrush, the same type of fungal infection I had seen in the mouths of so many AIDS patients – the quintessential sign of immunodeficiency. In that unforgettable instant, I realized I had contracted AIDS.

I sat through the remainder of the conference experiencing the full force of this revelation and went immediately to a dark place. In my mind, I played out the movie of my future life – the confirmation of my diagnosis, the public announcement of my plight, the subsequent progression of illness, and the onslaught of fevers, infections, and mental and physical debility.

Hospitalization. Ineffective treatment. Physical decline. I had seen it all before. Then, inevitably, death. This was the dramatic, fateful, heart-breaking tale of a doctor-in-training caught up in a most unfortunate coincidence of timing and bad luck. By the end of the conference, I was a mess.

I ran out of the conference room and rushed to the Dermatology Clinic where I found a sympathetic senior resident willing to address my concerns. He examined my hands, flashed them with an ultraviolet light, and then sat me down to give me the news, plain and simple – the unadorned truth. I had a bacterial infection that would require daily treatment with an antibiotic ointment. If I stuck to the treatment it would completely clear up in a few weeks.

Then he drew silent while waiting for me to respond. It seemed that he was avoiding the elephant in the room, so I gave voice to my anxiety. "So...um... is this an opportunistic infection?" He hesitated, perplexed by my query. "I mean...Is this a sign of AIDS?" With my second question, his puzzled expression broke into a reassuring smile. No, this was not a sign of AIDS. It was a trivial infection that occurred in healthy people and was easy enough to cure. I did not need to worry about any further implications.[4]

I can vividly recall the massive wave of relief that came over me with those comforting words. The tragic film of my future life evaporated in an instant. However, I was not to achieve full relief of my AIDS anxieties until 1988, two years after I completed my residency training, when I finally summoned the courage to test my own blood for Human Immunodeficiency Virus (HIV), the AIDS pathogen that was first discovered in 1983. This test had loomed over my career plans as a persistent, menacing shadow. My result was negative.

Vigo was not so fortunate. His repeat blood test confirmed he had serious internal bleeding, so we moved him to the ICU and gave him blood transfusions. Naturally, no surgeon wanted to open up his abdomen, which would be full of AIDS-contaminated blood, perhaps spurting like a fountain out of the puncture wound in his liver, so he was treated with repeated blood transfusions until he stabilized. Nonetheless, multiple complications ensued, and he died without ever being discharged from the hospital.

This course was too often the case for all my AIDS patients. A serious infection would land them in the hospital, mysterious complications would ensue, then a downward spiral of unpreventable medical events would lead to their inevitable demise. It was like watching a runaway train picking up speed on the tracks and being completely helpless to halt its advance. Along the way, there would be heartbreaking setbacks and dozens of tiny insults.

Apollo Greene was a young Black man from Georgia, who became short of breath during a visit to New York City and appeared in our Emergency Department. We quickly diagnosed his condition as pneumocystis pneumonia (PCP) – which was proof positive that he had AIDS.

His chest X-ray showed classic increased markings, "snow flurries," throughout his chest, and the diagnosis of PCP was confirmed by a sample of fluid from his lungs. For his treatment, we employed a simple cocktail of standard antibiotics that would hopefully cure this particular infection even though we knew in the long run he was doomed.

Apollo's strong southern accent was an oddity on a ward populated by lifelong New Yorkers and first-generation immigrants. As were his polite demeanor and genteel manners. He accepted his diagnosis with equanimity and had just one request. We should never let his family find out about his true diagnosis of AIDS. As they would never accept his homosexuality, they would certainly disown him. In that moment I solemnly vowed that I would honor this simple entreaty, not realizing that we would spectacularly fail to deliver on this, the only request he ever made of us.

Apollo's hospital course did not go well. He did not improve with treatment; he just got worse. As was usually the case with AIDS patients, he was confined to his room. Any such patient who dared to go out into the hallway was always shooed back into his room by anxious staff. Vital signs were checked less frequently on AIDS patients. Food trays were left on the floor outside the room. The call bell went answered.

Yet, I was proud that we the housestaff maintained close contact with our AIDS patients, even touching them with our bare hands as we probed for enlarged lymph nodes or abdominal tenderness – a welcome breach, no doubt, of the institutional sterility that marked the hospital's standard approach. However, to be completely honest, even some attending physicians would find an excuse to pass over the AIDS patients on daily rounds: "Let's not disturb this patient while he is resting. Who else do you have to present this morning?"

One afternoon, I entered Apollo's room to find him leaning forward, severely shortwinded, frantically trying to tell me something. Between the deep gasps of air, he eked out the following statement, one word at a time. "They....are....trying....to.... kill....me."

Who? How? Why? With some further coaxing I got the full story. He felt terribly short of breath and had been ringing his call bell all day long. No one had answered, and he was desperate for assistance.

Apollo felt completely abandoned by the staff and assumed it was a purposeful attempt to do him in. He was truly in a state. He was actually not so far off the truth, but the staff behavior was simply motivated by an impulse for self-preservation. It was an eerie foreshadowing of the public response to Ebola, which would play out 30 years into the future.

Apollo did not respond to our treatment, so we moved him to the ICU. There he continued to worsen until the end of my clinical stint. So I moved on to my next rotation. I learned later that he languished for an additional two weeks before finally succumbing to the effects of his lung infection. Shortly before his death, Apollo's family arrived to visit from his Georgia home. They were shocked to see a large sign in block letters on the door to his ICU cubicle on 16 South: AIDS PATIENT. USE FULL PRECAUTIONS.

The ostracization that Apollo feared from his family was all too common. Seth Feyland was a young gay man who presented with the other pathognomonic (tell-tale) sign of AIDS – Kaposi's Sarcoma. This form of skin cancer appeared as purplish spots virtually anywhere on the body.

Seth was a slender, pale man who was wasting away like all the others. He had the worst case of KS I had ever seen – purple lesions everywhere, including his face, arms, and chest. To make matters worse, he was not actually aware of the extent of his skin cancer because he had another devastating outcome of AIDS, a cytomegalovirus eye infection that had left him completely and permanently blind. And, of course, he had AIDS. Which meant he did not have long to live in any case.

Seth had a wonderful disposition. He was calm, deferential, and well composed – never a cross word or a stray tear. He spoke barely in a whisper. He did not complain about his plight. Nor did he wallow in misery. But he was alone. When his family learned he had AIDS, they realized he was gay.

From that point on, he was completely disowned by his parents, brothers, and sister. He was dead to them. Gone for good. Buried in the cellar. When I reached out to discuss his care, they would not even speak to *me*. And they were most certainly not willing to bring him home.

In this respect, Seth reminded me of so many of my other Bellevue patients – utterly alone in the world without family, friends, or even a single visitor. It hardly mattered why: homelessness, drug use, mental illness, alcoholism, homosexuality, abject poverty. These were society's castaways. Its misfit toys. Literally, the *Untouchables* – sheltering at

Bellevue, their final refuge. Thus, Seth remained tethered in place, blind and bedbound for his final months, and then passed away quietly in his hospital bed.

Given the public hysteria, social rejection, and health worker anxieties stemming from the disease, it was an uphill battle to achieve any degree of normalcy, to preserve the familiar trappings of a physician-patient relationship. So we the housestaff struggled to find equilibrium in our approach to each case. It seemed that we were making up the rules as we went along.

In the early part of my third year of training, I was back on the inpatient unit, now a supervising resident on a 36-hour shift, admitting new patients to the hospital. Early in the evening, I was paged about a new patient who was admitted to the ICU under my care.

He was a known AIDS patient with a typical presentation; he had an abnormal mental status. In fact, he was completely unresponsive – fully comatose. Undoubtedly, he had a serious brain infection, possibly meningitis, and would require treatment in the ICU. I would see this patient together with Eddie, one of the two interns I was supervising overnight.[5]

When I entered the cubicle, I noticed a lumbar puncture tray sitting on a cart at the bedside. This was a thoughtful gesture, as I would need the instruments on this tray to perform a spinal tap, an essential diagnostic test to diagnose the infection that was likely affecting his mental state.

As I turned to the patient, I drew back in a spasm of recognition. This was Juan Verdad, my clinic patient! The one with nine lives! The one who had decided on no more heroics, who had taken me into his confidence, who had elicited my promise to let him go when his time came. By some miracle he was now my *in*patient.

He appeared to be sleeping peacefully but did not respond at all to my voice or touch, not even when I pressed hard with my knuckle over his breastbone. His breaths were deep, irregular, and slow, about ten seconds apart. By now I could recognize the telltale sound of agonal respirations – the breathing pattern that shortly precedes death. Juan was in the final throes of his prematurely shortened life. Above all else, I was sure of one thing. This patient would not last the night.

But I knew exactly his wishes, so I sprang into action. I sent the lumbar puncture tray back to central supply, unopened. I instructed the nurses to move him to a regular room outside the ICU. I met with the nurses on his new unit and updated them on the plan. Juan was to be left alone. No vital signs, no tests, no procedures. I was determined that, for once, I was going to deliver on a promise to an AIDS patient.

I reviewed the plan with my intern. Eddie was actually not on my "day team." I was merely supervising him overnight as I did every three nights during our call cycle. By the next morning, he would continue his care of our newly admitted patients under the supervision of his regularly assigned resident. So he needed to fully understand our unconventional approach.

It was unusual to pull back like this without even a fresh diagnosis. Who knew whether we might discover a cause of his current mental condition that might be treatable, even curable? Juan had experienced his share of setbacks, but he had always responded to treatment and survived to tell the tale. Perhaps that would be the case this time as well. But this time was different in one important respect. Juan had made an explicit personal appeal to let him go, and I was bound to respect that.

One more thing. Based on my two years of Bellevue experience, I had a piece of advice, a pearl, for Eddie. Since he undoubtedly would be called in the middle of his busy night to make the death pronouncement, it would be helpful to get a head start. I advised him to complete the burdensome death certificate in advance, leaving only the time of death blank. When the big moment arrived, he would be able to complete his duties with minimum effort. Just one of those survival tips a resident likes to pass on to his intern.

Contrary to my prediction, the night passed without a call by the nurse. Juan had survived the night. This meant that Eddie would present the case to his attending supervisor at morning conference – to describe our findings and defend our treatment (or lack thereof) without my assistance or moral support. It did not go well. Eddie presented the saga of his patient, gamely wading through his previous hospitalizations, his expressed wishes to me in clinic, and the story of his current admission in a comatose state.

When Eddie got to the point of explaining why we did not do the spinal tap, his attending erupted in a furious reprisal. What?! No diagnosis? How could we just let him go? Not lift a finger! Not make the least attempt to identify the cause of his new symptoms. Something that might be treatable! The patient's blanket request could not possibly account for the nuances of a particular situation. Only *physicians* could make that determination!

Eddie was on the defensive trying to explain a decision that he did not even make himself. And, of course, I was not there to defend him. I was on morning rounds with my own team and my own attending. Worst of all, they had to go meet Juan together at which point Eddie would bear the brunt of another attack on his passive response to this patient in dire need.

As they entered Juan's room, Eddie was braced for the worst. Imagine their surprise when they found Juan sitting up in bed, wide awake, eating breakfast. "Hiya doc!" he exclaimed with a grand wave and a beaming smile. He was unquestionably alive and most definitely well. There was no residual evidence of his "deathbed" presentation the previous night.

As it turned out, Juan was not on the brink of death after all. He had merely overdosed on Valium, temporarily rendering him unconscious and markedly, but not completely, suppressing his breathing. By morning, the effect had fully worn off. He was back to his old irrepressible self.

Eddie was embarrassed, his attending was apoplectic, and I, the one whose dismal prognosis was so spectacularly wrong, was nowhere to be found. Juan was unceremoniously discharged as soon as he finished his breakfast. After that day, I never saw or heard from him again. Nor did he return to clinic. I fear that our interesting episode may have been his ninth and final life.

As the AIDS epidemic peaked over the next decade, the HIV virus became less selective, affecting women, children, heterosexuals, and even health workers. We yearned for that magic wand, but a cure eluded us. Only more recently, through effective antiviral treatment, have we finally become able to check the advance of immunodeficiency, which is the hallmark of disease. In those early years, however, we really had only one thing to offer – the same thing we have offered throughout our history.

Bellevue Hospital is 284 years old – practically as old as the grand traditions of Medicine in the United States. It has a rich history of education, research, and public service. Most important is its time-honored role as the destination of choice for New York City residents with deadly infectious diseases, regardless of their station in life.[6]

No one was ever turned away – not even those at the final stages of incurable infections such as smallpox, yellow fever, typhus, and tuberculosis. As waves of epidemics hit the city, the wards of Bellevue Hospital would swell and overflow with dying patients, for whom no treatment was possible or even expected. In those days, then, the principal role of the hospital was to provide a warm bed, three square meals, physical comfort...

And compassion.

For the first twenty years of the AIDS epidemic, Bellevue returned to this familiar role – to offer sympathy, comfort, and dignity – a safe haven in the final months of life. I wish I could say that we did so without fear or prejudice, that our empathy and professionalism prevailed over our darkest thoughts and impulses, but that was not fully the case.

Nonetheless, while a rage of hysteria gripped our nation, as families excommunicated their children, as schools expelled their students, and as communities exiled their members, health care professionals accepted the burden and risk of AIDS and provided compassionate care to its victims.

Alas, we have not done away with human suffering, and it is not limited to AIDS. As I advanced in my career, I learned that physical and psychic pain are bound up in the life story of nearly every new patient. Indeed, every physician who has formed longstanding relationships with patients has learned this same lesson. They suffer.

They suffer from mental anguish and physical pain. They suffer from childhood abuse and parental neglect. They suffer from adulthood compulsions and lifelong addictions. They suffer from soul-crushing disappointments – broken families, foundering relationships, and failed aspirations. And they suffer from losses – parents, friends, and, unimaginably, children.

In most cases, the suffering is balanced by the positive – success, friendship, joy. Nonetheless, one has to barely scratch the surface to discover the well-guarded secret, the hidden burden, the psychic pain that almost everyone carries. I have always appreciated this special privilege of my profession – the unrestricted access we have to the deepest and darkest refuge of mind and heart – which is the travelling companion of trust.

In any case, it is an honor to hold the sacred key that unlocks the magic door to reveal the inner sanctum, permitting open entry to that secret place sometimes even upon our first encounter. From this privilege arises an essential attribute of my profession – compassion. And our most fundamental purpose – to relieve suffering.

Why did I add this strand to the braid? What is the lesson from the bedside for politicians? They must recognize that they, too, have a special privilege – the immeasurable power to change lives. And not, as in the case of physicians, one patient at a time. On the contrary, national leaders can change the experiences of countless thousands, even millions, of individuals simply by the stroke of a pen.

Through thoughtful decisions, based on solid evidence and with clear goals in mind, our national leaders – presidents, senators, and representatives – can relieve or cause suffering on a massive scale. I cannot help but think that this is how future generations will ultimately judge the performance of our democracy – by the yardstick of compassion.

Indeed, America's distinguished 20th century was marked by monumental decisions of our leaders to relieve enormous suffering. Our interventions into two World Wars ended catastrophic human loss across the globe. Our incomparable diplomatic corps pressed the cause of peace on every continent. Our foreign policies checked the advance of totalitarian governments and promoted human rights in every corner of the earth.

Here at home, Social Security and Medicare erased an epidemic of poverty in the elderly and protected their health. Labor laws curtailed abuses of workers. Civil rights laws diminished the impact of abhorrent practices of discrimination. And, of course, legislation to promote banking, finance, and free enterprise improved the lives of millions by advancing the goal of broad-based economic prosperity.

Thus, throughout the 20th century, despite a few unfortunate, well-documented missteps, America's leadership had a pretty good track record of addressing the needs of the many, relieving suffering, and improving the lives of Americans and people across the globe. By and large, the free world trusted our intentions. We were the *good* guys.

Are we still? Are the decisions of our leaders still based on improving the lives of the many? Relieving suffering, protecting the vulnerable, and caring for the unfortunate? Do we still continue to listen? Understand? Empathize? Do the oppressed around the world still see us as a beacon of hope? Charity? Kindness? In other words: are we *still* the good guys?

This is a question best left for the reader, but I will note, as an experienced physician, that we have not cured suffering. It is invisibly sewn into the fabric of human life and will remain so for the foreseeable future.

In our review of attributes of leadership so far, we have learned four important lessons in the art – silken tresses for our weave. Two of these lessons are fundamental to institutional performance: a leader must be able to acknowledge and learn from her mistakes and must support a Just Culture to encourage honesty and transparency in others. The lessons that naturally follow – trust and compassion – are essential to the relationships that a leader must cultivate with her colleagues and constituents.

It is also worth highlighting, once again, the role of the systematic approach, even in advancing the *art* of leadership. As I noted earlier, atonement and the Just Culture require a playbook. Ditto for trust, which relies upon a steadfast commitment to the principle of integrity. Likewise, compassionate leadership calls for a systematic approach to address the needs of the underserved, as America has done historically.

As we progress through these examples, our conclusions continue to reinforce our first primary theme – the symbiotic connection between art and science. While an evidence-based approach to decision-making must be complemented by trust and compassion, those attributes are, in turn, reinforced by a systematic approach. This is just as true in politics as it is in Medicine. We need the Yin *and* the Yang.

Acceptance:
Conquer the Bias

We don't see things as they are, we see them as *we* are.

Anaïs Nin (1903-1977)

October. It is the final debate and Hillary is once again on point. Coifed and composed, she speaks in measured cadence – perhaps too much so. I am impressed by her experience and command of facts, yet they are still hammering away at her e-mails. I wonder why she doesn't offer up an ample sacrifice: a full-throated, unconditional, no-excuses apology. A generous dose of public atonement could go a long way toward putting this burden to rest. Or perhaps not. The electorate is fickle this year.

Trump stands heads above the competition. He makes his opponents seem small, diminishing their stature by quips and barbs. The disparaging nicknames are oddly effective: Lyin' Ted. Little Marco. Crooked Hillary. They roll off the tongue and seep into the subconscious, tarnishing their victims by repetitive inference. Before long I am singing them to myself.

Now I am replaying the sequence of the past year. How did we get to this place? Not by ruse. Not by deception. Trump has been forthright, authentic even, about his target state. He will make America great again. His America. Not the one we know, built by immigrants such as his paternal grandparents, his mother, and his wife. His new America will be fresh and pure. Safe. Insular. A world apart. This is a popular idea. Trump beckoned, and the voters followed.

Deep in my subconscious are unformed ideas about attributes of leadership, months away from palpable expression. But even now, I am painfully aware that Trump fails to meet the standards: atonement, compassion, integrity. He prattles from the parapets of his narcissistic palace, and I am trying to imagine the impossible.

I spent my early childhood in Berea, Ohio, a bedroom community on the outskirts of Cleveland. My memories of that period are dominated by my obsession with the Indians, Cleveland's professional baseball team. My Dad and I used to watch the games together on a small black and white RCA television in the family den. The Indians were a fairly ordinary team, but you would not know that by my loyalty and admiration for their players, especially Rocky Colavito, their slugger ace, who was, in my mind, not only an incomparable hitter but a moral icon.

On June 10, 1966, when I was eight, Dad took me to my first live game at the venerable Cleveland Municipal Stadium. I well remember the acute apprehension I felt walking along the vertiginous catwalks coursing through the upper reaches of the aging structure, then the rush of adrenalin when we entered the stadium and were greeted by the lush green fields laid out in dazzling splendor. The black and white images of our RCA were no match for this seemingly accidental collage of brilliant color. I had landed in Oz.

The game was fairly uneventful except for one notable achievement. Sonny Siebert, the Indians pitcher, tossed a no-hitter. I was not fully aware of the significance of that feat, but I sensed the growing tension in the stadium as the game wore on. I have rarely seen my dad as excited as he was in the final inning when Siebert retired the final three opposing batters. The ride home was pure bliss as I basked in the glow of my team's great victory. It was as if I had pitched the no-hitter myself.

I couldn't be prouder of my team. These were my people, my family, my tribe. Yes, my *tribe*. Oddly enough, one of the anachronistic nicknames for the Indians was "the Tribe." I knew them all intimately – their stories, their stats, their strengths. They were heroes, and for that they had my admiration, love, and undying loyalty. We were bonded for life.

Then we moved.

Almost exactly one year after that game, our family relocated to Dayton, 150 miles to the southwest, and just an hour drive from Cincinnati, home of the Reds. Within the first week, I became acquainted with new and unfamiliar names: Rose, Perez, Pinson, and May. Once again, I threw myself into the task of learning all about my new family: reading the sports pages, perusing the box scores, and memorizing the stats of the lineup soon to be known as the Big Red Machine.

As for my beloved Indians? Suddenly, they weren't so attractive any more. They were fairly mediocre, after all, and they played in the American League. That was practically a foreign country. Out of sight, out of mind.

How bizarre was the swiftness and intensity with which I bonded to this new group of unfamiliar men who had nothing to do with me except to play a popular sport in a city near my home! The degree to which I attached myself to, identified with, and pledged loyalty to these perfect strangers.

And the impact the success of the team had on my own self-esteem. As if I were on the team myself. As if their success was *my* accomplishment. As if their skills were my own. And finally, the naked ease with which I dumped one for another, just by moving across the state with my family.

My loyalty to my team was not much different than everyone else's. We all had our favorite teams, not just in sports but in every walk of life. Our teams were sports organizations, scout troops, high schools, local communities, and even states. I was so proud to be a Buckeye!

Our teams were also defined by personal identifiers: race, religion, and gender. I remember the intoxicating thrill of competition I experienced whenever the boys were pitted against the girls in any grade school activity.

And by nation. The Olympics were a time of great national pride as I rooted unabashedly for anyone wearing the stars and stripes. I identified with so many different teams, I cannot even name them all. But nothing I experienced in childhood could match the vast and varied array of teams I encountered at Bellevue Hospital in the great city of New York, a melting pot within a melting pot.

Bellevue Hospital is a remarkably diverse institution. The staff come from widely disparate ethnicities and backgrounds: White, Black, Hispanic, Filipino, Indian, and Chinese. Our patients even more so – as first and second-generation immigrants from all corners of the earth. More than 100 languages are spoken in the hospital's outpatient clinics and inpatient units, forever testing our phenomenal interpretation capabilities. Wolof, Tagalog, Fukienese, Creole, Russian, and Japanese. This could be our motto: *all languages are accepted here.*

As in society overall, staff diversity is reflected in the salary hierarchy. Physicians are mainly White. Nurses are primarily White, Black, Asian, and Filipino. Housekeepers are mostly Black, White, and Hispanic. By and large the staff work well together in the day-to-day interactions of patient care.

However, under stress, racial tension does sometimes rise to the surface as employees may sense bias in hospital communications, personnel policies, or disciplinary actions. And, in any serious incident, staff members will typically come to the defense of fellow employees of the same background – a natural coalescence of like with like.

A similar phenomenon occurs by job title. Physicians associate with physicians, support each other, defend each other. Nurses band together with nurses. Lab techs with lab techs. And so on. Raise a controversial issue, and the staff will likely organize themselves along party lines, looking for support by their representatives. Woe be to the nurse leader who does not stand up for her staff in a labor dispute.

Likewise, there is a remarkable group identity among physicians according to *specialty* as they array themselves by department: Medicine, Surgery, and Psychiatry. It seems that everyone's world view, everyone's version of right and wrong, everyone's ethical paradigm is profoundly influenced by the "team" they belong to.

In this sense, the microcosm of our hospital exactly reflects society. Our natural identification with the groups in which we associate profoundly influences our perceptions and behaviors. The powerful bonds we feel to our peers may outstrip reasonable attempts to overcome differences, build bridges, and assemble coalitions across those boundaries. Not infrequently, group dynamics can completely obstruct progress. Why is this so?

Our tendency to identify as members of groups, on teams, and by social classes is a powerful human trait. One aspect of this has been studied by sociologists for decades and is known as the minimal group paradigm. The essential concept is that humans have a powerful tendency to identify in a group, even if the group is defined by minimal or trivial characteristics. Once identification takes place, an individual will display typical features of group behavior – loyalty, favoritism, and discrimination – to an astonishing degree.

One of the early studies of the minimal group paradigm was published by Henri Tajfel in 1971.[1] In a classic experiment, 48 teenage boys were recruited to participate in what they believed to be a study of art appreciation. Once enrolled, each boy was shown a series of unlabeled paintings in pairs and was asked to identify which painting of each pair he preferred.

Once finished, the boys were told that one picture in each pair was painted by Paul Klee and the other by Wassily Kandinsky, two well-known European painters. Half the boys were falsely told that they had consistently shown a preference for Klee paintings, and the other half were told they preferred Kandinsky. Actually, the researchers had *randomly* assigned the boys into the two groups in a way that had *nothing* to do with the paintings.

But in each boy's eyes, he belonged to either a Klee group or a Kandinsky group. The fictional artist preference was the "minimal" characteristic that defined the groups, an absurdly trivial distinction that wasn't even true. Instantly, each boy developed a powerful association with his own group, an identity that was then tested in a second part of the experiment.

In this part, the boys were asked to allocate monetary rewards to two boys selected from each group. They were not told who the boys were, only which group they were from, and they were additionally assured that their allocation would have no impact on themselves.

In the allocation of rewards, each boy clearly favored members of his own group, and disadvantaged members of the other group. This favoritism became known as the minimal group bias and was repeatedly confirmed by countless experiments conducted over subsequent decades. It hardly mattered how one defined the groups, or however trivial the selection process. Flip a coin – heads vs. tails, dress up the subjects – blue shirts vs. red shirts, make up a pretend counting game – overestimators vs. underestimators.

In every case, the subjects would favor their own team, the "in-group," with rewards, positive impressions, and compliments. And they would predictably discriminate against the out-group with penalties, negative opinions, and insults. The tendency to discriminate based on minimal characteristics appeared across a broad range of ages, even in children under the age of four.

The power of this trend was tested by additional experiments to see how far individuals would go to distinguish between the in-group and the out-group. One highly revealing example was a more recent experiment in which 186 White undergraduate students from UCLA were asked to complete a questionnaire, then given an allocation task.[2]

They were told that the Regents of the University of California would be donating a yet-to-be-determined sum of money to support both

White and "minority" organizations. The actual allocation between the two types of organizations had not been set, and the students were asked to choose from seven distinct possibilities.

At one extreme, the subjects could select an option in which both types of organizations would be highly compensated, but the White organizations would receive somewhat *less* ($19 million) than the minority groups ($25 million). At the other extreme, the funds would be severely limited, but the award assignments would be flipped; White groups would receive substantially *more* ($7 million) than the minority organizations ($1 million).

In this way, the study was designed to learn what was more important to the White college students: maximizing the return for their own organizations or maximizing the *distinction* between the two groups by limiting payouts to both of them.

The second option went by the nickname "Vladimir's Choice," the tendency to seek maximum differentiation at one's own expense. The name derived from an old Russian fable in which God granted Vladimir, a peasant, a single wish for anything he wanted. The only catch was that his wish would be doubled for his neighbor, Ivan. Vladimir was quick to respond. "In that case, take out one of my eyes."

In the student experiment, only 11% of participants chose to maximize their income (which would also mean giving the minority groups an advantage). The most common choice, actually, was the middle one – to allocate $13 million to each group. Of course, this meant that they accepted less for themselves so as not to give their "rivals" the edge.

But 16% of students made Vladimir's Choice, accepting *much* less for themselves to maximize the *distinction* between the groups. In further analysis, the tendency to make Vladimir's Choice was correlated with being male and being economically conservative.

Wow! There is much to digest here, so let's summarize. We all want to be in a group. We will jump at a chance to identify with a group, no matter how trivial the entry requirement. Once we identify with a group, we will immediately develop powerful positive impressions of our fellow members, whom we will favor, and we will express negative impressions of outsiders, whom we will discriminate against.

We will seek to maximize the edge the in-group has over the out-group by limiting rewards to the out-group, *even at our own expense*, in order to maintain dominance. And we will express these tendencies early in life, even when we are barely past the toddler stage.

That sounds a lot like my fanatical bias about professional football teams. I do love the Philadelphia Eagles, my home team, but I also despise the Dallas Cowboys. Their players are overrated, and their fans are a bunch of hooligans. All this is a complete fiction, of course, but I would almost rather see the Eagles lose than see the Cowboys win. Just call me Vladimir.

Above all, it is absolutely crucial for the Eagles to close out the year ahead of Dallas in the standings – to maintain our dominance over these archrivals. All based on the trivial distinction of where I happen to live. As for the Reds? I forgot about them a long time ago – as soon as I left Ohio.

Group bias, then, is a fundamental human trait – confirmed by decades of evidence. It is within all of us, sometimes right on the surface, other times buried deep in our bones – lying dormant until the moment of truth, when a specific stimulus elicits the predictable response.

When one recognizes the role of group bias in sports it is easy to imagine how powerful this force must be in identification with groups that *really* matter race, religion, and gender. This is a most disturbing realization and one that explains a great deal of the dark side in human history. So how should we react to that revelation? Should we be ashamed? Repentant? Should we gnash our teeth and whip ourselves?

Of course not. It is not our fault we are born this way, and we cannot help how we feel – only how we *behave*. It is enough to recognize our undesirable tendencies and work to resist them. If we are aware of our predispositions, sense when they arise within us, and consciously regulate them, we can steer clear of the worst consequences.

Furthermore, our group identities deliver many positives. They provide a sense of community by association, a feeling of belonging through shared experience, and the comfort of security through group loyalty. Long ago, no doubt, there was an important survival advantage to being the member of a group. There is surely a good reason why we are built this way.

It is not surprising then, that group conflicts drive politics. They certainly pervade the daily life of the workplace and simmer in the background, waiting to boil over with the slightest provocation.

As an American-born, White, male physician I am subliminally aware of all the ways my patients are different, cautiously incorporating those differences into the ways that I interact with them – my communications, responses, and medical decisions – to the degree that I am able. Yet in all the ways that my patients are distinct from me – gender, religion, and socioeconomic status – none seems so powerful as race.

In my experience, race generally trumps other attributes in terms of group dynamics perhaps because it is the most visually identifiable characteristic or has had the deepest impact in human history. When amplified by a stressor, racial differences can dominate any interaction between two parties and set up explosive and unfortunate outcomes.

I have learned my lessons through incidents large and small – accumulated over a lifetime. But the greatest lesson of all, I learned through an intersection between two lives that took place across a fifteen-year span.

This story picks up mid-stream during my final year of residency training. By this point I was a competent and confident physician on the inpatient service, the leader of the team. On each monthly assignment, I supervised two interns and four medical students. Every day as we visited each patient on morning rounds, I would establish the daily plan and dole out the tasks at hand to my team members. Along the way, I would also help develop these learners – guiding, advising, and teaching them to the best of my ability as others had done for me.

On the first morning of a monthly rotation, I met my new team in the conference room. I was eager to size up the recruits, to assess their personalities and capabilities, as these would have a large impact on my own experience. I glanced at the students and was astonished to see Will Thomason, the Black pre-med major we had barred from joining our fraternity. What a shock! Unbelievable! Here he was, in the flesh, a complete surprise – and for now, *my* medical student. He would be a member of my team, working with me daily in the care of our patients for the next month.

This was unreal! I had not seen or heard from him since the fateful encounter on the Butler campus in the backyard of my fraternity house eight years earlier and 700 miles away. Somehow, fate had conspired with a time machine to join us on a team at the same time in the same hospital – to be intimately connected for the next four weeks. I could scarcely believe it.

It turned out that Will had left Butler and completed his college degree elsewhere. He then matriculated to NYU and was now a medical student in his fourth and final year. Neither Will nor I had any inkling we would be thrown together in this most unexpected circumstance.

He greeted me with a tentative smile, signaling recognition and nothing more. We did not verbally acknowledge our past connection, but we were both obviously familiar with our shared history. And I still felt a sense of incompleteness. So, in my mind, this unexpected development was the perfect opportunity to achieve closure.

I would broach the subject cautiously, then draw him into a discussion of the events that led to his rejection from our fraternity and departure from Butler. I would finally share the inside story, which would unburden my conscience and satisfy his curiosity. I would settle this affair once and for all.

But I did nothing of the kind. Day after day, we conducted our business. Will followed a cohort of inpatients, directly responsible for their care under my supervision. We would round on his patients together at the bedside, and he would present their progress for my comments and suggestions.

I would teach and mentor him, and he would glean the valuable lessons of a fourth-year medical student practicing the role of an intern, which he would become within the next year. Never in our numerous interactions and conversations did either of us mention Butler or our unfortunate past.

Will was an excellent student and performed with distinction. I learned to trust his judgment and capabilities, and he learned to trust my advice and guidance. We bonded to the degree one would expect in a short-term mentorship, but neither of us confronted the elephant in the room, the ever-present shadow that would forever define our relationship. His clerkship ended without either of us approaching the subject. We said good-bye with a handshake, and I soon thereafter submitted a positive evaluation of his performance. Opportunity missed. Case closed.

Years passed.

Sometime later, I was seized by an inexplicable urge to close the loop on our interaction and decided to reach out to Will. I still had a troubling sense of incompleteness. But I had no idea where he had landed. By now he would have finished his residency training and would be in a full-time practice. But where?

On a whim, I contacted the NYU alumni office, which provided me the name of the hospital in another state where Will was now an attending physician. They even gave me a contact. It was his work phone number, and I went so far as to dial it from the safety of my office. After three rings, I lost my nerve and hung up.

More years passed.

In the meantime, I graduated from residency, became an attending physician in the Bellevue medical clinic, married, and had a child. In 1990, our young family spent the year living in Kenya as my wife, Anat, and I worked on a public health project in a community on the outskirts of Nairobi. Upon our return to the U.S. in early 1991, I returned to Bellevue Hospital as an attending physician in the outpatient department. On July 1, President George Bush, Sr. nominated Clarence Thomas for a seat on the Supreme Court.

The Thomas nomination was controversial from the moment his name was offered. As a Black Justice, he would be expected to step into the shoes of the highly esteemed Thurgood Marshall, a pillar of the civil rights movement. But Thomas was extremely conservative and would likely push the court to the right. Most notably, he was opposed to affirmative action and was noncommittal about his stance on abortion, setting the stage for a strong backlash from liberals. In October, a bombshell dropped.

Anita Hill, a former special assistant to Thomas, came forward to testify that he had made sexually provocative statements to her as her boss. He allegedly had graphically described scenes from pornographic movies and bragged about his own sexual prowess. For his part, Thomas offered a vigorous denial and claimed to be the victim of a "high tech lynching." The televised hearings offered spell-binding drama as additional witnesses testified on both sides.

I was mesmerized. I could not stop watching the hearings, which went on for several days. I took those days off from work and stayed at home glued to the television. I was offended by the questioners. I was agitated by the witnesses. I was tortured by the testimony. By the time Thomas was confirmed on October 15, I was a basket case.

The hearings were dramatic, to be sure, but no one else I knew had the reaction I experienced. No one else watched the racially charged hearings from gavel to gavel. No one else was emotionally wrenched by the events. I realized that I was overreacting, and I knew why. I had unfinished business.

Shortly after the hearings, I made the fateful decision to visit Will and clear the air. I would take advantage of a conference I was planning to attend in the city where his hospital was located. I would call him in advance to set it up. I just needed to break the ice, and this time I felt the resolve to follow through.

When I called, I waited for the answer. Will was certainly surprised to hear from me. I explained that I would be traveling soon to the conference and would like to meet him for lunch at his workplace. I wanted to discuss the events that took place at Butler and wished to share some details that he was not aware of.

He was quiet for a moment. "Okay," he answered. "You were decent enough to me during my medical rotation. I guess I can do you the favor." We completed the arrangements, and then I hung up.

I was unsettled. *You were decent enough? I guess I can do you the favor?* What did *that* mean? Didn't he realize that I was doing *him* a favor? I was going out of my way to share information that he had probably wondered about for more than a decade. I was about to give him *closure*. What a strange thing for him to say!

A few weeks later I made the trip. We had arranged to meet at Will's office in the hospital and then have lunch together in the cafeteria. He greeted me with a polite nod, shook my hand, and invited me to accompany him to the lunchroom. We walked down to the bustling cafeteria, grabbed our trays, made our selections, and sat down across from each other at a long table amidst other diners.

We made small talk as we ate. We each filled in the time gaps since we last met. As we came to dessert, I launched into my spiel. I took him back 15 years to Rush Week in the fall of 1977. I explained everything that had happened behind the scenes: about my genuine interest in him as a pledge candidate, the discussion during which he was blackballed, what was said about him, how I had protested to no avail, and the strategy to break the news to him. I confessed pure and simple that it was an act of racism, and I thought he deserved to know the real truth. Will was quiet for a moment as he reflected upon my story. Then he responded in a soft voice.

"What you guys did to me..." he started. *You* guys. Ouch! That smarted. Up until that point, I had never lumped myself together with my wayward fraternity brothers. "What you guys did to me is something I have experienced plenty of times before. It was really nothing special."

This was feeling ominously adversarial, but he was soft-spoken. His voice was not tinged with anger, just a hint of resignation. "You don't realize that we know it's racial, but we do. We always do. And we know that you don't really know that we know. But we do. We always know."

He was on a roll now. He was the teacher and I was the pupil. This was *my* lesson. He explained that he was accustomed to acts of racism, and he had learned not to fall too hard, not to crumble in the face of it, but to put his head down, find a new path, and move on.

Will had left Butler because he had found it to be inhospitable to a young Black man from New York City, but he had landed on his feet. He made it to medical school and was a successful physician. No harm. The prejudice he had experienced was obvious and routine, part of the background of his life. He wasn't going to lose sleep over it.

It was a class act. His response was so elevated, so mature, so above my station, that I felt ashamed. I wasn't really surprised by any of this except that he didn't seem resentful. But he didn't let me off the hook either. I was simply one of the offenders, and there was no distinction in his mind between the friendly offenders and the unfriendly ones. We were one and the same.

Then Will made his appeal. One simple request. A plea for action. He maintained that Black Americans had learned to become self-sufficient together. They did not need anyone else to own their plight, lift them up, or solve their problems. All they needed from White people was one thing – an accomplice. A partner. Someone on the *inside*.

Someone inside the citadel, inside the chapter house, inside the boardroom. Someone with access who is brave enough to raise his hand, blow the whistle, or otherwise stand up against prejudice. Someone within the enclave to introduce the chink that becomes the crack that grows into the rift that opens the door. Black people are often stuck on the outside without access to the inner sanctum and sometimes simply cannot gain the traction they need to penetrate the barriers – without an accomplice.

With that he finished. We stood up, took our trays to the counter, shook hands, and parted. At no point in our brief encounter was he anything but polite and matter-of-fact. There was no anger, resentment, or regret. Or forgiveness. I believe in his mind Will had a message to deliver, and that was it. A simple lesson plainly told. I didn't feel as satisfied as I had hoped. Frankly, I wish I had just apologized.

It took some time for the full message to sink in, but I eventually came to understand why I carried this burden for so many years. I had failed Will. Despite my initial protestations at the blackball session, I had fully accepted the end result. I was not the inside man. The partner. The accomplice. I did not raise my hand, blow the whistle, or stand up to prejudice. I did not introduce a chink, or a crack, or a rift. I became the institution. A follower of the rules that barred Will entry. *A part of the problem.*

Moreover, our brand of racism (yes, now I can say "our") was a soft version. We did not don bedsheets, dangle a noose, or burn crosses in the yard. We did not shout epithets, block the lunch counter, or lie under oath to shield a perpetrator. Our racist act happened insidiously, behind locked doors, and it left no visible trace. Yet an aspiring and highly accomplished young man found a door closed and had to uproot himself to find a path forward. The harmful impact of the event was real, potent, and durable.

Most of the great lessons in life come from personal failures. The sequential process of denial, shame, and acceptance powerfully imbeds these lessons and forever changes us to our core. As I personally resolved the case of Will Thomason, I incorporated this experience into my moral framework. I forgave myself for failing to measure up when the opportunity presented itself to take the honorable path, for falling short in the indelible moment that separates the ordinary from the great. In sum, I absorbed the lesson. And this lesson holds an important message for national leaders.

Underlying the fabric of the society they govern are constant tensions that emanate from group characteristics, tug at our shared identity, and resist our collective purpose. Those tensions can be eased by wise leaders who emphasize common ground, foster shared goals, and promote mutual interests, or amplified by self-serving kingpins who highlight differences, exploit discrepancies, and pit one group against another.

Indeed, at their extreme, group dynamics fuel our worst impulses. Racism begets discrimination. Extremism breeds hate. Nationalism leads to war. In perhaps the most distressing example of modern history, an ill-advised but well-timed media campaign in 1990s Rwanda set a match to kindling to generate an uncontrollable forest fire of violent ethnic cleansing, a ferocious genocide of neighbor against neighbor and friend against friend, which did not dissipate until the fuel was spent. The fuel was 800,000 Tsutsis who were brutally slaughtered in 100 days.

The tendency for individuals to fall into the trap of class affinity, group alliance, and team loyalty is so inbred, so powerful, and so irresistible, it takes very little effort to tether it toward almost any nefarious end. Such an appeal to our base instincts, then, is simply fuel to the flame.

In so many examples in history, Stalinesque, Hitlerian, and Amin-like despots rose to power by harnessing this natural wellspring of support to bring eventual catastrophic harm to themselves and the people they governed. They just didn't realize they were standing in a pool of kerosene when they lit the match.

In present-day America, the signs and symptoms of group tensions are unmistakable and disquieting. Ferguson, Missouri, the Muslim Ban, and the Mexican Border Wall remind us that race, religion, and region continue to define us, separate us, and hinder our progress as a nation. After every incident, the population arrays itself along the usual fault lines, each faction supporting its team, protecting its own, and defending the in-group. The group bias is as predictable as it is destructive, sabotaging any attempt to find common ground.

Is it an exaggeration to link Ferguson and Rwanda? Of course. When it comes to the specifics and scope of these disparate events, they are worlds apart. But what they have in common is the source. Both events tapped into the unfortunate human trait of group identity and its attendant loyalties and prejudices. *On all sides*. As determined by experiments in the minimal group paradigm, this trait is prevalent and biological. It is baked into our DNA.

For this very reason, it is best to consider group bias as a "system defect," requiring a *systematic* response. It is intrinsic to all of humanity and lurks in the back of our consciousness, affecting almost everything we say or do. Blaming individuals for their biased feelings would be no more effective than firing Natalie for failing to address the alarm. Instead, we must constantly work together to overcome this destructive tendency, and curb its harmful impact in our quest for coalescence.

Possibly the most important leadership trait, then, is the ability to find the common ground, the national purpose that binds us together. Unfortunately, this is not a strength among America's current leaders, some of whom rose to power through McCarthy-like exploitations of natural prejudice. Indeed, President Trump makes no apology for his repeated attempts to tug and poke at the fault lines of race, religion, and country of origin.

But collaboration requires a prodigious effort to stifle this impulse across the electorate. It is a gifted individual who can restrain even his own inborn loyalties to govern equitably and fairly. Even less common is the remarkable leader who can suppress antagonism among all his disparate constituencies. Rarest indeed is the exceptional figure who can rise above all to conquer the bias.

Coalescence:
Bridge the Divide

THESE are the times that try men's souls. The summer soldier and the sunshine patriot will, in this crisis, shrink from the service of their country; but he that stands by it now, deserves the love and thanks of man and woman...I call not upon a few, but upon all... lay your shoulders to the wheel...Let it be told to the future world, that in the depth of winter, when nothing but hope and virtue could survive, that the city and the country, alarmed at one common danger, came forth to meet and to repulse it.

From *The Crisis*, Thomas Paine, 1776

November 8, 2016. There is no point to tuning in before seven, when the first polls close in the East. The initial reports are disconcerting. Virginia is surprisingly and strongly tilting toward Trump. We are reassured that the early returns always favor the rural red areas of this state.

As the evening wears on, I sense the margins in the firewall states are failing to materialize. The announcer's tone has ominously shifted to neutral. I feel like the nervous patient who divines she is about to learn bad news just by the twitching brow of her oncologist. I am not prepared to hear that the cancer has spread, so I go to bed early with the race still open. At two am, I wake up and check the internet. I barely sleep again for the rest of the night.

I finally arise from my bed in a daze and check the news to confirm that I haven't been dreaming. The train ride to New York is interminable. Now seated at my desk in a dark space, I am distressed, agitated, restless. I cannot find a comfortable position. I cannot think about work. I cannot even describe what I feel. Unmoored. Vaguely anxious. Unbearably nauseous.

I struggle to remember feeling this bad ever before. I recall my severe homesickness at summer camp, when the world closing in around me was alien and hostile. This feels similar but worse and without an apparent endpoint. My daughter calls me on my cell. "Are we going to be okay, Daddy?" I can't even fake it. For the first time in her life, my answer is this. "I don't know, Lani. I really don't know." It is, without a doubt, the perfect storm.

A principle challenge of national leaders is to overcome inborn differences among the people – to align disparate interests so that everyone pulls in the same direction to achieve collective goals. In the previous chapter, I described the powerful forces that resist this aim. In present day America, given the petty disputes between parties in power and the growing divide between regions, races, and religions, this end seems hopelessly beyond our reach. But it was not always so.

On many occasions in our history, our nation has come together as one to meet intractable challenges and face down external threats. After all, the sheer force of our collaboration won the Revolutionary War, survived the Great Depression, defeated Nazi Germany, outlasted the Soviet Union, cleaned up our environment, and landed Americans on the moon. These examples serve to strengthen our spirit and illuminate the path forward.

Yet the specter of disunity constantly threatens any organization, however large or small: an army platoon, a modern-day corporation, or a sovereign state. In each case, a successful leader must overcome natural prejudices, unwarranted mistrust, and blatant self-interest to instill allegiance to a common purpose that captures the imagination, loyalty, and support of all members.

This is no less true in a hospital, where employees of varying race, economic status, and professional discipline must work together to keep patients safe. Our combined efforts must overcome the powerful human dispositions that work against the shared aim, constant headwinds that demand unceasing vigilance and continual interventions to maintain the alignment that is fundamental to success.

Indeed, sometimes it takes an extraordinary event, a common foe, or an existential threat for us to overcome the natural divisions that separate us all. To bundle the talents. To align the interests. To coalesce a disparate group into a single, powerful, cohesive force. When that happens, the sheer strength of that unified response is a breathtaking sight.

On the eve of Halloween, 2012, I was witness to a most remarkable testament to that truth, in a fateful challenge through which natural boundaries dissolved, class distinctions melted away, and a diverse group of individuals banded together as one to accomplish a monumental achievement.

As residents of the northeastern United States may recall, the path of Superstorm Sandy was predicted with remarkable accuracy by the European Meteorological Service, which projected, four days ahead of schedule, a direct hit upon New York City on October 29. Brooding in the Atlantic for more than a week, Sandy had stalked the eastern seaboard, attaining hurricane intensity two days before landfall.

For our hospital, the implications of a direct hit from a storm this size were most alarming. The likeliest scenario was that the ocean tides would swell in New York Harbor to the south, causing water levels to rise dramatically in the East River. This would shut down all the bridges and tunnels, leaving the island of Manhattan completely isolated from the world outside, and making it impossible for many of our staff to commute to work.

The nurses would be especially impacted by a public transportation shutdown, as many of them lived in the outer boroughs: Queens, Brooklyn, Staten Island, and the Bronx. Our physicians would not be so affected, as most of our housestaff resided within walking distance of the hospital, but in this particular instance, the ferocity of the storm would bring about a complete lockdown for the better part of 24 hours.

Fortunately, we had done quite a bit of advance preparation and so maintained a highly organized command structure for events just like this. Moreover, after Hurricane Irene in 2011, our facilities department had installed a submarine-style door to shield vital equipment in the basement. This door would provide a watertight seal so that we would maintain power connections even if the basement flooded.

We had suffered severe storms before, so we had a well-rehearsed strategy to keep everyone safe. We would call in extra employees and keep them in the hospital during the entire period of the storm, platooning some staff on shifts while others slept. In this way, we would maintain operations continuously in our isolated hospital to provide round-the-clock care to our patients until the weather eased and the bridges and tunnels reopened.

The logistics of this were daunting. We would provide cots in several large "dormitories," requiring advance reservations for sleeping shifts, and we would contract with the food service to maintain provisions on site to last us throughout the event. In effect, we would simultaneously function as a hospital for our patients and a hotel for our staff.

On the Sunday evening before the Monday storm, all requisite staff came to work and began organizing. Service chiefs, attending physicians, and housestaff set up mini-command centers – local hubs of leadership and communication – within their respective departments. Nursing leaders, unit managers, and staff supervisors organized the thousand-plus registered nurses into their appropriate shifts and settled down for a long restless night. Likewise, housekeepers, transporters, and facilities personnel were all sequestered in place – in uneasy anticipation of the approaching hurricane.

Meanwhile, we opened our incident command center, a battle station on the ground floor near the Emergency Department that always becomes the nerve center of leadership and communications during a crisis. When an emergency alert is activated, executive leaders of the hospital will retire to this modern-day bunker and remain tethered there until the All Clear.

The centralization of leadership in this space always facilitates clear communication and good decision-making. Moreover, during an activation, we will perform our duties following a highly scripted protocol, each of us with a well-defined role to play. For example, my job as "Medical Branch Director," is to be responsible for the clinical care of patients throughout the hospital.[1] Thus, even in emergencies – *especially* in emergencies – we rely heavily upon a systematic approach.

To the same end, other hospital leaders will assume specified roles in operations, logistics, and planning – all under the able command of our Executive Director. We had practiced this organizational structure during drills and actual activations repeatedly over the previous decade, including 9/11, the New York City blackout of 2003, and Hurricane Irene in 2011. In truth, we were quite comfortable in our roles and ready for the challenge.

Sandy slipped into New York Harbor at midday on Monday. To me it all seemed rather anti-climactic. The command center was preoccupied with logistics of feeding and sleeping all the extra staff, so I wandered outside at one point to observe what seemed like the start of a typical Nor'easter. Windy to be sure, but nothing like what we had been warned about.

As the afternoon went on, however, the weather really started getting rough, and I became duly impressed. By 4 pm, it was impossible even to stand upright on the sidewalk. At one point, I observed debris swirling furiously in a vortex until a large piece of metal slammed against a concrete pillar with tremendous force. Bam! Game on!

As reports came in that all transportation channels had been shut down, I felt that familiar sense of foreboding that portends all disasters. While sitting idly in the command center, I asked one of my colleagues what he thought the worst-case scenario would be.

"Well," he started, "The worst-case scenario is that the East River will overflow its banks, cross over the FDR Drive, and flood our basement. The submarine doors will fail, and all of our power feeds will be completely incapacitated, forcing us to go on emergency power for the duration of the storm. Fortunately, our backup generators are all on the 13th floor."

In other words, if the storm breached our defenses we would have to implement Plan B: backup power. This was actually not very reassuring. Having suffered through this before, I knew it would be a most unpleasant experience. When the hospital is on backup power, all lighting is dimmed, only some outlets are functional, and elevator service is greatly limited.

Indeed, backup power is not a luxury; it is designed merely to keep our patients safe. Moreover, it is psychologically uncomfortable for a full-service hospital with 700 inpatients to be on emergency power, the last resort. After all, there is no backup to the backup. Even still, at that moment, I did not realize that just a few hours later, I would be desperately longing for that specific "worst case" scenario.

Some time later, one of my colleagues came into the command center, highly excited. "You have to see this," he said. "Come with me." He led me upstairs to the second floor and guided me to the windows facing eastward. There before me was the East River in its mighty glory. It had risen by at least a dozen feet and overflowed its banks – submerging the FDR Drive, which had now completely disappeared – and had advanced to the very foundation of the hospital. Bellevue Hospital was now *in* the East River.

That was a sight to behold. Although I was vaguely aware of the danger of the storm surge, I had not fully grasped its consequences until this moment. I went back to the command center, which was abuzz with eyewitness accounts of the astonishing power of the storm.

Bellevue was a peninsula now, surrounded on three sides by water. It was just a matter of time when we would go on backup power. Practically on cue there was a flicker and then a few seconds of darkness before the lights came back on in a muted glow. This was the tell-tale sign that we had lost our power. We were now completely dependent on our backup generators.

Plan B.

At that point, several facility engineers entered the command center ashen-faced. They had gone into the basement to do an assessment and had terrible news to report. The basement was chest-deep in water, limiting their ability to do a full assessment, but they could see the elevator shafts were flooded at their bases. This meant we had lost *all* elevator service.

More important, the submarine door had been breached, and all vital equipment was incapacitated. The power feeds had shorted out. The ventilation systems were toast. And, most important, the fuel and water pumps had been knocked out. The *fuel* pumps? These supplied the backup generators on the 13th floor! It seemed our hospital was now suffering, like a septic patient, from total body malfunction – an incestuous collaboration between all her failing systems to do her in. The harbinger of death.

An engineer spelled out the situation with remarkable poise. Our fuel supply was completely compromised, and the 13th floor generator tanks had only two hours of fuel remaining. At midnight, we would all turn into pumpkins. This had now become a classic Hitchcock suspense thriller. Something very bad was about to happen, and the audience was in on it because the time bomb was ticking in open view. The countdown had begun.

To the credit of my colleagues in the command center, everyone instantly grasped the significance of this announcement. Throughout the hospital, many patients were dependent on electrical power: intravenous medication pumps, chest tubes on suction, and mechanical ventilators.

A patient on a ventilator required electrical power for *life* support. For every such patient, when the power failed at midnight, we would have to disconnect the hose from the breathing tube and attach an "Ambu bag," a device that would allow someone to literally squeeze each breath into the patient by hand, somewhat like pumping the bellows to feed a fire.

We called that "bagging" the patient. There were 17 patients on ventilators, and each one would need to be bagged. We had barely two hours to set up oxygen tanks and implement a schedule of the staff to do the bagging. Unfortunately, we would be setting this all up in the dark.

Well, not completely in the dark. At this point, the command center went into hyper-drive. The director of logistics unlocked a cabinet and handed everyone a walkie-talkie and head lamp, stored just for this purpose. And then we did what previous events and drills had trained us to do. We planned. We deliberated. We problem-solved.

We did this in a remarkably calm state, unlike our usual interactions, which could be heated, boisterous, and rife with conflict. On this occasion, luckily, everyone seemed to realize that our success depended on full cooperation. So we reviewed likely scenarios and potential responses, then quickly came to consensus on a plan of action.

First, we would visit each mini command center in person to alert all our clinical leaders as to the situation and the midnight deadline. We would initiate a process to identify all patients at risk from the power loss and plan for contingencies for each one. In the meantime, we would work on a brilliant idea suggested by one of our engineers. If this idea worked, we might not lose power after all.

According to the engineer, the electrical closets on the southwest corner of every floor in the hospital were linked by a vertical "riser," putting them all on the same power feed. Because of the unique layout of the hospital, it should be possible to connect this riser to a backup generator in the adjacent ambulatory care building, which was not so severely impacted by the storm. In this way, power could be maintained for emergency outlets but only in the southwest corner of each floor.

This seemed like an attractive option. It would, of course, be Plan C: the backup to the backup. Not the perfect solution but a decent fallback position and much better than having to bag all the ventilator patients. So we all agreed to move patients dependent on power to the southwest corner of their respective floors. With any luck, the electrical feed would be maintained in those spaces.

As I grabbed my walkie-talkie and headed up the stairs to share the news, I could immediately see the backup power had plunged the building into a state of semi-darkness and the stairwells even deeper into shadow. Fittingly, on the eve of Halloween, Bellevue had become a haunted hotel, inhabited by sinister forces that threatened our patients and tormented our staff. I could just imagine a flock of Potteresque dementors flitting about in the stairwell, preparing to pounce on unwary staff climbing in the darkness.

My first stop was the Medicine Department mini-command center on the 16th floor. The leaders were gathered around a desk in the dim light facing a large whiteboard where they had already entered patient locations and diagrammed rescue strategies, much like a locker room chalkboard, for their vulnerable patients. They were already two steps ahead of me.[2]

I shared the plan and instructed them to move all patients dependent on power to the southwest corner. Patients on IV pumps would likewise need to be relocated or switched to another mode of medication administration. This team was so well organized and self-motivated, I would never have to visit them again on this night.

My next stop was the 14th floor to check in on the Pharmacy, and I could not believe what I was seeing. For some reason, the lights did not run on the emergency power system. There were extension cords everywhere, but none of them seemed to be powering anything. It would have been pitch black if not for the muted glow of flashlights, by which dim light a dozen pharmacists toiled, hunched over a common table, diligently counting pills into small plastic containers for the inpatients. These pharmacists would work just like this, crouched in the semi-darkness, all night long.[3]

On the 10th floor, I met with the ICU staff. They, too, had already done some advance planning. Not surprisingly, they had the sickest patients and the greatest number on ventilators. The Director of Critical Care pulled me aside. "I just want you to know," she began. "We have pulled together an ad hoc ethics committee to prioritize the patients."[4]

"Whatever for?" I did not understand what this had to do with ethics.

"Just in case," she replied. "Just in case we don't have resources for everyone. Maybe there will be a limited power supply or only a certain number of outlets. I just need a good process for deciding who gets first shot."

Yikes! This was something I hadn't anticipated. That we would not be able to protect all our patients equally. That we would have to make some life and death choices through rationing. I was grateful someone was thinking ahead, planning for every possible contingency, even the unspeakable.

It was like this on every floor. Well ahead of my communication, departmental leaders had already addressed local issues that I had not even considered. They were working in cohesive teams – anticipating, planning, and problem-solving. Likewise, the doctors, nurses, and staff on each unit were fully collaborating, working in tandem, and completely responsive to directives from above. This did not look like the hospital I was used to.

On the 8th floor I ran into a snag. The senior Pediatric resident was skeptical of the plan to move the patients to the southwest corner. "I have a very sick baby in the PICU," she asserted. The PICU was the Pediatric Intensive Care Unit. "He is on a ventilator in a fragile state. If we lose power, I will not be able to maintain him safely by bagging."

"Well that's why you need to move him to the southwest corner," I countered. I had already checked the electrical closet. There was a space nearby for a hospital bed, in this case, a crib, and the closet had open connections for extension cords.

"I'm sorry but I can't risk it," she continued, her voice rising. "I have to get him out of here. As soon as the storm begins to die down, I will take him myself to Cornell, by ambulance." At this point, I attempted to assert myself as Medical Director, and firmly insisted that she follow our plan.

"I don't trust you," she retorted. "I'm taking this baby out of here!" This was frank insubordination, but I was getting nowhere, so I moved on.

On the 11th floor, I learned a chilling piece of news from the Cardiovascular (CV) Surgery fellow, a cardiac surgeon who was in his final year of training.[5] In the CV post-surgical recovery room, there was a patient who had undergone open-heart surgery two days earlier. He was fully dependent upon a left-ventricular assist device (LVAD), a mechanical pump that was augmenting the strength of his heart and was needed to maintain an adequate blood pressure. His survival was dependent on the LVAD, and the LVAD was dependent on electrical power. The fellow warned me that the patient would not last beyond a few minutes if we lost all power.

Again, I explained the plan. The CV operating room, the very room where the patient had undergone surgery, was fortuitously located in the southwest corner of the 11th floor. We would move the patient back into the OR so that his LVAD could be plugged into the nearby electrical closet, preserving the device's power and the patient's life. The fellow was grateful but still concerned. "I think we need a buffer," he suggested. "I know where there is a backup battery over at Tisch. It will buy us an extra hour."

Tisch was NYU's private hospital, two blocks to the north. Two *outside* blocks. In essence, the fellow was offering to go out into the teeth of the storm, cross those two blocks, and retrieve a battery from one of the upper floors. Actually, he was not offering; he was insisting. Within minutes he descended the stairs, exited our ambulance bay, and headed north to Tisch.

Over the next half hour or so, all the preparations were carried out, floor by floor. The command center was humming with activity, and all the leaders present were carrying out the tasks at hand. Although communication with the upper floors had to occur face-to-face, we had runners making the trips up and down the stairs. Meanwhile I had reached out to the Chief of Pediatrics to discuss the PICU baby.[6]

He reassured me that it made perfect sense for the resident to transfer the child, and he would vouch for the plan. Sure enough, later in the night when the storm had subsided, the resident, accompanied by a nurse, walked down eight flights of stairs in the dark with the baby in her arms, bagging him the entire way, went out the back of the ED, climbed into an ambulance, and transported him safely to Cornell.

One special concern was Adult and Child Psychiatry, two of our largest departments. In the upper reaches of the building, on floors 18 through 21, there were 250 adult and child psychiatric inpatients, including 50 inmates, maintained on a locked forensic unit.

Our Chief of Adult Psychiatry was concerned about the impact of a complete loss of power on these large units of mentally ill and possibly restless patients. There was no telling how they might respond if they were plunged into darkness. Hopefully, most of them would be asleep and not even notice. I asked her to keep me posted on any new developments.

At 11:30 pm, I went back up to the 16th floor where I quickly found my way to the southwest corner. To my dismay, the rooms in that section were completely dark. There were extension cords everywhere on the floor and several lamps were set up in rooms next to the electrical closet. But they were dark as well. A nurse happened to walk by, so I grabbed her arm.

"What happened to the power," I demanded to know.

"Didn't you hear?" she responded. "The plan didn't work. When they hooked up the power, the generator failed. They said it can't be fixed."

What a crushing blow! Plan C, our one and only chance to maintain power, was a bust. We would have to bag the ventilator patients after all. I sure hoped everyone was prepared for that. Then suddenly I remembered the LVAD patient. I raced down the stairs to the 11th floor OR. The CV fellow was standing in the hallway with the backup battery in hand.

I broke the news about the failed generator. Our last hope had failed us, and we were now on our own. "Well, we have an extra hour because of the battery," he started hopefully. "After that..." His voice trailed off. We both knew what he could not put into words. After that, his patient would die within a few minutes. The clock of doom had restarted, and there was barely more than an hour left. I looked down at my shoes.

"Let's talk about your other patients," I offered. *The ones we can save*, were the words I did not say. This was my lowest point of the Sandy experience, the depth of my despair, the moment when all hope was lost.

As I have shared previously, the death of a patient from a system defect is just as devastating to a hospital leader as is a fatal error to a responsible physician. It is an indefensible lapse, an unspeakable calamity – a *never event*. Still, it sometimes happens. On rare occasions, despite our best efforts, our systems betray us and harm our patients. Thus, we must make every conceivable effort to prevent such an occurrence.

But in this case, for the first time in my leadership career, I had an *advance* warning that a system defect was about to take a life. The institutional gap, lack of electrical power, was evident. The impact on the patient was equally clear – a straight line from input A to outcome B. And the time course was immutable. We were down to the last hour.

In effect, I had a sneak preview of the movie that was about to play out about the unexpected demise of this cardiac patient caught up in a most unfortunate coincidence of timing and bad luck. I knew exactly when the patient would take his last breath, yet I was powerless to stop it. Unable to rewrite the script. Impotent against the irresistible force of fate. Above all else, I was sure of one thing. This patient would not last the night.

I trudged back down 11 flights of stairs and returned to the command center, ready to share my dreadful news. Unexpectedly, I found my fellow leaders smiling, actually radiant. "What's going on?" I asked in surprise.

"Come with me." One of my colleagues took me by the hand and led me out of the command center. We threaded our way to the north end of the ground floor to the main stairwell.

There, in the stairwell, was an awesome sight to behold. It was packed with hundreds of hospital staff milling about on the steps winding upward as far as I could see. Doctors, nurses, dietary aides, respiratory therapists, housekeepers, and transporters. They were all there in the stairwell, chatting, laughing, socializing. They appeared to be waiting. But waiting for what?

Then I saw it. The fuel canister. A single plastic container being handed from person to person, winding its way up through the stairwell in a continuous spiral. Not just one but many. One after another, countless canisters of kerosene were being passed from one person to the next, hand over hand, in a giant human chain that was lifting a steady supply of fuel skyward more than 150 vertical feet to the backup generators on the 13th floor.

It was a bucket brigade. Just like days of old. Except in this case, they were not passing water buckets to quench a fire. They were hauling fuel canisters to feed a generator. There was the Chief of Medicine, wearing a surgical mask, positioned between two housekeepers, leading the charge.

In this space there was no hierarchy, no division, no fault lines of envy, disrespect, or mistrust. Everyone was one and the same, all contributing to the overarching goal: keep the generators running. In an instant, I recognized this amazing, bustling scene exactly for what it was. This was *Plan D.*

I learned later that the National Guard had been activated on our behalf. They had brought a fuel truck, canisters, and a large number of strapping young guard members. They were filling canisters outside just as fast as we could empty and return them.

The bucket brigade ran all night and into the next day. It was to continue for four days, hospital staff eventually being replaced by National Guardsmen, as kerosene fumes permeated all areas of the hospital. But it did its job. During our entire Sandy experience, we never lost backup power. Two months later, we would celebrate our own version of the Chanukah story: the night when two hours of fuel miraculously lasted for four days.

Wry note to self: next time, call the National Guard *first*.

By next morning, the eye of the storm had passed, giving way to a day of bright sunshine, the staff had changed shifts, and our leadership team had snatched a few hours of sleep. There had been no decision yet about whether to evacuate the building, but we knew we had to make a start. We were, at that point, blissfully unaware of the growing predicament that would soon force our hand.

We started by identifying all the ICU patients, dialysis recipients, inmates, women in labor, children, and newborns – nearly two hundred in all. These were the ones who would go first. By now we were in full communication with our Central Office,[7] the Office of Emergency Management (OEM), and the city and state Departments of Health.

We spent all day Tuesday engaging these external partners to identify recipient hospitals, and then having phone conversations with clinical counterparts to do a proper handoff before sending them each patient. Nonetheless, the sheer volume of decisions to be made and conversations to hold were staggering.

The command center was hot, noisy, and hectic – a cacophony of conversations and interruptions. There was a parade of hospital physician and nurse leaders presenting urgent problems requiring split second decisions, but it seemed impossible to string two thoughts together.

On the upper floors of the hospital, the staff were scrambling to meet their patients' needs, yet there was a surprising sense of normalcy as everyone seemed willing to help in every conceivable way. Food was delivered, medications were administered, vital signs were checked, and the world went on.

By now, the National Guard contingent was 150 strong. Not only did they haul fuel *up* the 13 flights of stairs, they carried patients *down,* as many as 17 floors, on molded plastic sleds specifically designed for this purpose. All day long, patients would emerge from the bottom of the south stairwell, staff would check their identification, and ambulances would pull up to the south exit door, load up, and pull away. This was to continue well into the night.

As the day went on, I became concerned about the risk to critically ill patients travelling unaccompanied to recipient hospitals, but it wasn't clear who could ride with them. I was standing at the exit door feeling acutely anxious about this dilemma when a half-dozen Emergency Department residents came striding in. Their unit had been closed since the previous night, and they wanted to help.

I am not sure if it was due to lack of sleep or unrelenting stress, but the arrival of the ED residents inspired an absurd vision. I imagined I was in J.R.R. Tolkien's Middle-Earth at the battle of Helms Deep. I was helping to defend the castle walls, which were about to be breached by Saruman's army of 10,000 Orcs. Just when all seemed lost, the Elves appeared. I imagined the ED residents to be those very Elves – bows, arrows, pointed ears and all – marching in to save the garrison just in the nick of time.

I was overwhelmed with gratitude and invited them to ride one by one with the sickest of the patients. Thank goodness they had appeared on the scene because one unfortunate patient lost his pulse and blood pressure while en route to another hospital. His intravenous line had become tangled and kinked, obstructing the flow of a critical medication. The alert resident diagnosed the problem and successfully resuscitated the patient, saving his life and preserving our perfect safety record in the Sandy evacuation.

By Tuesday afternoon, most of the high-risk patients had been evacuated, but a new problem now captured our attention. We had run out of *water*. In addition to the fuel pumps, the water pumps in the basement had been compromised by the flood. The roof tank was now empty, and the taps were dry, not to mention the toilets, which could no longer be flushed. This was the shortfall that spelled our doom.

The staff were restless. Many had spent two solid days in the hospital, which was becoming less hospitable by the hour. The stench of kerosene hung in the air, but that was no match for the toilets, which were being used multiple times in a row, unable to be flushed. By Tuesday night it was obvious that we would have to evacuate the hospital completely.

The psychiatric patients were still of concern, especially the children. The Chief of Child and Adolescent Psychiatry spent all day Tuesday arranging a transfer that was to take place by bus to another facility. However, the bus did not show up until midnight. Here, the director put her foot down. She was not about to wake up her kids to pack them on a bus in the middle of the night. Their evacuation would have to wait until the next day.[8]

Likewise, the Chief of Adult Psychiatry was consumed by the task of finding suitable receiving hospitals for her patients. She spent much of the day on the phone with various public authorities including the state Office of Mental Health (OMH). It was not clear who would be willing to handle our challenging palette of homeless schizophrenic patients.

At one point it was suggested that they be sent to a warehouse in Poughkeepsie, which could be quickly outfitted as a makeshift hospital.

This chief, too, put her foot down. If the patients were going anywhere it would be to a proper inpatient unit in a real hospital, she insisted. The following day, her expectations were met.[9]

On Wednesday morning, the announcement was made that we would complete the evacuation. Not a boutique operation, one patient at a time, as we had done the previous day, but a mass exodus. This would be handled by the public authorities, who would identify receiving hospitals on our behalf and arrange the transportation. We were grateful to turn the responsibility over to our capable governmental partners.

Our job was simply to prepare transfer documents to accompany each patient: a discharge summary, a medication list, contact information of the sending doctors, and personal advice for the receiving hospital. We were concerned about losing the documents, so we put them in a manila envelope, safety-pinned to each patient's bedclothes, a memento of sorts from their Sandy experience.

Meanwhile, our hospital was overrun by governmental emergency personnel who directed the entire operation. No more pussyfooting around. This was going to run like a factory assembly line. The national guardsmen would enter a ward, starting at one end, and work their way down, room by room, to the other end, until the ward was vacant.

Hundreds of patients were carried out this way on sleds, down 17 or more flights of stairs, out the south entrance, and into waiting ambulances that were stretched in a long line around the block and down the street. It was a continuously moving conveyor belt of people.

The evacuation continued until well after dark, when, finally, the hospital was empty. Or nearly so. There still remained two patients, including our LVAD patient, who were too fragile to be carried down the stairs. Two days later, both patients were successfully evacuated when a single elevator finally became operational. At this point, the staff went home, the hallways darkened, and the alarms fell silent. Bellevue Hospital was completely vacant – for the first time in 276 years.

We had one more task to perform in the service of our patients. We set up a call center in the now-deserted Psychiatric Emergency Department to handle clinical queries and circulated the number to all the receiving hospitals. For several days, the desk was staffed by physicians who sat in front of computers that displayed the Bellevue records.

This was fortunate because some of our patients reportedly arrived without their documents tethered to their bedclothes. Oddly enough, they all seemed to have come from the same Bellevue ward. It was some time before we solved the mystery. One of our medical records staff had noticed the envelopes pinned to the patients and had been dutifully unpinning and collecting them to be sent to where they obviously belonged: our own medical records file room. She was just doing her job.

Our interlude was short lived, however, as services began to reopen in just one week, starting with the Emergency Department, then the outpatient clinics, and finally the inpatient wards three months later. In between was a most remarkable and successful effort to repair, relocate, and replace the vital electrical equipment that had so catastrophically failed during the storm. But that is quite another story.

It is an interesting tale, a story of unexpected challenges met by teamwork, dedication, and heroism. Sandy brought out the best in us, no doubt. And there is an important thread that runs through the narrative. It is the uncommon way in which the hospital staff joined as one to meet an external threat. Along the way, I learned several vital lessons in leadership.

First, singular events can bring out superhuman qualities in people. The adrenalin rush, the communal aim, and the singleness of purpose all combine to stir the soul, fortify the body, and concentrate the mind. Each person becomes three with astonishing focus, strength, and endurance.

Second, a common threat blurs natural divisions, bringing forth a remarkable alignment that greatly simplifies and amplifies the organization's ability to overcome any challenge. As we all put our shoulders to the collective wheel, group dynamics that normally impede progress just melt away, and the massive wheel grinds with incredible power.

I will never forget the scenes of everyday people doing the extraordinary; the images come back to me in a rush. The cardiovascular fellow who went out into the storm, the Pediatric resident who defied my order, the ICU Director who convened a committee, the Chiefs of Psychiatry who took a stand, the dedicated pharmacists who hunched over their tables, the National Guardsmen who did their duty, the Emergency Medicine resident who saved a life, the medical records clerk who was just doing her job, and the hundreds of employees who joined in the bucket brigade.

In every one of these examples, a member of the team rose above their station. None more so than my leadership colleagues who manned the command center and made courageous decision after decision in a remarkable display of collaboration and camaraderie.[10]

So that's it. That's what unity feels like. *Coalescence.* Think of times we felt unified as a nation: World War II – when young men stormed the beaches while their families at home bought war bonds, rationed rubber products, and staffed the assembly lines; the Moon Landing – when pajama-clad children across the nation listened with pride to Neil Armstrong's words as he stepped onto the lunar surface; and 9/11, when we collectively gasped in horror as the World Trade Center collapsed, and mourned together for the fallen without regard to race, religion, or gender. All as one.

We should not be surprised by these historical examples. Just as the human body requires symbiotic interactions between microscopic cells, specialized tissues, and complex organs, the body politic depends upon the harmonious interplay of compliant citizens, cohesive families, and cooperative communities to achieve a healthy state. When coalescence rules, the organism thrives. All as one.

How about now? Does our modern state feel that way? Unified? Are we all pushing in one direction? Aligned? Have we come together as one? Coalesced? Quite the contrary. It is difficult to recall any time in the past century when America has seemed so divided on so many fronts. Health care, immigration, community policing, gun control, Mideast policy, and climate change have all become highly polarized issues that seem to offer no middle ground or room for compromise.

Like the septic patient on the verge of death, we are working at cross-purposes. We have no consensus on our current national direction, much less the ultimate destination. And our leaders are not helping to bridge the gap. Whenever one political party gains control, they declare victory and undo the work of the other. It is not clear that our elected officials wish to collaborate at all. Or that the electorate even wants them to.

Moreover, as we will soon see, income and wealth inequalities have restored a class hierarchy not seen since the 1920s, pitting owners against workers, rich against poor, and haves versus have-nots, in an extreme version of a zero-sum game. A nation turning on itself.

Finally, as perhaps the most distressing sign of all, current leaders are successfully mining these divisions, exploring every fault line to gain an electoral advantage – *and it seems to be working.* Consequently, our elected officials have no incentive to behave differently, no reason to compromise. Unquestionably, these are the most distressing symptoms of our ailing democracy, our patient in extremis.

Is there a clear lesson here for national leaders? Yes, and it is a simple one. The strength of a nation comes from a unity of purpose. An alignment of the people. A coalescence of forces. An ethical leader will never exploit natural divisions for personal gain. A disciplined leader will resist those temptations to channel the power that resides in the collective whole. A truly great leader will bridge the divide.

Interlude:
The Ghosts of Presidents Past

When Scrooge awoke, it was so dark, that looking out of bed, he could scarcely distinguish the transparent window from the opaque walls of his chamber...the curtains of his bed were drawn aside; and [he] found himself face to face with the unearthly visitor who drew them...

"Who, and what are you?" Scrooge demanded.

"I am the Ghost of Christmas Past."

"Long past?" inquired Scrooge; observant of its dwarfish stature.

"No. *Your* past."

From *A Christmas Carol*, Charles Dickens, 1843

In these three sections, I have explored attributes of the art and science of Medicine, qualities that I suggest would enhance leadership performance. This is the perfect time to take a break, review our progress so far, and summarize. Most important, I need to answer a question I often ask myself when I am deep in the middle of a case: is this making sense?

Here is a simple check. Let's test our lessons, the strands in our braid, against the ghosts of presidents past. In particular, let's assess three of our favorites: Washington, Lincoln, and Franklin D. Roosevelt (FDR). They almost always lead the register of America's greatest presidents. Did they exhibit the traits we have just discussed? You can decide for yourself.

When you equate trust with integrity, our first president certainly attained an unearthly stature. He was, of course, the subject of the iconic tale of honesty: confessing to his father that he cut down the cherry tree.

Mythical as it was, the story exemplified Washington's unimpeachable integrity, which was further validated by his insistence, as president, that America repay all its war debts – a minority view in his administration. Here was a man you could trust.

"Honest Abe," likewise, was a man distinguished by his transparency. Mary Todd Lincoln once wrote that her husband was "almost a monomaniac on the subject of honesty."[1]

When you liken compassion to concern for the lost and forgotten, Lincoln and Roosevelt undoubtedly rise to the top. Lincoln's compassionate view toward suffering *on both sides* in the Civil War even made its way into the Gettysburg Address. "But, in a larger sense, we cannot dedicate – we cannot consecrate – we cannot hallow – this ground. The brave men, living and dead, who struggled here, have consecrated it, far above our poor power to add or detract." Similarly, FDR aimed to ease the nation's suffering in the Great Depression, and the New Deal was his plan to do so.

What about the spirit of self-reflection, learning from one's mistakes, and promoting the Just Culture? Washington was a confident military leader, but as president he was full of self-doubt, which he openly expressed in his letters. Lincoln, of course, was the paragon of humility. He constantly fretted about the wisdom of his choices as he was a man "wracked by uncertainty, doubt, and psychological pain."[2]

FDR, likewise, was refreshingly open to feedback and known for continual experimentation, always learning from his mistakes. "It is common sense to take a method and try it: if it fails, *admit it frankly* and try another. But above all, keep trying." No one ever said it better.

When it comes to coalescence, though, these three really set the bar. Washington motivated a ragtag band of soldiers to overthrow a mighty occupation, Lincoln rallied the North through a brutal civil war for a lofty moral purpose, and FDR inspired a nation to emerge from the Great Depression and defeat an evil empire. In his second inaugural address, Lincoln put coalescence into words in a most remarkable speech.[3]

> With malice toward none, with charity for all, with firmness in the right as God gives us to see the right, let us strive on to finish the work we are in, to bind up the nation's wounds, to care for him who shall have borne the battle and for his widow and his orphan.

So it *does* make sense. We *do* value these traits in our leaders. We *do* recognize the value of relationships, the soft, squishy center, in the art of leadership. And when we combine these interpersonal skills with a systematic approach, we can round out our description of a great leader through the characteristics that our examples have illustrated.

In my profession, we would collectively call these features the *phenotype*: the observable traits that define an individual. The phenotype of a great national leader, then, includes the following nine attributes:

- A secure sense of self to permit *honest reflection*, admission of error, and learning from one's own mistakes
- A systematic and fair-minded approach to the mistakes of others, leading to transparency, forgiveness, and *the Just Culture*
- A solid foundation of integrity to *encourage trust* by colleagues, counterparts, and constituents
- A frank and impartial *acceptance of facts* to support accurate and objective assessments
- A *methodical approach* to problem-solving to promote faithful and steady progress toward the target state
- A capacity to fully consider and objectively interpret *all available evidence* to ensure the best possible decisions
- A *compassionate heart* toward the less fortunate to inspire the benevolent application of the levers of power
- An appreciation of the dark forces that drive group dynamics and the *capacity to overcome inherent bias*
- An ability to transcend natural divisions in the electorate to achieve unity of purpose and a *coalescence of forces*

It is worth emphasizing once again the importance of the systematic approach. Even for such intangible aims as compassion, trust, and coalescence. After all, we did not make our hospital safe by telling everyone to be careful. We gave them rules to follow. We did not improve the patient experience by telling everyone to be nice. We gave them standard work to do.

Likewise, we do not promote compassion by telling everyone to be sympathetic. Only by addressing the needs of the many in our target state, gap analysis, and solution approach will we truly establish the practice of compassion. Indeed, only by embracing the principles of integrity will we earn trust. And only by systematically bridging our differences will we achieve coalescence. All planned. All implemented. All on purpose.

It should be clear by now that these attributes of governance cover a lot of ground. They draw from all aspects of the intellect and require a wide range of abilities. Have I set the bar too high? Perhaps I have. What single person could possibly be proficient at all of these skills?

My first response is to acknowledge that nobody is perfect at everything, but we can still use our great leader phenotype as an assessment tool to help us select candidates for higher office. It will remind us what we are aiming for – our leadership target state. My second response is that the best physicians I know actually do well in every one of these attributes. Why should we expect less of our national leaders?

Indeed, we do have some wonderful historical role models who combined natural gifts in art and science. Leonardo da Vinci, for example, was a grand master of the canvas, yet also a proficient scientist and engineer. From the Mona Lisa to flying machines and anatomical treatises, da Vinci was perhaps the most famous artist-scientist of all time.

And then there was Vladimir Nabokov, author of the highly praised novel, *Lolita*, a native-born Russian who perfected poetry as prose in English to world-wide acclaim, and who peppered his masterpiece with puns, anagrams, and spicy wordplay. How many of his enraptured readers knew that he was a world-class lepidopterist, a prolific contributor to our scientific understanding of butterflies?

A final example comes from my young adult life. As a medical student at Washington University, I was mesmerized by Douglas Hofstadter's Pulitzer Prize-winning work, *Gödel, Escher, Bach: An Eternal Golden Braid*.[4] This witty, self-referential, boundary-crossing weave of mathematical philosophy, art, and music transported me to paradise as a dazzling coalescence of ideas.

In any case, we are not talking about museum art or laboratory science. We will settle for the interpersonal and decision-making skills that translate from the bedside to the podium. The point here is that leaders as well as physicians have great responsibilities that require a multitude of interconnected talents. It is not unreasonable to demand exceptional abilities in those we select to meet those challenges.

I am pleased to report that our lessons are ready to be tested, as it is time to shift our focus from the corridors of the hospital to the chambers of government. Does it seem fair to cross this line? To trespass this boundary? To translate stories from my world into advice for national leaders? I would say most definitely yes. This foray into politics makes perfect sense.

I noted in the Prelude that American hospitals have borrowed heavily from the outside. As the aviation, automobile, and hotel industries taught us about safety, quality, and customer service, it only stands to reason that an enterprise with as much at stake as health care would have the standing to inform our nation's leaders. To prove my point, in the chapters that follow, we will put our attributes of leadership through an audition of sorts by reviewing them in the context of contentious challenges facing America.

The first of these will be income inequality, a high-profile issue that trains a spotlight on the middle class and carries enormous implications for our nation's predicament. This is the perfect test of the evidence-based approach as we will learn whether there is such a thing as objective truth hiding among the toxic weeds of all the fake news.

Next, we will examine the topic of health care, which is, of course, familiar terrain for me. In this chapter, we will assess how Obamacare stacks up against our attributes of leadership. Then we will move on to a pair of hotbed issues: gun control and abortion.

Why examine two of the most excruciatingly divisive and intractable issues facing our nation? Because they live in the land of competing rights – the epicenter of our nation's illness, the site of origin from which our cancer spreads. Because that is precisely where the symbiosis of art and science is best demonstrated, where great leadership is most vital, and where our lessons face their greatest challenge.

After that, we will re-examine our great leader attributes in the context of three recent American presidents – as the ultimate test of their relevance. In the stories of Ronald Reagan, Barack Obama, and Donald Trump, we will better understand our lessons from the bedside and their impact upon leadership performance.

Rest assured that I have not forgotten the primary mission of this book: the diagnosis and treatment of the patient – our ailing nation. I have reserved that exercise for the final three chapters.

Curiosity:
Follow the Trail

"I had," said he, "come to an entirely erroneous conclusion which shows, my dear Watson, how dangerous it always is to reason from insufficient data...I can only claim the merit that I instantly reconsidered my position when, however, it became clear to me that whatever danger threatened an occupant of the room could not come either from the window or the door...Having once made up my mind, you know the steps which I took in order to put the matter to the proof."

From *The Adventure of the Speckled Band,*
Sir Arthur Conan Doyle, 1892

December. I am thinking about the five stages of grief. I have already exhausted three phases of denial: My first initial hopes for a recount in the firewall states. My farfetched back-up plan for electoral college defections in deference to the popular vote. Then, perhaps, some sort of judicial intervention over Russian interference. Each of these seemed tantalizingly possible at the time, but they were mainly carried aloft by the magic carpet of wishful thinking. Like most fantasies, each vanished, one by one, in an agonizing instant. Three pricks of the bubble. Snap, crackle, pop!

Now that I am past denial, I don't see much point in anger. Just disappointment – that nearly half of American voters would fall under the spell of the magician. Would stay focused on the right hand while the left palmed the silver dollar.

But maybe not. Perhaps they were fixated on the left hand all along. The one with the shiny coin. This was not a magic trick, after all, but a vaudeville act. A song and dance routine in open view with the full engagement of a rapt audience.

This is the part I need to work on. This is the question I will obsess about for months. Why? How? What on earth were the voters thinking? This mystery will require a deep dive into the inner workings of popular sentiment. Trump is not the one out of touch with the truth. I am.

In Chapter 6, I described how evidence drives out myth in the field of Medicine to provide a solid foundation in our search for the truth. Now, I feel compelled to address the question of transferability to the secular world of governance. Which begs the question: what *is* the current state of evidence in the political realm?

I think it is rather obvious that our political discourse has nothing remotely approaching an evidence-based approach or even a common base of understanding about how to *get* to the truth. The foundation is more like quicksand. Hence, all the finger-pointing about fake news. Hence, the rise of websites that exist solely for the purpose of shaming political leaders who tell falsehoods. Hence, our growing concern about the elusive nature of objective truth itself. In my profession, we would say the truth is *friable*. Like fragile tissue, every time we nearly have it in our grasp, it seems to disintegrate at our very touch, crumbles to pieces in our outstretched hands.

I can't help but feel that fragility of truth is the greatest threat to our democracy. If we don't know what to believe, how can we agree on the facts? If we cannot agree on the facts, how can we make collective decisions about *anything*? The lack of an evidentiary foundation is utterly paralyzing in the practice of Medicine and equally toxic to the conduct of leadership.

So the transferability of the evidence-based movement to the political sphere is crucially important. What would be our litmus test? Can decisions of our leaders rest on an agreed-upon foundation of understanding? Would this even improve the condition of the nation, our patient?

Fortunately, several of the hot political topics of this decade *do* lend themselves to a quantitative approach. Income inequality, fiscal integrity, and economic performance are topics that can be measured, tracked, and studied "by the numbers."

So here is the nugget: Does the political arena foster ill-conceived notions, elaborate myths, and utter falsehoods that rest on fancy, speculation, or even outright fabrication? Does the evidence exist to bust those myths, counter the lies, and set the record straight? In other words, is there any hope for the truth?

In short, the answer is yes, and in this chapter I am going to prove it.

In recent decades, economists have claimed that there are growing disparities in wealth and income across America. Some suggest that rising inequality erodes the American dream for the middle class and harms our democracy. I would like to spend this entire chapter on three simple questions about this assertion: Is it true? If so, why did it happen? And... does it matter? The purpose of this discussion is to test whether there is an objective standard upon which we may rest our conclusions. In the spirit of an evidence-based approach, we will rely heavily upon facts.

To answer the first question, we must embark on an ambitious journey across the economic landscape to track the flow of income, taxes, and wealth. We will don our deerstalker cap, manicured moustache, and spinsterish persona to join the tradition of three great detectives in literary history – Sherlock Holmes, Hercule Poirot, and Miss Marple – to follow the clues wherever they may lead. In other words, we will follow the money.

For the record, this is exactly what I must do when faced with doubts about a *medical* decision, such as for Candice Staner, Gerald Menard, or Stan Loritan. I must decide in advance what facts I need to answer the question, and then go looking for them. In this search for the truth, I am driven by intense *curiosity*, one of the essential qualities of a skilled clinician.

But here is the deal – our binding contract. Once I gain the evidence, I must let the chips fall where they may. As did Sherlock Holmes in *The Adventure of the Speckled Band*, I must accept the new truth if facts disagree with my preconceptions. Then I must reconsider my position and redirect my strategy. This is a worthwhile test of the evidence-based approach.

We will start by outlining our parameters. First, I propose we should categorize Americans into five quintiles – 5 equal baskets of 20% layered one on top of the other from lowest income to the highest. I would then define the middle class as encompassing the middle three baskets (quintiles) out of the five – i.e., from the 20th through the 80th percentile.

As we can see, this is a 60% broad band that extends from lower to upper middle class, and which represents the majority of American households. Please also note that it is commonplace to express economic units of people as households because this brings children into the fold and takes into account that households typically function on a combined budget.

We will begin with a simple question. What has happened to middle-class household incomes over time? But let's be careful here. The obvious caveat is that household income does not tell the whole story. We really should be focusing on *net* income – what is left over *after* taxes and benefits. And here is the reason: we have a progressive tax system. High earners pay higher taxes than low earners. They should get credit for that. Furthermore, low income people are more likely to receive government benefits such as food stamps. Some would say they are the "takers." Moreover, government health benefits *also* represent a form of in-kind income that narrows the gap between rich and poor.

In the spirit of pure evidence, a true measure of household income should take into account these four factors: 1) employment income, which includes the value of health coverage; 2) government cash benefits, such as Social Security, unemployment, and welfare benefits; 3) government *non-cash* benefits, such Medicare, Medicaid, and food stamps; and 4) taxes paid. That would be the Full Monty – the true final measure of household income that incorporates all the giving and all the taking.

This, then, should be the gold-standard comparison between rich and poor – our ideal metric. It turns out that the Congressional Budget Office (CBO) has done just that. In 2011, the CBO put out a report tracking household income from 1979 to 2007, after adjusting for taxes and benefits. The following table displays the results by percentile, just as we prefer. All figures are expressed in 2018 dollars to control for inflation. In political science, this is what we call *evidence*.

US Real Household Incomes *After* Taxes and Benefits: 1979 and 2007[1]

Percentile	1979	2007	Gain
20th percentile:	$ 18,647	$ 22,965	23%
40th percentile:	$ 27,650	$ 36,020	30%
60th percentile:	$ 36,713	$ 51,064	39%
80th percentile:	$ 49,701	$ 73,274	47%
99th percentile:	$140,313	$305,654	118%

In this table, one can see that middle-class household incomes in 2007 ranged from $22,965 to $73,274. That sounds about right. However, it is striking to see how modest the gains were for the middle class compared to the upper class. For example, over 28 years, folks at the 99th percentile gained 118% or $158,000 per household (i.e., doubled their income), while those at the 20th percentile gained only 23%, or $4,000 each. That's less than 1% per year. Not very impressive for a world class economy!

Since these data reflect household income *after* adjusting for all the ways that employers and government mitigate disparities, I would say that the case is convincingly proven that income inequality is getting worse. This is most definitely an *evidence*-based conclusion. And all those government benefits have *not* neutralized the growing disparity. Myth busted.

I am curious to know how this disparity impacted the *distribution* of the income pie, the size of the portions flowing to each basket. First, the bottom quintile, the lowest 20% of households, who earned only 7% of all income in 1979, saw their portion *shrink to 5%* by 2007.[1] That means the bottom 20% are now fighting over 5% of the pie.

The shares of the three central quintiles, our middle-class Americans, also shrank by 2-3% each. The upper 20%, on the other hand, saw its portion *grow* from a 43% share to a 53% share. Thus, the top fifth ended up with more than half of all the national income.

What about the infamous top 1%? Their share more than *doubled* in 28 years. They went from an 8% slice in 1979 to 17% in 2007. In a single generation. Now that is really astonishing. That means that the share of the pie gained by the top 1% almost exactly equaled *all* the losses of the lower 80%. Middle-class Americans are losing ground, all right. But not to the poor. Not even to the near-rich. Their share is going to the *ultra*-rich. All of it.

So far, we have been talking about *income* – annual earnings by a household. What about accumulated *wealth* – total assets? Is the wealth pie becoming more unbalanced as well? The answer is a resounding yes. Even more so than for income. For example, let's look at the bottom 90% of American households with respect to wealth ownership. This group owned 20% of America's assets in the 1920s. Their share expanded to 35% by 1978, then dropped back down to 23% by 2012.[2]

On the other hand, the top 0.1% (one *tenth* of a percent) had the opposite experience. Their share, which was a quarter of the pie in 1928, dropped to less than 8% by 1978, and then nearly tripled – to 22% by 2012. This elite group, literally one in a thousand, consisted of the top 160,000 households in America, each possessing at least $20 million in wealth. In plain English, 0.1% of Americans now own 22% of the wealth.

Did you notice the striking comparison? Check the current wealth share for the top 0.1% compared to the bottom 90%. For every 1,000 American households, the one at the top has about the same amount of wealth as *the bottom 900 households combined!* Can this be true? Can this possibly be a good thing for democracy?

The golden age of equitable distribution of wealth and income in America peaked at around 1980. Beginning with the Reagan administration, there has been a growing disparity in prosperity for some strange reason. And now the level of inequality looks like it did nearly a century ago.

What do our nation's people think about wealth disparity? When 5,500 Americans were surveyed about their ideal distribution of wealth, they were invited to slice the pie any way they liked. The average proposal was to have the top quintile owning 32% of the wealth, and the bottom quintile owning 11%.[3] This was far removed from the astounding truth, which was that the top quintile owned 84% of the wealth, and the bottom two quintiles *combined* owned just 0.3%. Not three percent. *Zero point* three percent.

When asked to choose between two anonymous pie arrangements, one of which was the American version and the other of which was the Swedish version, 92% of American respondents preferred the Swedish version. Interestingly, the answers did not vary significantly between Republicans and Democrats.

Let's summarize the evidence so far. From about 1980 onward, there has been a markedly growing disparity of income and wealth between rich and poor, with the ultra-rich increasing their share of the pie at everyone else's expense. When surveyed, Americans favor a much more equitable distribution of wealth than currently exists anywhere in the world, yet Americans have the worst degree of equity among industrialized nations.

That is not based on speculation. It is grounded in facts. Most disturbing is this observation: what the voters want is not what their leaders are doing. I cannot imagine a more telling symptom of an ailing democracy.

Now I must return to this question. Where *did* the money go? We have already discovered that the money did not go to the poor. The lion's share went to the rich. Who are other possible recipients of this largesse?

One plausible offender is Mexico. Because of the North American Free Trade Agreement (NAFTA), it is commonly believed that Mexico is responsible for the plight of our middle class. We should clearly see this in a rising trade deficit with our southern neighbor, so let's test this theory with facts.

Indeed, statistics show that in 1993, the year before NAFTA, we had no deficit in our trade balance with Mexico. By 2019, the deficit had grown to $102 billion.[4] That certainly supports the point. But that deficit represents just 0.5% of our gross domestic product (GDP), practically a rounding error. Are we making Mexico the fall guy for a more sinister culprit?

Perhaps a stronger argument against Mexico is that our trade agreement allows low-cost foreign workers to drive down the prices of foreign products. Stiff competition then squeezes the profit margins of American companies, forcing down the wages of American workers. If that were true, the profit margins of American corporations should be looking pretty skimpy by now. But American corporate profits are not getting squeezed; they have *soared* over the past three decades – soared to stratospheric heights.

In 1988, Reagan's final year of office, corporate profits after taxes were $535 billion (in 2018 dollars). By 2018, they surpassed $1.9 *trillion*.[5] This 250% real increase is not a typo. Corporate profits have nearly quadrupled even *after* adjusting for inflation. Thus, in a head-to-head comparison, the trade deficit with Mexico went up by $102 billion while corporate profits went up by $1,400 billion. There really is no contest.

More important, corporate profits as a share of the overall GDP have *doubled*, from roughly 5% in the 1980s to 10% in the 2010s, an all-time high.[6] Corporate profits, then, must have taken a 5% chunk of the pie from someone else. Who do you think that was? Now compare this amount to the Mexico trade deficit, a paltry 0.5% of the GDP, and try not to snicker.

Here is an interesting thought. What if corporations redistributed their *extra* share of the pie *back* to their employees? In other words, turned back the clock. Kept their old 5% share. Behaved like they used to. What would be the impact on their profits? The math is easy. Their profits would be cut in half, to $950 billion, which is still nearly double what it was in 1988.

And what would be the impact of sharing the remaining $950 billion in excess income – industry's *false* profits, if you will – with America's working class? Astoundingly, this share of corporate profits, along with recouped taxes on those profits, would be enough to nearly double the income of the bottom half of all workers.

That's right. The cumulative earnings of 84 million American wage-earners (50% of all workers) making less than the median income of $32,800 in 2018 was about 1.2 trillion dollars.[7] This payout could be nearly doubled by the excess profits that corporations are paying to their shareholders instead of their workers. I am not suggesting that we should do this. I am just pointing out how much money there is and where it went. Not to the poor. And not to Mexico. It is still right here in the U.S., in corporate coffers.

Besides the rich, the poor, foreign countries, and domestic corporations, are there any other possible culprits? One obvious remaining suspect is the health care industry. In 1979, national health expenditures equaled 8.9% of the GDP. By 2018, this share had doubled to 17.7%.[8] The additional bite is a huge chunk of the pie, which must have come from somewhere and can be seen in two ways.

In the table I presented earlier, increasingly expensive health care benefits are counted as a contributor to growing incomes of workers because they are considered part of the compensation package. In other words, when the cost (i.e., value) of your health care goes up, the employer considers that a raise, even if your wages remain exactly the same.

What if workers don't see it that way? To a worker, health care is all the same regardless of price. The employers' growing health care expense doesn't feel like a rising income; it feels like a necessary cost to preserve a stable benefit. What we really care about is the size of our *paycheck*.

I am coming to a sobering realization. What if even the meager 35% growth in median household income over 28 years is a complete fiction? What if this modest increase is primarily due to the growing expense of health insurance and other benefits, which counts as a "raise" – on paper.

Now, suddenly, I am not so interested in total household compensation as I am in *wage rates* for individual workers. Do we have anything on file about that? Of course we do! From 1979 to 2019, real (inflation-adjusted) median weekly earnings for full-time wage and salary workers rose from $862 to $914, an increase of just 6%.[9]

Once again, we must rub our eyes and remind ourselves that this is the *total* increase over the entire span. The real pay of American middle-class wage earners went up by only 6% in 40 years! During those same 40 years, America's real GDP per capita rose by 92%.[10] In other words, overall *output* per person nearly doubled while *wages* per person barely budged.

And we haven't even mentioned the calamity at the *lower* end of the spectrum. In 1978 the federal minimum wage was $2.65, which was the equivalent of $10.21 in 2018 dollars. In 2018, however, the minimum wage was actually only $7.25. Thus, folks at the bottom end of the pay scale were effectively slammed with nearly a 30% real pay cut over four decades.

Here we must recall a principle of evidence-based decision-making: focusing on the important outcomes. What really matters in this discussion is the prosperity of the *people*. Our miserable return on lower and middle-class incomes is all the evidence we need to confirm the abject failure of our economic strategy over 40 years.

It is time to sum up. We have followed the money. We have gathered all the suspects in the parlor and are ready to identify the perpetrators: the "Great Reveal." Yes, middle-class Americans have lost ground. They have completely missed out on the growing GDP of the past four decades. While the pie is getting bigger, their share is getting smaller, so take-home pay has remained stagnant. No wonder they are angry and resentful.

And where did the money go? Not to where Republican leaders told us it went. Not *down*. Not to the poor, not to inner cities, not to minorities. Not to "takers," "welfare queens," or immigrants. Not even to Mexico.

No, my dear Watson. The money went *up*. Up to the rich, up to corporate profits, and up to the health care industry. In fact, most of it got swallowed up in three ill-fated ventures in Supply-Side Economics. Let's go there now to find out why.

To understand what happened to start the ball rolling toward greater inequality, we must reflect upon President Reagan's introduction of Supply-Side Economics in 1981. The concept was simple: feed the economy at the top. Cut taxes for wealthy Americans and corporations. These, after all, are the "job creators." Slash capital gains taxes to encourage investment. Scrap regulations to permit unconstrained growth. Then let the magic begin.

The growth in investment will expand the economy. The thriving corporate sector will hire more workers, and increasing revenues will fill all the coffers, including the pockets of labor. As the money flows down to all sectors of the economy, the rising tide will lift all the boats. Sound familiar? Best of all, the expanded economy will more than make up for lower tax rates, so the budget deficit will *melt* away. So what actually happened?

Exhibit 1: Reaganomics. First, the predicted increase in tax revenues did *not* materialize, and the deficit spun wildly out of control. Second, the rich *did* get richer, as the facts have proven. Nonetheless, this bounty did not flow downstream, as Americans in the bottom half gained no ground in household income over eight years. This was a massive redistribution of wealth and income *upward* through the food chain.

Exhibit 2: Bill Clinton *reversed* Supply-Side-Economics. He *raised* taxes on the wealthy to the dismay of his Republican opponents, who warned that he would wreck the economy. As a result, he turned a $290 billion dollar deficit into a $236 billion *surplus*. Along the way, 23 million new jobs were created, an all-time record for a two-term president. Some wrecking job!

Exhibit 3: In 2001, George W. Bush *reinstituted* Supply-Side Economics. He cut taxes once again in a way that catered to the wealthy.[11] While the middle 20% of Americans received just 9% of the cuts, the top 0.2% received 15%. By 2004, the budget surplus had become a $413 billion *deficit*. By 2006, corporate profits had tripled. Two years later, the bubble burst.

Sometimes, when a physician is curious about a treatment, she performs a three-phase trial. She introduces a medication to test its impact. Then she withdraws it to test the reversal. Then she introduces it a second time – the *rechallenge*. Between these 3 phases, the impact of a treatment is usually clear – a beautiful demonstration of the evidence-based approach.

In the history of Supply-Side Economics, we have the physician's dream: a natural experiment in three phases. Phase 1 was Reaganomics. Phase 2 was the Clinton Reversal. Phase 3 was the Bush Rechallenge. By the end of Bush's second term, with the economy in tatters, 700,000 jobs disappearing every month, and a budget deficit rising to $1.1 trillion, it was clear that Supply-Side Economics was a flop. Then came the coup de grâce.

Believe it or not, after Obama had recovered the economy, partially reversed supply-side policy with a tax increase on the rich, and wrestled the deficit down by more than 60%, Republicans added one more experiment that proved to be the final nail in the coffin – the Trump Tax Act of 2017.

This was a supply-side tax cut of *gargantuan* proportions – $2.3 trillion in total costs.[12] And, once again, this was money we didn't have. In truth, we borrowed every penny – enough to provide $1600 annually for every American tax unit (typically one per household). That's how much we borrowed. Is that how the money was distributed? $1600 per family? Let's take a peek at the evidence.

Once again, imagine all American households are equally divided into five boxes. The bottom box holds the 20% of households with the lowest annual income and the top box holds the 20% who make the most. The middle three boxes are the in-between groups. If the tax cuts were distributed equally, every family in each box would have received a $1600 tax cut. But that's not how it happened.

First, the group at the bottom received just $60 per family per year.[13] Not sixteen hundred. Not even *six* hundred. Just sixty. The next box up, which includes many senior citizens relying on Social Security, got $400. What happened to the other $1200? The next box up, the middle one, got $900. Not sixteen hundred. *Nine* hundred. The next box got eighteen hundred. But where are the missing shares from the first three boxes?

When we get to the top box, we find all the missing shares concentrated here. In this tier we find a payout of $7,600 per family, more than four times what would have been an equal share. And what about the infamous top 1%? What was their share of the tax cut?

Believe it or not, the average share of the tax cut for the top 1% was *$51,000* per year. Per family. A thousand a week. While the folks in the bottom box got $60 apiece, the folks at the top got $51,000. *That's* where the missing money went. *Up* the ladder. Up to the very *top* of the ladder.

In the usual lopsided way of supply-side tax cuts, the bottom 20% of families shared 1% of the money while the top 1% shared 20%. Even worse, the massive federal borrowing required to pay for these tax cuts completely undid Obama's progress on the deficit and is projected to send our shortfall soaring back up to $1.1 trillion by 2022.[14]

Just for fun, let's take a look at the impact of the Trump tax cuts on jobs growth. Surely there was a spike upward in jobs growth after giving such a massive boost to job creators.

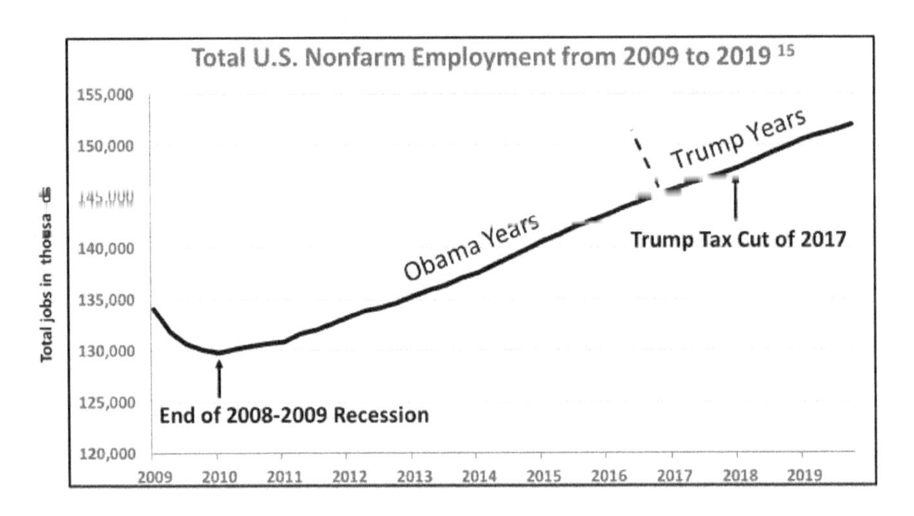

In this graph, we see a remarkably steady rise in jobs over the past nine years, about 2.2 million jobs per year – like clockwork – without any visible impact by the Trump tax cuts.[15] The first six years were under Obama, and the final three years were on Trump's watch. If we compare jobs growth in the year *before* the tax cut (2.36 million) to jobs growth in the year *after* the tax cut (2.14 million), we are stunned to learn that jobs growth actually went slightly *down*. The tax cut, it seems, was a big flop as far as jobs growth. And, of course, in 2020, the COVID pandemic would send U.S. employment spiraling downward in a response that had nothing to do with tax policy.

When we sum up our forty-year experiment, one can clearly see the devastating impact of supply-side tax policy on the federal deficit. In the graph below, the vertical bars represent the annual federal budget deficit or surplus expressed as a percentage of the GDP.[16] The deeper the bar, the worse the deficit. Each application of supply-side tax policy (by Presidents Reagan, Bush, and Trump) is captured by a black box. Presidents Clinton and Obama raised taxes for the rich in 1993 and 2013, respectively.

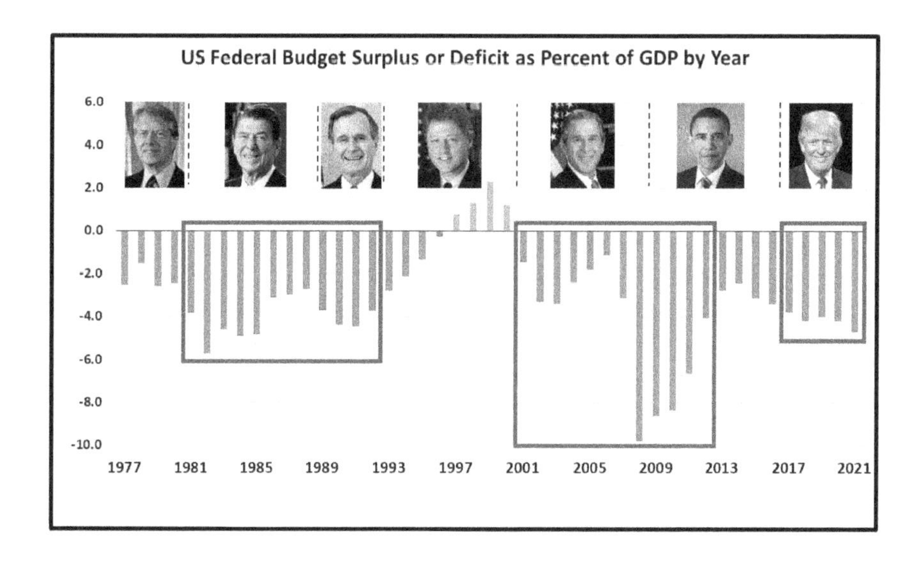

Incredibly, by 2022, our federal debt accumulated over 230 years will be nearly $20 trillion, and 71% of that will have come from our supply-side boxes outlined above.[14,17] As for income inequality, one can only speculate how much worse this will become over the next decade.

These results simply reinforce a point already made by economists. In capitalism, it takes money to make money. Hence, wealth begets wealth. Hence, money naturally rises, like heat. Hence, affluence concentrates in the upper tiers, just like the air we warm with our furnace. Feeding the rich makes no more sense than installing heating ducts in the ceiling.

Cutting taxes severely expands the deficit and lines the pockets of the wealthy. Rising corporate revenues do not flow downward into workers' paychecks. The hyperstimulated economy enrichens everyone at the top, leaving the middle class on the outside, and may even build a huge bubble that leads to a crash. This natural experiment is the convincing evidence we need to drop Supply-Side Economics from our political vocabulary – *forever.*

At this point we have completed the evidence-based portion of this chapter, which should have answered several questions by now. Is inequality rising? Where did the money go? And...Why? Now let's answer the final question – So what? The "so what" question is perhaps the most important of all. It is a question we often ask about medical decisions we are making.

The new medication lowers my patient's blood pressure by 30 points. So what? The chest x-ray shows an infiltrate in the right lower lung. Who cares? The cardiac cath reveals an obstruction in the coronary artery. What does it matter? It is not enough to show one thing leads to another. It is necessary to go one more step, to identify the impact of that result. Once again, this is a lesson from the bedside.

The starting point for answering the "so what" question is to ask ourselves what is the goal of the economy, after all? Is income inequality intrinsically a bad thing? An economic conservative might disagree. She might argue that economic output is maximized by creating a meritocracy, an environment in which talent and effort are rewarded by success, and laziness and incompetence are punished by failure.

In this world, inequality is actually a good thing – a motivator. For an outstanding summary of this argument, I suggest reading *Equal is Unfair: America's Misguided Fight Against Income Inequality* by Don Watkins and Yaron Brook.[18] This incisive and well-written book will make you stop and think, especially if you are a liberal.

That would be a fair game – with rules that do not favor outcomes but channel acceptable income to the many, and massive wealth to the few – the geniuses among us who think up great ideas to make the world a better place and prove themselves by their creativity, persistence, and hard work. Such an environment would maximally incentivize innovation, investment, and wealth creation to produce the highest possible economic output (GDP).

However, I beg to differ on a key point. I would argue that the ultimate goal of the economy is not to produce the greatest possible economic output, but rather to produce *broad-based prosperity*, to maximize the greatest good for the greatest number. Not complete equality, but broad-based success. A world in which all Americans would have a chance to earn a decent living to provide for their families and achieve their aspirations.

In this world, *which is overwhelmingly favored by American people in surveys*, the incentivization of talent and effort would be merely the means to an end, not the end in itself. And, if the rules of the game resulted in maximal rewards that were experienced by only a few, then we would *not* have attained the target state. Let me explain my point through a hypothetical example. Imagine these two potential outcomes for the U.S. economy:

Option A: The national income is $20 trillion, and 80% of it ($16 trillion) goes to the top 10% of households, leaving only $4 trillion for the lower 90%. **Option B:** The national income is only $10 trillion, half as large, but the lion's share, $8 trillion, goes to the lower 90%.

Which is preferred? It depends on your point of view. Option A is a massive pie but so badly skewed in its distribution that there is little left for the great majority of Americans. If the goal is simply to bake the biggest pie, this is best. Option B is a much smaller pie but so much better distributed the great majority of people enjoy *twice* as much annual income. If you are looking for the greatest good for the greatest number, this is the preferred choice and the one that most Americans favor. By the way, our current state of *wealth* is option *A*. The top 10% of Americans share 78% of the pie.[2]

What about the argument that the current distribution of income is desirable because it is based on the *purity* of a free-market economy? That the government has no right to meddle. That it will just distort the laws of supply and demand and corrupt the natural flow of goods and services.

This is a modern myth. The underlying American economy is *not* a model of pure capitalism. It is *not* a "natural" state of economic forces governed by an invisible hand. It never was. For an exceptional treatment of this topic from the other side, I recommend Robert Reich's insightful book *Saving Capitalism: For the Many, Not the Few.*[19] This is a required read that will make you stop and think, especially if you are a conservative.

In truth, our entire economic structure is a synthetic paradigm of government regulation, which defines the very elements and processes of economic exchanges. Take the modern corporation, which is completely defined by legislation. The main purpose of this entity is to shield owners from personal liability for financial obligations. As a result, if the corporation I own goes bankrupt, its creditors may not come after my personal assets.

Case in point? Donald Trump's corporations went bankrupt a half-dozen times. Six times his organizations went belly-up. Six times he reneged on payments. Six times he scampered away from egregiously poor business decisions, unscathed. Meanwhile, his banks, his investors, and even the blue-collar workers who built his casinos, bore the full burden of the losses that were never repaid. All perfectly legal. The record speaks for itself.

For more on these topics, read Paul Krugman's collection of insightful essays, *Arguing with Zombies: Economics, Politics, and the Fight for a Better Future.*[20] Nobody does evidence-based analysis better than Krugman, Nobel Prize-winning economist who is drawn to the truth like a moth to a flame. I marvel at his ability to make plain sense of all this madness.

We have covered extensive territory in this chapter, and it is time to wrap up our review of evidence-based principles. First, we identified convincing proof that income inequality is growing at the expense of the middle class. Then we followed the money to see that it did not go to the poor, to the inner cities, to immigrants, or to minorities. Not even to Mexico. Instead, the money went *up* to health care, corporate profits, and to the ultra-rich. The evidence spoke for itself. We just followed the trail.

Then, we examined the mechanism of growing inequality and exposed the perverse impact of Supply-Side Economics on the American middle class by way of a classic three-phase historical experiment. Finally, we realized that there really is no such thing as a pure, unfettered economy. Another myth shattered by a hundred years of contradictory evidence. Which leads to confirmation of our diagnosis and a plan for treatment.

Growing income inequality is bad for America, our patient, because it corrodes democracy at its core: the all-important middle class. Government policies caused this mess, and government policies can fix it. We need to reverse the disease process by raising the minimum wage and redirecting tax cuts from the upper tier to the middle class.

Perhaps the time is ripe to experiment with a new idea: *demand*-side economics. Feed the economy at the middle and lower end, and watch the proceeds flow *up* through the system, just like the heat in our home or the biological food chain in our natural world. If that doesn't work, try something else. As FDR would remind us, "Above all, keep trying."

Finally, we need to continue to regulate our "free market" to maintain the vitality of capitalism as a wealth-creator for everyone. These collective polices will undo the redistributive intent of Supply-Side Economics and set our sails toward our ultimate goal: broad-based prosperity for *all.*

Whew! I think we need to take a breather. This chapter was a wild ride through a dense array of facts and statistics. A policy wonk's dream come true. Why on earth did we do this? For what possible reason did we take this winding detour far afield from our opening chapters? To be frank, I wanted to make a simple point: facts matter.

One of the most distressing symptoms of our nation's malady is the endangerment of truth, which at times is merely a faint signal buried in all the noise – a cacophonous din of political flak, competing claims, and fake news. All too often the first response to an uncomfortable truth is to launch an information bomb, a competing barrage of made-up facts to crowd out, cover up, and otherwise obliterate the truth that lies beneath. Sorting through this pile seems like a hopeless task.

But it is not. In my evidence-based world of medical science, there *are* sources of truth. There are biological measurements, diagnostic tests, and randomized trials, each with well-established standards for reporting. While not completely infallible, the results are not intended to mislead or cover up the truth – but rather to enlighten. And good decisions are usually easy to make when you have all the facts. Every physician knows this.

The same is true in *political* science. As demonstrated in our review of income inequality, there *is* one truth underlying our discourse, and that truth can be uncovered and displayed for all to see. Just as in medical science, there are standards for collection, assimilation, and distribution of political facts that should be the foundation for all our executive, legislative, and judicial pursuits.

Our collective aim, then, is to promote evidence-based *politics* as a discipline to counter opinion, speculation, and false assertions. The judge, jury, and bailiff for this benchmark are the American voters, who must hold their leaders accountable to "follow the trail" of verifiable facts as they make crucial decisions affecting our nation. By enforcing the evidence-based standard, Americans can ensure that their leaders build a path to a future that rests on the immutable bedrock of truth.

Courage:
Take the Risk

> If one advances confidently in the direction of his dreams...he will meet with a success unexpected in common hours. He will put some things behind, will pass an invisible boundary; new, universal, and more liberal laws will begin to establish themselves...and he will live with the license of a higher order of beings.
>
> From *Walden*, by Henry David Thoreau, 1854

January. The nights are long and the days unforgiving. My acute symptoms have subsided, and I am in the grip of a chronic illness. The signs are nonspecific, yet unmistakable: I cannot sleep. I am unable to concentrate. A pervasive listlessness erodes my spirit. The future is bleak.

I have read the textbooks. I know what I have and why. I am aware that this does not bode well for my health but am powerless to address it. The transition is underway. Obama is packing it in and Trump is all over the news, selecting his new team. Pruitt, climate change denier, for the EPA. So much for facts. Flynn for National Security Advisor. There goes trust. Sessions for Attorney General. Say good-bye to the Just Culture. Bannon is riding shotgun. This does not bode well for compassion. Or coalescence. This is even worse than I feared.

One morning, I arise at three am for no apparent reason. I give in to wakefulness with a cup of coffee, then pace fretfully back and forth across the white-tiled kitchen floor. I am feeling edgy, a sense of unease. Suddenly, I am ripe with an irresistible impulse. I sit down at my laptop and begin to type. My first words are the chronicle of Natalie Ghintino and the ICU alarms. I have a story to tell. The first of many.

I have not written before, not like this. Not the delicate revelations of timeworn memories and long-kept secrets. Not in the meandering path of an itinerant preacher. I am most comfortable thinking of this as a personal journal, the private memoir of a late-career physician leader for his own amusement. Not to be shared with anyone else, of course. No need to take a risk.

Debbie Shault was a 57 year-old woman with a previous diagnosis of asthma, who was admitted for severe shortness of breath. Because of a lapse of insurance, she had run out of her medications. When I listened to her lungs, I expected to hear wheezing, the most conspicuous sign of asthma. Instead, she had very quiet breath sounds, and it seemed to take forever for her to push the air out. Each breath was oddly asymmetrical: a quick, easy inspiration, and a slow, labored exhalation: classic emphysema.

Further testing confirmed the diagnosis of emphysema and a low oxygen level in the blood – so low that Debbie would need supplemental oxygen at home. But without insurance, that was impossible. The best we could do was to send her home on her usual medications – supplied by the Bellevue pharmacy on a fee-scale basis.

Therèse Vorot was a 45 year-old woman with a terrible problem. She could not swallow. She was born with an abnormal narrowing of her lower esophagus so that food would get stuck there, unable to pass into her stomach. She had taken extreme steps to compensate for her condition by cutting food into smaller and smaller pieces, using a blender to puree fruits and vegetables, then limiting her diet to nothing but soup and oatmeal.

Yet her problem kept getting worse. She had lost 80 pounds in six months. Not only could she not swallow food, she could not drink liquids either. In fact, she could not even swallow her secretions. When she came into our hospital, she was dehydrated, exhausted, and absolutely miserable.

After our failed attempt to relieve the obstruction with an endoscope, Therèse continued to struggle, so the new plan was to send her home for a few weeks to improve her nutrition with intravenous feedings, and then bring her back for a surgical procedure to offer full relief. On the day of discharge, we learned her health insurance had just elapsed, and we would not be able to provide the nutrition she needed to prepare for surgery.

Keith Tasker was a 28 year-old man who was paralyzed in his lower body from a spinal cord injury two years earlier. Because he had no feeling below his waist, he had developed a dreaded complication of paraplegia – a sacral decubitus ulcer. In the lower part of his back, just above the tailbone, there was an opening in the skin about one inch in diameter, which had tunneled through the skin and muscle layer all the way to the bone of the spine. Keith was being admitted because this deep ulcer was infected.

Keith had been taking care of the ulcer by packing it daily with gauze and covering it with a bandage. Each morning, he would remove the gauze and replace it with fresh packing using his cell phone camera on selfie mode – as a mirror. What was unusual about Keith was that he performed this self-care at home – on the sidewalk.

You see, Keith was homeless. He lived in his wheelchair on the streets of New York, sleeping each night in a sitting position above a warm, vented grate. When the ulcer became infected, he delivered himself to the Bellevue ED – wheeling his way in through the front door under his own power.

This trio of my recent patients faced challenges in breathing, swallowing, and just staying alive.[1] What they also had in common was they had fallen through the cracks, had slipped unnoticed through the fingers of our health system. This was why they came to Bellevue – a safety net hospital. The need for hospitals like Bellevue is a sure sign that our health care system still has gaps, and was the main reason for the birth of the ACA.

The Affordable Care Act (ACA), affectionately (or derisively) known as Obamacare, was the most politically charged topic of Barack Obama's presidency. While there are many details to discuss in this legislation, it was designed very simply to advance health care coverage for uninsured Americans. Nonetheless, the venture was an enormous political risk that passed by a single vote in Congress, nearly collapsed under its own weight during the rollout, and barely survived a Supreme Court challenge. It was by no means a simple birth.

It is quite surprising that, as of 2008, the richest nation with the most advanced health care system in the world had not yet found a way to guarantee universal coverage as all other industrialized nations had done. Yet, for the previous four decades, from Richard Nixon to George W. Bush, no presidential administration had successfully addressed this intractable problem.

So, when Obama set out to solve the dilemma, the path was not clear. America's crazy patchwork of coverage – Medicaid for the poor, Medicare for the elderly, the VA system for veterans, and employment-based insurance for most, but not all, workers, had left nearly 50 million Americans falling through the cracks. The challenge of closing this enormous gap was not for the faint of heart.

Given the astronomical costs of health care, the intricacies of the insurance market, and the lack of national consensus in how to proceed, it did not seem plausible that a solution was achievable, especially in the wake of a huge recession that had nearly burned down the house.

Quite frankly, it was a political suicide mission – an enormously risky undertaking by a young and inexperienced president. Health care reform, then, could be seen as an indefensible political gamble that would threaten Obama's credibility, taint his legacy, and diminish his clout for the remainder of his term. Nonetheless, he took the plunge.

The principle tenets of the ACA are well known. American citizens who do not already have health insurance through their employer or some other means are eligible for coverage via Medicaid for those at the lowest income levels, or through the health care exchanges for those of greater means. The exchanges are run by the states and allow purchasers of health care to compare private health insurance offerings side by side.

The ACA provides for federal subsidization of insurance purchased on the exchange – based on income from 100% up to 400% of the federal poverty level (FPL). Everyone must contribute according to his or her income, and the difference is paid by the federal subsidy. For example, a family of four with an annual income of $44,000 is required to spend $2,800 for their annual premium, and the government covers the rest.[2]

Several elements of Obamacare have proven to be quite popular. The ACA prohibits insurance companies from denying care to applicants with pre-existing conditions. The ACA also forbids insurers from dropping coverage of patients who exceed a certain level of cost in a given year or over a lifetime. These provisions make insurance available to people who need it most and give them confidence that they will retain it no matter how sick they become. In short, these features allow health care to be truly universal.

The ACA further prescribes a required minimum benefit package that includes emergency care, inpatient stays, drug benefits, maternity care, and mental health visits. This provision prevents insurance companies from shaving costs by excluding benefits. The ACA also provides for coverage of young adults by requiring insurance companies to include them on their parent's policies until the age of 26 – thus addressing a point in life when insurance coverage is notoriously unreliable.

In summary, these are the popular elements of Obamacare:

- Universal coverage
- Comprehensive benefits
- Subsidized premiums
- Prohibitions on denial of coverage for pre-existing conditions
- Prohibitions against annual or lifetime caps
- Extension of coverage for young adults to age 26

These two elements have not been so popular:

- High costs of premiums, deductibles, and co-pays
- Individual mandate

The high costs of ACA premiums and co-pays are simply a reflection of the high costs of American health care, of course – a fact well known to employers – and are mitigated by subsidies for premiums. These are the natural consequence of supply and demand in the marketplace, and not the fault of Obamacare. On the contrary, much of the content of the ACA is focused on *reducing* overall costs of health care in the U.S. The success of those measures will be addressed shortly.

The second source of discontent was the individual mandate, which I now speak of in past tense since it was removed by legislation in late 2017. This feature stirred up the most strident opposition and nearly brought down the ACA in the Supreme Court case of 2012. Since the mandate was the primary focus of opposition to the ACA, I will tackle this in depth.

The ACA individual mandate required everyone to purchase health insurance or pay a federal "shared responsibility fee," which was a penalty to encourage participation. The argument against the mandate was that this curtailed personal freedom. By not permitting some Americans to freely opt out, the ACA overrode personal preferences and compelled participation. Some would say that this limit on personal choice was distinctly un-American. Nothing could be further from the truth.

The primary purpose of the mandate was actually to prevent freeloaders, or health care "moochers" – those who can afford to purchase health insurance but choose not to, knowing full well that their costs will be picked up by their fellow citizens. Americans do not typically tolerate moochers, so how is it possible to mooch in health care?

Let's start with an example. A free-lance landscaper who is self-employed and earning $70,000 per year can afford to purchase health insurance. A typical premium for a low-cost Bronze plan on the exchange might be about $4,000 per year for this 35 year-old, healthy, non-smoking male. Since his income is above the upper limit, he does not qualify for a subsidy. The plan is certainly expensive, but not beyond his reach.

Nonetheless, he might reasonably choose *not* to purchase health insurance and spend $4,000 per year on new car payments instead. In this sense, he is taking a risk. Or is he? Can he possibly be safe without health insurance? In America, the answer is yes. He would be safe.

First, he would take into account that he is currently healthy. If he does not have diabetes, hypertension, or any of a host of chronic medical conditions, he would have no need for regular physician visits or ongoing medications at his age.

Second, he would know that if he were to develop such a condition in the future, he could pay into the health care system at that time, and would receive full coverage. Since denial of coverage for pre-existing conditions is prohibited, it is never too late to buy into coverage. By waiting until his first health event, he could save many years' worth of premium payments.

Third, he may know full well that if he has an unexpected emergency in the meantime, he will be fully treated by our current health system as required by law. This means that if he were to have a heart attack, develop severe sepsis, or be struck by a car, he would be taken to an emergency room and admitted to the hospital without question – as a charity case. His bill would be picked up by everyone else: taxpayers, who support public hospitals, and insured patients, whose payments are invisibly inflated to cover patients without insurance.

So it is easy to be a moocher. If you choose not to pay into the system now, your emergency needs will be covered financially by your fellow citizens. If you subsequently develop a chronic illness, you can always join the system at *that* point because the current rules allow it. Imagine the poker player who does not ante into the pot, then joins the game on the third hand, hoping to reap all the winnings. That is our moocher.

It is analogous to waiting until a car accident to buy your car insurance. Or waiting until your house burns down before purchasing home owner's insurance. One can reasonably ask why *anyone* would purchase health insurance up front when *everyone* can join in at the back end. For that reason alone, the ACA included a mandate.

One other example is worth noting, best described through a thought experiment. Imagine a *mandatory* national health insurance program in which all working citizens are required to pay annual premiums that are deducted from their paycheck. Those who cannot afford the full price pay only what they are able to, according to their income, and those who have no income are completely covered by the government.

But no one can opt out. Participation is fully *mandatory*. For that reason, when the time comes, everyone will have complete and total coverage with a specific package of benefits that are heavily regulated by the government. Imagine that this health care program is so vastly popular it becomes the third rail of politics. No candidate for public office from either party would dare challenge it. Could this happen in America? Most definitely, yes. It already has, and we have a name for it.

Medicare.

Indeed, Medicare is a mandate since everyone with income must pay an annual premium (tax), which is deducted from their paycheck by their employer. Call it a premium, fee, or a tax. It is all the same. Mandatory coverage with mandatory participation. There really is no other way to do health care. Moreover, it is ironic that Republicans consider Medicare, a mandate to purchase *public* insurance through *taxes*, more palatable than Obamacare, a mandate to purchase *private* insurance through *premiums*.

Now let us turn to the science. What does the evidence tell us? How has Obamacare fared by the numbers? There is no denying that the main goal of the ACA, to improve insurance coverage, was a solid success. In March, 2016, the U.S. Department of Health and Human Service (HHS) reported that 20 million Americans had gained coverage under the ACA. These gains crossed age and racial lines: 6 million young adults, 9 million White people, 4 million Hispanic people, and 3 million Black people.[3]

Further, according to HHS, the percent of uninsured non-elderly adults decreased from 22.3% in 2010 to 11.9% in 2016. When *all* Americans (including children and senior citizens) are included in the calculation, the proportion of the uninsured dropped from 16.0% to 8.6%, which is the lowest rate in America's history.

What about the costs? As stated previously, much of the content of the ACA was designed to slow the overall growth of health care costs. The first five years following passage validated this approach as the inflation-adjusted annual growth in per capita health care spending was only 1.8%.[4] This compared favorably to the decades of the 1980s, when it averaged 6.1%, the 1990s (2.9%), and the 2000s (3.7%).

Let me repeat this amazing fact: while the ACA was expanding universal coverage to an additional 20 million Americans, the overall growth in annual health care spending actually slowed down! If only this trend could continue. Alas, health care costs are expected to accelerate in the coming decade, eroding the gains of the past five years. This is no fault of the ACA; it is the natural tendency of American health care.

Indeed, health coverage overall is remarkably expensive in the private insurance marketplace with annual premiums for *employees*, the healthiest segment of the population, reaching $7,188 for individuals and $20,576 for families in 2019.[5] The sticker shock experienced by anyone comparing prices on the exchanges is a result of decades of price increases above and beyond the natural rate of inflation. These rates are reportedly so high they threaten the viability of the ACA.

But remember, these prices are set by *private* insurers in the marketplace. They are the result of free-market competition *without* government interference. They represent the *natural* cost of health care based on the private insurance model. How do they stack up against Medicare?

As noted earlier, Medicare is our highly popular federal single-payer system for senior citizens. For many years, it has been noted that administrative costs of private insurance, which include operational costs, marketing, and profit, are much higher than for Medicare. For example, the Congressional Budget Office has reported that administrative expenses for private plans clock in at 15% of premiums, while similar expenses for Medicare are less than 2%.[6]

Further, multiple studies have shown a long-term trajectory of slower growth in Medicare compared to private health insurance in costs per beneficiary. Over an 11-year period, Medicare costs grew by 2% per year less than private plans, which gave it an added 20% edge.[7]

Thus, it seems that Medicare can offer the same coverage for 30% to 40% less than a private plan, which would result in a similar discount on the annual premium payment. Further, Medicare offers much more attractive deductibles and copays than private offerings on the health care exchanges.

So, on balance, Medicare is not only cheaper but better. I think we just figured out how to solve the exorbitant costs of health care choices – the plan we need to add as an option on every exchange.

Medicare.

That's right. Add a Medicare choice to every exchange as an option. The rules would be simple. The insurance would work just like the Medicare we know – same reimbursement rates, same deductibles, same coverage. Same everything. Just use the infrastructure already in place. The premium would be adjusted for age according to the rules of the exchanges, and the federal government would offer the plan at actual cost for each age group. This boat would have to stand on its own bottom.

And why is Medicare so less expensive? There are many reasons for the Medicare advantage: an economy of scale based on its massive size, favorably negotiated hospital payment rates (for the same reason), much lower administrative costs, no marketing expenses, and no shareholders to pay. And if Medicare *were* able to offer a fantastic discount, why shouldn't everyone using the exchange be allowed to benefit from that discount? Do you know who would save the most? American taxpayers, who would save billions on subsidies if consumers were to select Medicare on the exchange.

While we're at it, why not also offer Medicare as an option to every worker with *employment*-based health insurance? And let the worker pocket the annual savings, which could be as much as $8,000 for family coverage. Nothing could be more American than letting a health care consumer make a free choice and then experience the financial consequences, for better or worse, of that choice. The government does not need to dictate the outcome of any competition between private and public health insurance. Americans can vote with their pocketbooks. Let the chips fall where they may.

In summary, Obamacare provided health insurance to 20 million Americans while slowing the rise of overall health care spending and coming in under budget – a most remarkable trifecta of success. A signature achievement for Obama and his legislative partners.

How did the rollout of the ACA mesh with our lessons in leadership? Certainly, it deserves an A plus in compassion. Moreover, it has been a remarkable accomplishment in coalescence. To be sure, the birth of the ACA was a divisive process, but a growing number of Americans now favor the legislation (especially if it is not called "Obamacare"[8]), and the improved access to care has crossed all social boundaries. Finally, the success of the program demonstrates the virtues of meticulous planning

– from actuarial calculations to experimentation with systems design – a nod toward *science*.

But above all, I submit that promoting the ACA took courage. Not the Churchillian "Let's unite to save the Motherland!" type of courage. Rather it was the courage to take a political risk – the risk of failure. Previous Presidents had pursued the challenge and fallen short, consuming massive political capital. Given the collapse of the political center, it was not even clear there was an open corridor between liberals who wanted a single-payer system and conservatives who wanted no system at all.

The ACA, then, had to pass through the eye of a needle, an all but invisible gap between warring factions, to pass by the slimmest of margins. So we must give huge credit to Obama and his legislative partners – Nancy Pelosi, Speaker of the House, and Harry Reid, Senate Majority Leader, who worked in tandem – for their resolve. For their courage. For boldly taking on the impossible – and succeeding.

How has the Republican Party responded to the ACA's success? It is no secret that congressional Republicans were implacably hostile to the ACA from its earliest beginnings. It would kill jobs, destroy businesses, and break the bank, they claimed. It was nothing more than a government takeover of health care, they charged. They could barely conceal their glee, rubbernecking at the grisly scene, when the website crashed during the rollout. Of course, none of the predictions came to pass. The website recovered, coverage expanded, corporations thrived, and job growth continued unabated.

Ironically, the most forceful objection to the ACA all along was about the individual mandate, an objection that finally led to its rollback in the Republican *Tax Cuts and Jobs Act of 2017*. It is ironic because the market-based approach of the ACA and the idea of a mandate to promote personal responsibility were born and raised in the conservative wing of the Republican Party.[9] Given the ACA's conservative origins, it is most surprising that Republicans rooted so enthusiastically for its downfall and have so persistently attempted to repeal it ever since.

Actually, it is more than surprising. To oppose a measure that expands health care according to the governing philosophy of one's own party and to attempt to sabotage an intervention that has improved the lives of tens of millions of Americans demonstrate a level of cynicism that rises above the usual unpleasant political discourse. In the health care arena, it is no longer apparent what the Republican Party actually stands for.

Compromise:
Find the Sweet Spot

Jesus wept.
Then said the Jews, Behold how he loved him!...
Then they took away the stone from the place where the dead was laid.
And Jesus...said, Father, I thank thee that thou hast heard me...
And when he thus had spoken, he cried with a loud voice, Lazarus, come forth.
And he that was dead came forth, bound hand and foot with graveclothes.

John 11:35-44, The Bible (King James Version)

"How long have we been at this?"
"Fifty minutes, give or take."
"Any point in continuing?"
"Hardly. He's been shocked six times already."
"Okay, check the EKG once more. What do you have?"
"No rhythm at all. Just v. fib. Always v. fib."
"What a shame. Okay, let's call it. What's the time?"

"Wait a sec! Did you just see that?"
"What?"
"Oh my God! He just opened his eyes!"
"No way!"
"And he tried to pick up his head. He looked right at me!"
"Stop it! That's not even possible!"

An unmistakable grunt emanates from the lips of the corpse lying still on the stretcher. The trauma slot breaks into excited conversation. "Oh, wow! That's some CPR you've got going there!"

"Call Cardiology, stat! We've got a live one!"

As a safety net hospital, Bellevue has always emphasized its rapid response to life-threatening emergencies, and it has long been our mission to save the life of any patient brought in from the street, without exception. One example of this was Thomas Spectes, a 66 year-old tourist from Ohio, who collapsed on a Manhattan sidewalk while sightseeing with his wife.

Emergency Medical Specialists (EMS) found Thomas lying at the curb and then followed their protocol. They checked his pulse (absent). They applied an electrical shock to restore his heartbeat (unsuccessful). They inserted a tube into his windpipe to sustain his respirations (done). They alerted the Bellevue ED to expect a case of cardiac arrest – more aptly known as "sudden death." And then they raced through Manhattan streets with lights flashing and sirens blaring to deliver their precious cargo.

The triage nurse was waiting at the entrance as the former Mr. Spectes was wheeled in on a stretcher with a paramedic performing chest compressions on his lifeless body. At this point, without a spontaneous breath or heartbeat, he was essentially a corpse. The nurse simply pointed to the trauma slot, where a care team was awaiting their new charge.

The trauma slot is a large immaculate space with bright lights and tiled floors, outfitted with every imaginable piece of equipment to save the life of a patient in extremis: a pedestrian struck by a taxi, the victim of a gunshot wound, or, as in this case, the casualty of a massive heart attack.

The trauma slot is Bellevue's crucible – the superheated vortex where life battles death in a cosmic tug of war. In this space, a patient enters purgatory, poised between this world and the next. In this space, physicians and nurses summon their time-tested skills and well-honed reflexes to coax the faint, flickering flame of life back into a roaring blaze, while the Angel of Death endeavors to snuff it out. Into this space, Thomas was deposited by EMS staff, who were fully aware that his odds were slim indeed.

The experienced ED team swung into action as an intern immediately took over CPR – standing on a stepstool, leaning forward over the chest, pressing down on the breastbone with one hand over the other, fingers clasped and elbows locked, engaged in the rhythmic pumping action that always reminds me of convicts in horizontally-striped pajamas, bobbing up and down on the handle of the small railroad flatcar, making their escape along the tracks in the old black and white movies of the 1930s.

Only the intern was not a convict; he was a surrogate heart. With each chest compression, he was squeezing blood forward through the circulatory system in the one-way flow dictated by the cardiac valves, to nourish the body with oxygen that was being piped into the lungs, to preserve precious brain tissue that would be required to run this body again if only the heartbeat could be restored. The primary mission of cardiopulmonary resuscitation (CPR), after all, is crystal clear: save the brain. As long as the brain survives, there is hope.

While the intern bobbed up and down, the assembled staff carried out the systematic routine known as advanced cardiac life support (ACLS). There was a script to follow, a rote sequence to be carried out – of diagnostic steps and therapeutic interventions. A systematic approach like every other in our profession. They had read from this script hundreds of times before.

Interpret the EKG, make a diagnosis, and treat accordingly. Analyze the blood – pH, hemoglobin, potassium. Assess the organs – brain, lungs, heart. Review the differential diagnosis – stroke, embolism, infarction. Infuse, inject, defibrillate. Administer medications to speed up, slow down, and stir around the heart. Be thorough, methodical, and precise. Think. Leave no stone unturned. Give this patient every possible chance.

And that is what happened. While a succession of interns and nurses took turns pumping on the chest, their back muscles cramping and their sweat dripping onto the bedsheets, the ED attending and residents worked desperately through every possible step in the algorithm. Down one blind alley after another. But all to no avail. After a half-hour of effort, it became clear that they were literally beating a dead corpse.

Yet, for some unknown reason, they continued. It is hard to fathom why they did not give up after several rounds of defibrillations and medical treatments. Why they did not throw in the towel while the opposing side was running up the score. Why they did not cry uncle when they were pinned to the mat. For some unknown reason, they slogged forward.

Perhaps the team was driven by a collective momentum that made it impossible to be the first to suggest failure. Perhaps the team leader was reminded of his own father in the final breaths of his life. Perhaps the patient's wife was standing in the wings in full view of the team, a reminder that this life mattered dearly to someone close at hand.

For whatever reason, the ED team continued to apply CPR for more than 50 minutes, way beyond reason and well beyond hope. Near the end of the hour, against all odds, and just when the team was about to give up, they were staggered by an astounding development.

Thomas briefly woke up, looked around, beheld his caregivers, and then slipped back into a state of unconsciousness. This astonishing display of preserved brain function, this unexpected flash of hope, inspired the team to continue CPR while paging Cardiology for urgent assistance.

The Cardiology team rushed to the ED, sized up the situation, and decided to make a heroic attempt to save the patient. They packed him up and transported him to the cardiac catheterization lab, all the while pumping on his chest. In the lab, a cardiologist inserted a catheter and discovered the patient had an obstruction of one of his coronary arteries, just like Stan Loritan, only worse. This was a massive myocardial infarction in progress.

The cardiologist cleared the obstruction and placed a stent to keep the blood vessel open. Miraculously, the heart began to beat. The patient was now gravely ill and still unconscious, so he was transported to the Coronary Care Unit to continue his care. Because of likely brain damage from lack of oxygen, he underwent a protocol to cool his body for 24 hours to protect his brain from further injury.[1]

Two days later, Thomas woke up from his coma. He was groggy and confused, but he recognized his wife. Over the next week his status improved, so he was transferred to a regular room, where I met him for the first time as his assigned attending physician. My patient was awake, but he had difficulty with attention and memory. He was irritable and could not focus on tasks at hand, the result of the brain injury sustained during his cardiac arrest. But he was improving every day. We finally discharged him into the care of his wife so that she could return him to their Ohio home.

One year later, Thomas and his wife returned to New York to thank the Bellevue staff who saved his life – especially the ED team who never gave up on him, and the Cardiology physicians and nurses who delivered such extraordinary care. Best of all, his personality and mental function had completely returned to baseline. He was functioning normally and had even returned to work part-time. He offered eloquent thanks to the staff, some of whom wept from his words of gratitude.

It is always a morale boost for the hospital to have an outcome like this, and it is not as rare as you might think. Up to ten times each year, our hospital receives an out-of-hospital cardiac arrest, quite literally a case of "sudden death," for which the goal is to roll away the stone and bring the patient back to life – a modern day Lazarus, raised from the dead.

It matters not who the patient is: a Wall Street broker, a tourist, a homeless person. In each case, we pull out all the stops and do everything in our power to save the life. In about half the cases, we are successful in reviving the patient and restoring vital functions of heart and brain. These are the success stories that motivate our staff and drive our hospital forward.

Not every hospital is this aggressive in treating sudden death. Such cases consume a lot of resources, diverting attention from other, more plausible opportunities for success. And no matter the effort, there is a high fatality rate, which affects the publicly reported outcomes of the cardiac cath lab.[2] It is a massive intervention at high cost, and many of these patients are uninsured. So why do we do it? Why do we make this leap? In our colossal efforts to save these lives hanging in the balance we are following a simple *principle* that guides every department of our institution.

Never give up.

As a safety net hospital, that has always been our mission in a nutshell. Save the life, no matter who, no matter what, no matter how. Drop everything, and save the life at all costs. It is an inspiring mission. Especially when you consider that some hospitals would not have continued CPR for an hour and would not have transported what was basically a corpse into the cath lab, a case that would likely "stain" the cath lab statistics with a fresh mortality.

"Never give up" is a wonderful example of a guiding principle, a foundational standard. That is not to say that the decision to intervene ignores all context, including the underlying condition, patient preference, or goals of care. For a patient with a terminal illness it is often *not* in her best interest to be resuscitated. But if going all out to save a life is the right thing to do, we will not hold back.

This is one of many tenets that guide our work: rules that may not be broken. A list of such principles, which are the bedrock of our systematic approach to patient safety, could go on for pages: Check two patient-identifiers before administering medications. Wash your hands before every patient encounter. Include patients in decisions that affect their health.

The list is endless...Give antibiotics before surgery. Remove the urinary catheter when no longer needed. Wipe down the probe before sending it back to central sterile processing. Use a checklist when placing a central line. Reconcile medications at discharge. Maintain patient confidentiality. Document your work. Disclose errors. Be honest.

Such principles are essential for the safe, effective, and ethical care of patients. So much so that every hospital aims to imbed them in the structure of the daily work. So much so that we employ guidelines, checklists, checkers of the checklists, monitors of the checkers, reviewers of the charts, and constant tweaking of all our processes to ensure no defects appear in the application of the principles. Hospitals that do this well are considered "high reliability" organizations, which is another way of saying that they are consistent in the application of their principles.

Why did I begin a chapter on compromise with a discussion of principles? Because I want to make a crucial point. Principles are essential. They are vital. They give us a solid foundation. They impart consistency. And they keep us on track. They are *always* the starting point.

Principles, then, become a scaffold for decision-making, a solid substructure that keeps us grounded, predictable, and transparent. Most important, they are the anchors. If compromise is a bridge between two points of view, principles are the two towers from which that bridge is suspended. I just wanted to make it crystal clear that principles are always the starting point.

But they are not the *final* word. Not every medical decision adheres to a fundamental principle, a rigid rule that cannot be broken. In truth, much of medical practice is about weighing options, considering pros and cons, comparing risks and benefits, and then finding the best possible path of many – a path that frequently represents a middle ground, a proper center among all the alternatives – in other words, a *sweet spot*.

This is a process of negotiation and compromise, which is an even more common approach in my profession than following a rigid rule book. This is where the *art* of Medicine becomes especially important. Finding the sweet spot, then, represents the intersection of art and science.

Recall my patient, Candice Staner, the woman who suffered the GI bleed after being started on an anticoagulant for a blood clot. There is a body of evidence on this topic that has led to a scientific consensus on the treatment of blood clots. Thus, national guidelines have promoted the use of anticoagulants as a general rule for the typical case.

But Candice was not a typical case. She was unusual in many aspects, especially in the severity of her multi-organ failure. The uniqueness of her situation called for special consideration, a personalized approach that would represent a compromise of the general principles of treatment.

The same was true for Juan Verdad, my memorable AIDS patient. The decision to back off when he was wheeled in unconscious was most definitely not from the playbook, not in conformance to a guideline, not even a standard of care.

It was a compromise – a departure from the treatment imperative in order to comply with a competing principle – patient autonomy. One more example of the nuance of doctor-patient relationships. As it turns out, I find myself almost always compromising in one way or another to achieve the best plan.

So that is an interesting point. When you take a deep dive into the evidence, you will find yourself standing on solid ground – a sturdy foundation of results from randomized controlled trials, our gold standard for research. You will have a clear understanding of the risks and costs of a treatment, as well as its benefits. The facts will speak loudly and clearly.

Even better, as we discussed earlier, treatment decisions may be boiled down into numbers. Numbers of lives saved or improved for every 100 patients treated. Quantity of harm and cost of care incurred by treating those same 100 patients. Benefits and Costs. Pluses and Minuses. Pros and Cons. All boiled down into a simple calculus, balanced on the cosmic scale.

And then you will meet the patient.

The worried well. The stoic sick. The non-compliant drinker. The life-long smoker. The short-tempered accountant. The fast-talking addict. The healthy, granola-crunching marathon-runner. The uninsured, risk-laden mother of three.

As soon as you meet the patient, you will realize that she is unique. She is not exactly the same as the subjects in the experiment you have just read about. This is when you realize that the evidence is merely the starting point – the solid runway from which your flight will soon depart.

Where you go from there depends on many other factors. Is your patient at higher or lower risk from her disease than the subjects in the study? If the treatment is a medication, will she be compliant? Tolerate side effects? Afford the costs? In the end, will the treatment be worth it?

That is the challenge of Evidence-Based Medicine. The science takes us only so far. Beyond that, we must rely on our skills of communication, trust-building, compassion, negotiation, and compromise to arrive at our intended destination. At that point, the art takes over.

Only then can we make the decision that is tailored to a unique, real person, the plan that is most suitable for this *particular* patient. Only then can we find our way to the sweet spot – combining what we know about the treatment with all that we have learned about the patient. That sweet spot is the holy grail of decision-making, the highest form of Evidence-Based Medicine, and the best combination of art *and* science.

I believe leadership works *exactly* the same way. Leaders must start with a solid base of experience, knowledge, and underlying principles. They must stand on a solid foundation of facts. From there they must bring in the nuance. The intangibles. The soft and squishy human factors that bear on almost any important decision.

This is especially true when there are competing factors coming to bear on a decision – as there often are. Or when one segment of the population seems pitted against another – as there usually is. Or when the facts are not perfectly clear – as is always the case.

In these situations, the leader must learn to strike that perfect balance between two sides, between the pros and cons, between the rock and the hard place. In short, the leader must find the sweet spot.

Nowhere is this more important than in the domain of personal liberty. Of course, our nation was *founded* on the concept of liberty – freedom to speak, think, and act as one wishes without interference by the government. Unfortunately, one person's liberty is another's shackles.

The literal example of this was the shameful practice of slavery, through which plantation owners exercised their "economic freedom" at the full expense of another class of people, completely within the bounds of our nation's founding principles. Indeed, the Civil War was fought exactly over this tradeoff: advancement of the basic human rights of Black slaves versus the economic well-being of White plantation owners.

But that is an extreme example. In a lesser vein, personal liberty bumps up against collateral damage in almost every sphere of American life. The classic paradigm is freedom of speech being checked by potential harm, such that it is *not* okay to yell "fire!" in a crowded movie theater or to slander your neighbor with malicious lies.

It is also not okay to drive on the wrong side of the road, smoke in a restaurant, blare loud music on your lawn, or go naked in public. But it is okay to drive within the rules, smoke outside, play music indoors, or visit a private nude beach. All within bounds.

At present, our public institutions have established a wide array of norms and expectations that are a compromise between personal liberties and their consequences. I would submit that in these examples the goal is always the same: to offset competing principles, to find the perfect balance between freedom and its consequences, to split the difference. In the other words, to find the sweet spot.

With this principle in mind, I would like to explore two highly contentious topics of our day: gun ownership and abortion. Before I begin, I fully recognize that I am entering a treacherous political mine field. Especially since I am going to strike a balance that will leave no one satisfied.

Even worse, I will make an outrageous comparison between gun enthusiasts and abortion rights activists. Just right there, I'm sure I will deeply offend a great many readers from both sides of the aisle. But if I am to be true to the spirit of this book, I feel I really need to take this head-on.

While there are many reasons to own a gun, I believe for some Americans the issue has deep *symbolic* meaning, whether or not they would ever choose to possess a firearm. They would say the freedom to own a gun represents an essential right to defend their family, secure their home, and protect our nation against the prospect of tyranny.

They might even consider that right to be a core freedom that must be guaranteed above all costs in a representative democracy-a fundamental right that supersedes all others, including freedom of speech and religion. Although I do not intend to own a gun, I fully understand why some people hold that belief so dearly.

Nonetheless, this right comes at a cost. In 2014, there were 33,600 firearm deaths in the U.S, almost the exact same number as deaths from motor vehicle accidents.[3] About 64% of gun deaths were self-inflicted, and 33% were due to homicide.

That adds up to more than 30 gun homicides per day. Every two years, more Americans die of gun deaths than the number of U.S. soldiers who died in the entire Vietnam War (58,000). Worst of all, our national epidemic of assault weapons is tied to unimaginable tragedies on a massive scale: Newtown, Orlando, Las Vegas, and Parkland. We cannot pretend that the right to gun ownership has no associated cost. You could do the math and easily conclude that firearms should be banned in their entirety.

And then you will meet the gun owner.

The law-abiding hunter. The dyed-in-the-wool survivalist. The tough-as-nails matriarch intent on defending her home. The upstanding citizen who respects the danger of firearms and the need to use them responsibly. And you will realize there is nuance to this topic that goes way beyond the numbers – a complexity that requires a balanced approach.

There is a wide spectrum of potential restrictions on gun ownership. At the most restrictive end would be a complete ban on private possession of firearms. As impractical as this may seem, there are some nations that have virtually done exactly that. At the least restrictive end would be a completely unlimited right to own any type or number of guns without a background check and without any restraint on their use.

In between are a host of possibilities ranging from a complete ban on certain types of guns or strict controls in certain geographic areas, or a variety of procedures to guarantee that guns cannot fall into the hands of certain classes of people, such as those with a psychiatric disturbance, criminal record, or membership on a terrorist watch list.

By comparison, abortion rights activists hold some parallel opinions about *their* topic. While there are many reasons to terminate a pregnancy, I believe for some Americans the issue has deep *symbolic* meaning, regardless of whether or not they would ever choose to have an abortion. They would say the freedom to terminate a pregnancy represents an essential right to control their own bodies and to make one of the most important decisions anyone will ever face in a lifetime: whether to bear a child.

They might even consider that right to be a core freedom that must be guaranteed above all costs in a representative democracy- a fundamental right that supersedes all others, including freedom of speech and religion. Although I do not intend to terminate a pregnancy myself, I fully understand why some people hold that belief so dearly.

Nonetheless, that right comes at a cost. In 2016, more than 620,000 legal abortions were performed in the U.S.[4] The majority (66%) were performed by 8 weeks gestation, 25% at 9-13 weeks, 8% at 14-20 weeks, and 1% past 20 weeks.

The rate has declined by more than 40% since 1980, but for those who consider the fetus to have the status of a newborn baby, there is an undeniable price being paid in the large number of abortions remaining. We cannot pretend that the right to abortion has no associated cost. You could do the math and easily conclude that abortions should be banned in their entirety.

And then you will meet the mother.

The unwed teenager. The pregnant grandmother, caught by surprise. The well-meaning housewife who is trying to responsibly plan a family. The childhood victim of incest who desperately wishes not to bear her father's child. And you will realize there is nuance to this topic that goes way beyond the numbers, a complexity that requires a balanced approach.

There is a wide spectrum of possible restrictions on abortion. On one extreme are those who would ban termination at any point after conception regardless of circumstance. They might also say that abortion should be prohibited in *every* situation, even when the mother's life is in danger or when the pregnancy occurs through rape or incest.

At the other extreme are a minority who feel that there should be no restriction on abortion at *any* point of pregnancy, even up to the natural time of childbirth. They would say that a woman owns her womb and everything in it. Period.

In between are host of possibilities, including exceptions for rape and incest, or setting time points beyond which the pregnancy may not be terminated. Current laws, of course, are based on the Supreme Court ruling in Roe v. Wade, that abortion is fully permissible but only during the first or second trimester.

Both gun control and abortion have one important aspect in common. They represent a battle between principles – the intersection of competing rights. In each example, the advancement of one right appears to infringe on the other. In the case of abortion, it is the right of a woman to control her body versus the right of a fetus to be born. In the case of gun control, it is the right of Americans to bear arms versus the right of Americans to be safe from gun violence.

It is especially interesting that the pro-choice position, which supports personal freedom with minimal government interference, is a *liberal* one, while pro-gun ownership, which also asserts personal freedom with minimal government interference is a *conservative* one. How is that possible?

I am sure the reasons are complex, but there appears to be a libertarian streak within each political party, as well as a counterweight. Neither side may appreciate this comparison, but I am just trying to point out the similarities. It is crucial for each side to gain some perspective on the other.

So where do we go from here? I submit that the extreme positions are unreasonable because they cater completely to one right at the expense of the other, as if there is no competing viewpoint. It is simply not sensible, or even realistic, to expect the other side to capitulate to one's own extreme position. So no one bends and our ailing nation continues to decline.

If we are to move forward as a healthy state, both sides need to move toward each other. Those on the extreme must inch forward along that bridge, across the divide, toward a reasonable compromise that accepts the legitimate basis for both positions.

What would this mean? First, we would all respect the fundamental right to own a gun but also agree to set limits on that right. Second, we would all respect the fundamental right to terminate a pregnancy but also agree to set limits on *that* right. The discussions that ensue would not be about adopting one extreme position or the other, but rather about agreeing where to draw the line. Of course, both sides would be advancing toward compromise from an anchoring principle, which they would continue to respect, but they would also be promoting another principle – national unity.

Once again, I must ask...Does this make any sense? Would the electorate agree to respect the fundamental rights at hand but still set limits? The answer to that question is a resounding yes. Based on recent surveys, 34% of Americans say abortion should be legal in most cases, while 26% say it should be *illegal* in most cases.[5] Fewer take a more extreme position: that abortion should be legal in *all* cases (27%) or illegal in all cases (12%). When it comes to abortion, a majority of Americans (60%) are standing somewhere on the bridge. They appreciate the nuance.

Ditto for gun control. In a 2015 survey, nearly 80% of Americans supported laws to prevent mentally ill people from buying guns, 70% supported the creation of a national database to track gun ownership, and 57% favored a ban on assault weapons.[6] On a general question, 50% of respondents said it was more important to control gun ownership, while 47% said it was more important to protect the right of Americans to own guns. In a related survey, only 9% of respondents favored a proposal to prevent all Americans from owning guns.[7] The rest are somewhere on the bridge.

I have presented both these contentious issues as zero-sum games, where one side can gain only at the other's expense. Is that completely true? Are there any solutions that allow *both* sides to gain? Are there any win-win propositions that can liberate us from the interminable battle zone? Indeed, there are!

The win-win proposition in gun ownership is advancement in firearm safety – technology to guarantee that a stolen gun cannot be fired or that a child cannot accidentally shoot a sibling. Such technology could save countless lives while fully preserving the rights of gun owners. Incredibly, our elected leaders have banned the expenditure of federal funds for this purpose. The Centers for Disease Control may not even conduct *research* on gun safety. We are, by law, like Gerry Menard, unable to *learn* about this topic.

The win-win proposition for abortion is prevention of unplanned pregnancies. The nationwide advancement of effective family planning could markedly reduce the number of abortions without encroaching on women's rights. Incredibly, there are powerful electoral forces resisting the provision of birth control education and contraception that could help men and woman avoid the dilemma of an unwanted pregnancy. The entrenched opposition to solutions that would advance the goals of *both* sides of these contentious issues surely reveal the advanced stage of illness in our political system.

We have focused on two especially controversial topics in this chapter. Are these the only ones? Most certainly not. Here are some additional two-sided propositions: corporate regulation versus free enterprise, free enterprise versus environmentalism, national security versus personal liberty, and free trade versus protectionism.

When you look at the important issues facing our country, they always seem to boil down to two sides. Two *strong* sides with securely entrenched positions. Two firmly planted, implacably stubborn, absolutely irreconcilable factions with a no-holds-barred, take-no prisoners, win-at-any-cost ethos.

This is a classic bimodal distribution, with humps on each end and a gap in the middle. The collapse of the *political* center is distressingly reminiscent of the decline of the middle class – our *economic* center. No wonder our government seems like a pendulum, swinging wildly from side to side as we progress from one election cycle to the next! Each election becomes an act of revenge for the previous one. There is simply no moderating force in the middle.

If we are to break the gridlock, shed our symptoms, and rise from our sick bed, we must learn to agree to disagree and then move on. To avow our principles as a starting point, then gather the facts to enhance our understanding, and finally to engage our opponents in a respectful discussion about competing rights, one that invokes the artful principles of trust, acceptance, and coalescence.

And then we must assess the costs and benefits, weigh the pros and cons, and find our way to a compromise that promotes respect, fairness, and balance – that best possible place somewhere on the bridge that values those competing rights. In other words, find the sweet spot.

These past three chapters have given us a chance to explore attributes of leadership in the context of real-life dilemmas facing our government. No doubt the political landscape is even more challenging than the hospital setting, so it is fitting that we have elaborated upon our lessons in this way.

Even better, we can test our leadership phenotype against actual presidential performances. To that end, the next three chapters will consider the life stories and political careers of Ronald Reagan, Barack Obama, and Donald Trump, three recent presidents who span the full spectrum of the political divide, and whose personal behaviors and outcomes further illuminate our understanding of great leadership.

Reagan:
Master the Art

> Nothing can hurt us now. What we have can't be destroyed. That's our victory – our victory over the dark. It is a victory because we're not afraid.
>
> Judith (Bette Davis) in *Dark Victory*, Warner Bros., 1939

Ronald Wilson Reagan was born in Tampico, Illinois in 1911 and grew up in a modest household. His father, John ("Jack"), was of Irish origin, and his mother, Nelle, was of English and Scottish descent. From year to year, his family moved around the local area, at one point inhabiting an apartment above the H.C. Pitney Variety Store – a humble beginning to an eventful life. After graduating from Eureka College in 1932, Reagan became a radio sports announcer. In 1937, he took an acting screen test, which landed him a seven-year contract with Warner-Brothers studios.

Reagan's movie career got off to a promising start with roles in *Dark Victory* (with Humphrey Bogart and Bette Davis), *Knute Rockne, All American* (from which he picked up the nickname "The Gipper"), and his personal favorite, *Kings Row*. After a military stint ended in 1945, Reagan returned to acting but not on his previous trajectory. His post-war films included such memorable classics as *The Voice of the Turtle* and *Bedtime for Bonzo.*

In 1947, Reagan ascended to the presidency of the Screen Actors Guild. In this position, he worked to rid the association of communist influence, an experience that deeply influenced his political orientation. During this period, he also addressed labor-management disputes, provided the FBI with the name of communist sympathizers within the movie industry, and testified before the House Un-American Activities Committee.

In the 1950's, Reagan became a motivational speaker at General Electric plants around the nation. In this lucrative role, he wrote his own speeches, honed his craft, and burnished his reputation as a defender of conservative values: free markets, lower taxes, and limited government. Over an eight-year period, his message became increasingly more conservative, even as he remained a member of the Democratic party.

In 1960, Reagan wrote a letter to Richard Nixon in which he warned that the passage of Medicare, which he equated to socialism, would be the end of freedom in America.[1]

> Shouldn't someone tag Mr. Kennedy's "bold new imaginative" program with its proper age? Under the tousled boyish haircut it is still old Karl Marx – first launched a century ago. There is nothing new in the idea of a government being big brother to us all. Hitler called his "State Socialism" and way before him it was "benevolent monarchy."

The next year Reagan switched to the Republican party. In 1966, he was elected Governor of California, elevating him to the national stage. As Governor, Reagan raised taxes, froze spending, and eliminated the budget deficit. He had no tolerance for student protestors against the Vietnam War and did not mince words when it came to his own opinion about the war.[2]

> It is silly talking about how many years we will have to spend in the jungles of Vietnam when we could pave the whole country and put parking stripes on it and still be home by Christmas.

Reagan won re-election in 1970 and served to the end of his second four-year term. Meanwhile, he twice ran for the Republican nomination for president, in 1968 and 1976, narrowly losing the second time to Gerald Ford.

His conservative message did not prevail until 1980, when he finally won the Republican nomination. During his presidential campaign against incumbent Jimmy Carter, Reagan continued to peddle familiar staples from his political pantry: smaller government, states' rights, and national defense. His message resonated with the American people as he won by a 10% margin in the popular vote and 489 to 49 in the Electoral College.

Throughout this period of political activity, it is most remarkable that Reagan never wavered from his core message of conservative values, low taxes, and limited government – regardless of how he was received. His ascendancy to national prominence, then, was not a result of pandering to the crowd. The American people came to him. In this sense, he was truly an authentic leader – rooted firmly in a cause that he articulated clearly and consistently. By 1980, he had convinced America he was right.

Immediately following his election, and only momentarily slowed by an assassination attempt ("Honey, I forgot to duck") and a brief but brutal economic recession, Reagan moved boldly to realize his vision for America. In his first year in office, he proposed a constitutional amendment to permit prayer in schools, fired 11,000 striking air-traffic controllers, and implemented Supply-Side Economics by lowering capital gains rates to 20% and cutting marginal income tax rates across the board. He also campaigned to restore prayer in schools, curtailed public housing, and cut the Community Development Block Grant program.

To the dismay of fiscal conservatives, the dramatic cut in tax rates, a mainstay of "Reaganomics," did not produce the predicted surge in government revenue. On the contrary, the federal budget shortfall swelled to 5.7% of the GDP, the highest peacetime deficit in American history. We are reminded of Reagan's own words castigating the Carter administration.[3]

> The head of the government which has utterly refused to live within its means and which has, in the last few days, told us that this year's deficit will be $60 billion, dares to point the finger of blame at business and labor, ...which have been engaged in a losing struggle just trying to stay even.

By 1982, Reagan's budget deficit had ballooned to $195 billion, more than triple the Carter figure that he had so severely criticized just two years earlier. It was a devastating blow to the theory underpinning Supply-Side Economics and left Reagan unable to ever regain control of the fiscal budget. Astonishingly, in just 8 years, the Reagan administration accumulated nearly twice as much debt as the previous 39 American presidents *combined.*

Nonetheless, deficit spending and its necessary consequence, federal borrowing, successfully stimulated the economy, producing respectable growth in jobs and the GDP, as government debt tripled over eight years. Reaganomics, it seems, had become Keynesian economics, completely dependent on the stimulus of government spending.[4]

On the international front, Reagan pursued a vision as bold as his economic plan by escalating American military capabilities in a show of force to confront the Soviet Union. He implemented a massive buildup in the armed forces, revived the B-1 bomber, introduced the MX nuclear missile, and deployed Pershing missiles to Germany.

Further, Reagan provided covert aid to anti-communist resistance movements around the world – an initiative known as the Reagan Doctrine, trained anti-Soviet resistance fighters in Afghanistan, and introduced the Strategic Defense Initiative (SDI). Derisively nicknamed "Star Wars," the SDI was to be a space-based shield to protect America from nuclear war.

In 1982, Reagan teamed up with Margaret Thatcher to denounce the Soviet Union in a provocative, bold, visionary speech, which he delivered to the British House of Commons.

> We see totalitarian forces in the world who seek subversion and conflict around the globe to further their barbarous assault on the human spirit. What, then, is our course? Must civilizations perish in a hail of fiery atoms? Must freedom wither in a quiet, deadening accommodation with totalitarian evil? ...What I am describing now is a plan and a hope for the long term – the march of freedom and democracy which will leave Marxism-Leninism on the ash-heap of history as it has left other tyrannies which stifle the freedom and muzzle the self-expression of the people.

In 1984, on the 40th anniversary of D-Day, the Normandy invasion, Reagan delivered what might have been the most stirring speech of his presidency, rechanneling the Gettysburg address in a modern setting and reminding us of his impressively inspiring, positively Churchillian, eloquence, one of the great attributes of his leadership.

> President Lincoln once reminded us that through their deeds, the dead of battle have spoken more eloquently for themselves than any of the living ever could. But we can only honor them by rededicating ourselves to the cause for which they gave a last full measure of devotion... These are the boys of Pointe du Hoc. These are the men who took the cliffs. These are the champions who helped free a continent. And these are the heroes who helped end a war.

Reagan's first term was one of the most successful terms of any president in modern history. He laid out a pure vision and then partnered with Congress to enact legislation that advanced his vision in vibrant, bold steps. Through his stirring rhetoric and deft use of media, he rallied Americans to accept his vision and join him on his journey.

Thus, Reagan ran for re-election on a strong first-term performance. It was "Morning again in America." His much younger opponent, Walter Mondale, was a former vice-president who performed well in the debates. Reagan, however, pre-emptively addressed concerns about his advancing age with a devastating quip. "I will not make age an issue of this campaign. I am not going to exploit, for political purposes, my opponent's youth and inexperience." Even Mondale laughed at that.

Reagan's first term success was validated resoundingly by the American people when he won re-election in 1984 by an Electoral College vote of 525 to 10, winning nearly every state – an all-time record. If not for Mondale's home state of Minnesota, it would have been a clean sweep. Reagan had completely won the admiration and support of the American people. He was king of the world.

Reagan's second term did not prove to be so successful. Perhaps due to the loss of James Baker, his incomparable chief of staff who switched jobs to become Secretary of the Treasury, or to the inevitable loss of steam that might follow such a whirlwind pace in the first term, or perhaps the aging of Reagan himself, the second term became a pale shadow of the first.

In 1985, Reagan made an ill-advised visit to a German military cemetery to lay wreaths on graves that included former Nazi SS officers. Although the controversial nature of the gravesite was brought to light beforehand, Reagan persisted in making the ceremonial visit. It was not his nature to reverse course, admit mistakes, or apologize.

In January, 1986, the administration was further rocked by the explosion of the Space Shuttle Challenger and the loss of seven American astronauts. In response, Reagan delivered some of the most memorable lines of his presidency.

> The future doesn't belong to the fainthearted; it belongs to the brave... We will never forget them, nor the last time we saw them, this morning, as they prepared their journey and waved goodbye and slipped the surly bonds of Earth to touch the face of God.

In 1986, Reagan signed two significant bills into law. The first was the bipartisan Immigration Reform and Control Act, which tightened restrictions in the employment of undocumented Americans but also granted amnesty to 3 million illegal immigrants who had entered the U.S. prior to 1982. The second was a drug enforcement bill that budgeted $1.7 billion to support the War on Drugs. The bill was criticized for a disparate impact on sentencing of minorities to prison for drug offenses but praised for decreasing drug use.

Meanwhile, AIDS, which appeared in the first year of Reagan's first term, spread across major American cities with explosive impact. Remarkably, Reagan did not directly address the epidemic until well into his second term. By then, more than 20,000 Americans had already died from effects of the HIV virus. By the time he left office, the number of deaths from AIDS exceeded 70,000.

Near the end of Reagan's second term, information surfaced on the Iran-Contra affair, a scheme in which the U.S. government illegally used proceeds from covert arms sales to Iran to fund Contra rebels fighting the Nicaraguan government. The scandal eventually resulted in 11 convictions among Reagan's staff. When questioned under oath, Reagan professed ignorance of the activities of high-level officials who operated within his inner circle.

Following Reagan's presidency, he and Nancy, to whom he had been married since 1952, retired to an estate in Bel Air, Los Angeles. In 1994, he was diagnosed with Alzheimer's Disease, which he shared with the nation through a handwritten note.

> I now begin the journey that will lead me into the sunset of my life. I know that for America there will always be a bright dawn ahead. Thank you, my friends. May God always bless you.

Over subsequent years, Reagan withdrew from public life. He died at home in June, 2004, at the age of 93. His state funeral was conducted in the Washington National Cathedral and was attended by Margaret Thatcher, Mikhail Gorbachev, Prince Charles, and many active world leaders.

So what kind of president did Reagan prove to be? To what extent did he exhibit the leadership traits I have endorsed in previous chapters? Let's begin with trust. Reagan undeniably won the trust of the American people as evidenced by the unprecedented landslide in his 1984 re-election. He earned his credibility through an unwavering commitment to consistent political themes that he could express in descriptive language with an impeccable delivery. And he never pandered. It was obvious that his opinions were his own, and he was willing to express them, popular or not. His moniker, "The Great Communicator," was well deserved.

Reagan's authenticity was further enhanced by his affable nature, his self-deprecating humor, and evident honesty – which built a reservoir of goodwill and disarmed his critics. The bloom did not come off the rose until the Iran-Contra affair surfaced in his second term. Even then, all accounts of the scandal indicated that Reagan's culpability was in lack of attentiveness, not malicious intent.

When it came to compassion, however, Reagan's record was decidedly mixed. Among his first decisions as president were several striking steps to slash the safety net. His inexplicable avoidance of AIDS was one of the great missed opportunities of his legacy, and his war on drugs led to disproportionate imprisonment of young Black men through disparate sentencing guidelines. Yet his immigration policies reflected a more balanced view and brought several million undocumented Americans out of the shadows.

As far as admitting mistakes is concerned, Reagan was also far from perfect, as he was stubbornly consistent and unapologetic. The devastating impact of Reaganomics on the federal budget, the delayed response to AIDS, and the sordid tale of Iran-Contra were all examples where missteps could be laid at Reagan's feet, but he did not apologize for any of them.[5]

When it came to coalescence, however, Reagan was the modern master. No president in American history achieved the geographic dominance that Reagan did after his first term – a stirring of the electorate that stretched from coast to coast, north to south, and across the Midwest. It was an electoral college rout.

His advancement of the image of America as a beacon of liberty, as a staunch defender of human rights, and as the international counterweight against the godless, malignant, totalitarian regime of the Soviet Union appealed to national pride and won the loyalty of his constituents. He built a trusting relationship with the American people and mined that rapport to bring them to a new place.

Of course, it has long been debated whether that new place was the right place. Reagan's early stances on Medicare and the Vietnam War were invalidated by history. And his prediction of the impact of Supply-Side Economics on the federal deficit was disproven by subsequent events.

Furthermore, Reagan's coalescence did not extend across racial lines. His open support for "state's rights" and his offhand tales about welfare queens continued the Republican tradition of speaking in racial code to southern conservatives. In the end, 90% of Black voters opted for Mondale. In this respect, there was an important strand missing from Reagan's braid.

Nonetheless, shortly after his second term, the Soviet Union collapsed under the weight of unsustainable military obligations and a failing economy, largely as Reagan and his staff had hoped and predicted. This was his dream, after all, the capstone of his 40-year quest to prevail over communism.

How might Reagan have summarized our triumph over the Soviet Union and its Communist regime? Most probably something like this: *"Nothing can hurt us now. What we have can't be destroyed. That's our victory – our victory over the dark. It is a victory because we're not afraid."*

What kind of physician would Reagan have been? In my view, he would have been a stereotypical surgeon.[6] His positions were intuitive, based on deeply held convictions. He knew what he wanted right from the start. He did not dither or falter. With immense self-confidence, and without any second-guessing, handwringing, or wavering, he executed his plan.

Moreover, he neither admitted failure nor apologized for his actions. He was John Wayne swaggering into the saloon – the confident surgeon who could breeze into the trauma slot and, through force of irrepressible personality and sheer self-confidence, take command of the case. In fact, he was sometimes right and sometimes wrong – but never shy or indecisive.

In the final analysis, then, Reagan mastered the *art* of the presidency. His clarity of purpose, his consistency in principle, his expertise in communication – all attributes of a great leader – won the hearts, minds, and votes of an unprecedented majority of Americans. He projected confident leadership and the people followed. They came to *him*, and he took them to a new place.

Together.

Obama:
Perfect the Science

If you can keep your head when all about you
Are losing theirs and blaming it on you...
If you can wait and not be tired by waiting,
Or being lied about, don't deal in lies,
Or being hated, don't give way to hating,
And yet don't look too good, nor talk too wise...
Yours is the Earth and everything that's in it,
And—which is more—you'll be a Man, my son!

From *If-*, Rudyard Kipling (1910)

February. The gray days lengthen as I continue to write. Every morning I am up by four, wide awake, with much to say. Two hours on the laptop by first light, an hour on the inbound train, another on the way home, and, if I am able, another round late in the evening.

In between, while driving to the station, attending meetings, and rounding in the hospital, the ideas continue to flow, captured as notes on my smart phone or as jottings in a memo's margin. Even beyond that, while lying still in bed waiting for sleep to overtake me, I am beset by distant memories that penetrate my consciousness and spill into my dreams.

My fingers cannot type as quickly as I can think of the words, impatiently tumbling out on top of each other, fighting for space on the page. The stories have become lessons, the message has become a prescription, and the nation has become a patient. I have the perfect title for this nascent manuscript – The Golden Braid: A Marriage of Art and Science. No, wait. There is yet a better one, and it is more to the point: The Ill Country.

I am surprised by the unrelenting pressure I feel to move this story along. I must repeatedly restrain myself, must check my pace. Best to take a dose of my own medicine: Tincture of time. Patience.

Barack Hussein Obama was born in 1961, almost exactly 50 years after Reagan, in Honolulu, Hawaii, the most disputed birthplace of any American president. And, by now, the best documented as well. Obama was initially raised by his Kansas-born White mother, Ann Dunham, after her divorce from his Kenya-born Black father, Barack Obama, Sr., in 1964. Dunham remarried in 1965 and followed her new husband to Indonesia in 1967.

Barack, who was known as Barry to his friends, returned to Hawaii in 1971, at the age of ten, to live with his maternal grandparents until he graduated from Punahou School, a private college prep school, in 1979. Obama saw his biological father only one more time, in 1971, before his father died in an automobile accident eleven years later. Obama's mother would also die prematurely, of cancer, in 1995.

Following high school, Obama entered Occidental College in Los Angeles and then transferred in his junior year to Columbia University, where he majored in political science. Two years after his graduation from Columbia in 1983, he became a community organizer on Chicago's South Side, working for three years as director of a church-based organization, where he set up a tenants' rights association.

In 1988, Obama matriculated to Harvard Law School, where he was selected as the first Black president of the Harvard Law Review – an event that garnered national attention and led to his authoring a personal memoir – Dreams from My Father – in 1995.

After law school graduation, Obama joined the faculty of the University of Chicago Law School, where he taught constitutional law from 1992 to 2004. Meanwhile, he entered politics, representing his local district in the Illinois Senate from 1997 to 2004. During this period, he became an outspoken opponent of the decision to invade Iraq.

Obama voiced his opposition most eloquently in October, 2002, the very same month that Congress authorized the invasion by broad majorities in both houses. His rhetoric was matched by an eerily prescient nod to economic instability, income inequality and health care access – national issues that would define his presidency.[1]

> I don't oppose all wars. And I know that in this crowd today, there is no shortage of patriots, or of patriotism. What I am opposed to is a dumb war. What I am opposed to is a rash war...What I am opposed to is the attempt by political hacks like Karl Rove to distract us from a rise in the uninsured, a rise in the poverty rate, a drop in the median income – to distract us from corporate scandals and a stock market that has just gone through the worst month since the Great Depression. That's what I'm opposed to.

> A dumb war. A rash war. A war based not on reason but on passion, not on principle but on politics.

In 2004, Obama handily won a seat in the U.S. Senate in an unexpected landslide with 70% of the vote. During that same year, he gained national prominence from his well-received keynote address at the Democratic convention, analogous to the impact of Reagan's highly influential concession speech at the 1976 Republican convention. The most memorable lines of this address reverberated throughout the remainder of Obama's political career and defined him more explicitly than any other.

> The pundits like to slice and dice our country into red states and blue states: red states for Republicans, blue states for Democrats. But I've got news for them, too. We worship an awesome God in the blue states, and we don't like federal agents poking around our libraries in the red states. We coach little league in the blue states and, yes, we've got some gay friends in the red states...We are one people, all of us pledging allegiance to the stars and stripes, all of us defending the United States of America.

In February, 2007, Obama announced his candidacy for the presidency. The competition for the Democratic nomination quickly narrowed to a single opponent, Hillary Clinton. Despite a close contest, Obama prevailed by June, 2008. Two months later, he selected Joe Biden as his running mate and delivered his convention speech to a crowd of 80,000 at Invesco Field in Denver, Colorado. In his own words, Obama described the void he intended to be filled by government. It offered a striking contrast to Reagan's vision.

> In Washington, they call this the "Ownership Society," but what it really means is that you're on your own. Out of work? Tough luck, you're on your own. No health care? The market will fix it. You're on your own. Born into poverty? Pull yourself up by your own bootstraps, even if you don't have boots. You are on your own.
>
> ...Ours is a promise that says government cannot solve our problems, but what it should do is that which we cannot do for ourselves: protect us from harm and provide every child a decent education; keep our water clean and our toys safe; invest in new schools, and new roads, and science.

To this rapt audience, Obama once again invoked the rhetoric of his stirring address four years earlier to call upon Americans to come together. Five months later he would be sworn in as the next president.

> The men and women who serve on our battlefields may be Democrats and Republicans and independents, but they have fought together, and bled together, and some died together under the same proud flag. They have not served a red America or a blue America; they have served the United States of America.

The period between Obama's acceptance speech and his inaugural address was a time of great economic turmoil. For the better part of 2007, the subprime mortgage market was roiled by increasing rates of homeowner defaults. By 2008, the rising tide of failures had become a tsunami of foreclosures, which threatened large banks and Wall Street brokerage houses.

By September, 2008, the bubble had completely burst and the nation's economy was in a free fall. American homeowners had already experienced a massive loss of value in their properties, and an alarming freeze in the credit markets was now threatening cash flow, the life blood of healthy corporations. This forced the government's hand.

On October 3, 2008, the Troubled Asset Relief Program (TARP) was signed into law by George W. Bush, pumping hundreds of billions of dollars into the financial sector to prevent a contagion of institutional failures throughout the banking system.

Meanwhile, the national economy was imploding as corporations tightened their belts in the face of decreasing consumer demand. By November, 2008, the S&P 500 stock market index had lost 45% of its value from the previous year. By January 20, 2009, Obama's inauguration day, the unemployment rate had risen to 8.2%, and jobs were disappearing at a blistering pace – 700,000 per month. Enter Obama, the freshly-minted 44th president of the United States.

As Obama began his term, there was no end in sight to the downward spiral. The vicious cycle of layoffs, foreclosures, and shrinking consumer demand, which weakened retail sales, reduced corporate revenue, and led to even more layoffs, was in full throttle. Every major economic player had rushed to the sidelines, leaving a huge gap in the middle of the field, a growing chasm that threatened to swallow whole the entire U.S. economy.

At times like these there is a natural temptation for the federal government to do the same – to cut spending, lay off workers, and batten down the hatches in preparation for the perfect storm. In other words, step on the brakes. But if national leaders joined corporate titans in slashing spending, cutting investment, and shrinking the work force, the downward spiral might gain overwhelming momentum. There was no telling where rock bottom might be. So, Obama resisted the temptation to join the stampede heading for the exit ramps. He did quite the opposite.

He stepped on the gas.

On February 17, 2009, Obama signed the American Recovery and Reinvestment Act of 2009, a nearly $800 billion stimulus package of federal spending. On March 23, 2009, the U.S. Treasury Department announced the Public-Private Investment Program for Legacy Assets – to provide liquidity for utterly "toxic assets" that plagued financial institutions.

During the same month, Obama intervened in the American auto industry to bail out General Motors and Chrysler. In June, he signed into law the Car Allowance Rebate System ("Cash for Clunkers"), which further boosted the economy. Meanwhile, the Federal Reserve was busy pumping cash into the financial markets through a program of "quantitative easing."

The feverish pace of the federal government to counteract the threat of a calamitous economic depression within Obama's first hundred days was quite remarkable. Yet, despite his best attempts, Obama could not convince other industrialized nations to do the same. Across the world, including the Eurozone, the prevalent attitude and collective approach was similar – step on the brakes. Or march in place. In the end, the U.S. was the only industrialized nation to adopt a such a bold stimulus strategy to counter the economic tailspin.

What was the reaction by Republican leadership? Predictably, there was intractable opposition. Conservatives warned that Obama's stimulus policies would not generate recovery. Rather, they would further wreck the economy by causing runaway inflation, a devaluation of the dollar, and uncontrolled deficits – all consequences of the federal expansion.[2]

So, what is our retrospective verdict on this approach? What does the jury say in the face of a decade's worth of evidence? Let's review the *facts*.

First, none of the feared outcomes came to pass.

- Runaway inflation never materialized. The inflation rate barely registered above zero for both of Obama's terms.

- The dollar did *not* devalue. In fact, it gained 21% against the Euro during Obama's tenure.
- The federal deficit steadily decreased from 9.8% of the GDP to 3.4%.[3]

More important, Obama's polices achieved their objectives.

- The unemployment rate peaked at 10.0% in his first year and then came down steadily to 4.7%, even better than Reagan's best rate of 5.3%.[4]
- Obama ended his presidency with 75 consecutive months of job growth, the longest such stretch in U.S. history.
- While worker's wages continued to disappoint, corporate profits boomed, reaching nearly $1.8 trillion in Obama's final year in office, which was more than all four years of Reagan's second term *combined* – even after adjusting for inflation.[5]

Some wrecking job! In fact, the U.S., which was the only country to adopt Obama's expansionist approach, had, by far, the most successful response to the recession.[6] By January, 2016, the Eurozone unemployment rate, which had peaked at 12%, was still mired at 9.6%, while the American unemployment rate had fallen to 4.8%. No other industrialized nation recovered from the recession as quickly as the U.S. did.

Thus, for the better part of Obama's first year, his administration was dominated by the economy. Yet, at the same time, he began to address one of the most vexing issues of the previous four decades: the growing number of Americans lacking health insurance – by then approaching 50 million.

During his first one hundred days, Obama called upon Congress to reform health care by expanding coverage for the poor, protecting insured Americans against the loss of coverage, and adding a government insurance plan offering – otherwise known as the public option.

House Democrats introduced the first draft of this legislation in the summer of 2009. Over the next six months, Obama participated in a national debate over its merits. It eventually became clear that the public option could not garner the necessary votes even though Democrats controlled both the House and the Senate, so it was stripped from the bill.

Even so, this most conservative approach to universal health care barely passed the Senate in December, 2009. The vote was 60-39, the absolute minimum to break a Republican filibuster, without a single vote to spare. On March 21, 2010, the Patient Protection and Affordable Care Act (ACA) was passed in the House by the whisker-thin margin of 219 to 212. Two days later, Obama signed it into law.

Thus, barely a year into his presidency, Obama had led a major federal response to the economic crisis and instituted a national program to address the epidemic of uninsured Americans that had eluded seven presidents before him.

At the time of Obama's inauguration, the dominant foreign policy topic remained the war in Iraq, as the U.S. military presence there still numbered 142,000 troops. Barely a month into his first term, however, Obama announced his intention to cease combat operations in Iraq while introducing 17,000 troops into Afghanistan. Thus, the military focus pivoted from Iraq to Afghanistan. This remained the theme of U.S. policy up until and beyond the shooting death of Osama Bin Laden by Navy Seals in 2011.

Throughout this period, however, the elephant in the room was Iran, our nemesis. Purveyor of terrorism, supporter of Syria, and incessant adversary hell-bent on establishing a nuclear arsenal, Iran was already a hot topic during the 2008 election campaign. In the presidential debates, Obama had acknowledged the danger Iran posed and expressed his intent to engage Iran's leadership in negotiations about the nuclear threat.

Following his election, however, Obama found Iran's religious leaders to be intransigent and still fully committed to the advancement of its nuclear program. Since sanctions imposed by George W. Bush had not impacted Iran's behavior, there was a growing drumbeat in support of Plan B – military action. Israel's prime minister, Bibi Netanyahu, in particular, was a forceful advocate for airstrikes against Iran's nuclear facilities.[7]

However, Obama was not so enthralled with the idea of Plan B. Airstrikes against Iran would almost certainly have to be followed by a full-scale invasion, since at least some of Iran's nuclear facilities would be protected from airstrikes in underground bunkers.

Earlier sanctions had not been successful because they fell short of the mark. Thus, Iran had been able to exploit lack of unity among all its trading partners in order to continue to sell oil and obtain military technology. For sanctions to work, then, *all* major powers would need to buy in to stricter controls – including Russia and China. For this to happen, Obama would need to win the trust of adversaries who didn't naturally support our foreign policy interests. And that is exactly what happened. He earned their trust.

When Iran failed to respond to Obama's good faith negotiating efforts, the UN Security Council passed Resolution 1929 on June 9, 2010. This new resolution severely tightened sanctions and was supported by all the permanent members of the Council, including Russia and China, which had become impatient with Iran's stubborn refusals to meet Obama halfway.

Equally important, the resolution specified a carrot: incentives for Iran to give up its nuclear program. This provision outlined a path toward relief of sanctions if Iran would meet certain requirements. With these measures in place, the world waited for Iran to respond.

Then, nothing happened. For three years, Iran balked. For three years, Iran endured the sanctions. For three years, Iran continued its nuclear program with no end in sight. But the new and improved sanctions took an enormous bite, sending Iran's economy into a prolonged slump. Further, the U.S. unilaterally continued to impose further penalties against institutions linked to Iran's nuclear program – and waited – while the noose tightened.

Finally, there was a break in the stalemate when, in 2013, the Iranian people elected a new president – Hassan Rouhani. Rouhani was a clergyman who had the trust of the mullahs but also had demonstrated an openness to negotiating in good faith over offers that had been lying dormant for years.

Almost immediately, U.S. officials began negotiating in earnest with Iranian leaders - intense talks that lasted two years. Finally, in April 2015, an announcement was made that a general agreement had been reached. Over the next three months, the deal was finalized as the Joint Comprehensive Plan of Action.

The key components of the deal were that Iran would agree to give up its entire stockpile of medium-enriched uranium, and eliminate 98% of its stockpile of low-enriched uranium. It would further agree to limit future efforts to enrich uranium, and would permit comprehensive international inspections to monitor compliance. In return, the sanctions would be lifted.

This was a most remarkable accomplishment. Seven years after Obama promised new efforts of engagement with Iran in the presidential debates, six years after a bellicose Republican Congress agitated for military action, five years after the new implementation of airtight sanctions, and two years after the beginning of negotiations, all the major states – Iran, Europe, Russia, China, and the U.S. – eventually came to full agreement. Plan A, the *non*-military option, had finally prevailed.

What is remarkable about Plan A is that it even had a chance, having failed once before under George W. Bush. In order to succeed, then, the plan required several essential ingredients. First, Obama had to hold the line on military intervention despite considerable political pressure to take action. This called for firm restraint.

Second, he had to win the cooperation of Russia and China, foreign policy adversaries who were skeptical of his motives. Fortunately, he earned their trust by demonstrating good faith in negotiations for a peaceful solution. By comparison, it was Iran who appeared unreasonable.

Third, and most important, Obama had to practice patience. He had to play the long game. In my world, patience is often crucial to the success of a treatment that requires nothing more than the natural process of healing to take effect. We have a name for this ingredient: *tincture of time*.

It is not easy to exercise patience when the stakes are high, the clock is ticking, and there is little visible progress. Nonetheless, that is sometimes exactly what a leader must do: Relax. Wait. Be patient. In the face of Iran's intransigence, Obama's patience was the key to his success.

In 2009, less than eight months into his young presidency, Obama was awarded a Nobel prize he did not deserve. The award was based purely on rhetoric: his *articulated* goals for diplomatic engagement, his *avowed* plans for international cooperation, his *declared* intent to draw in friends and foes alike to advance the cause of peace. At that point, there were no tangible accomplishments. Even Obama seemed surprised to receive the honor.

By 2015, Obama had finally earned his prize. The seven-year effort to avoid a cataclysmic war with Iran required restraint, cooperation, trust, persistence – and patience. Tincture of time. It was a remarkable display of leadership at its best. It was, plausibly, Obama's most important contribution to the world during his eight-year presidency.

In this chapter, we have reviewed Obama's ascendancy to the Oval Office and three major accomplishments of his tenure: economic recovery, the Affordable Care Act, and the Iran nuclear deal. Unfortunately, we have not allowed time to discuss his many other leadership exploits: equal pay for women, gay marriage rights, Wall Street reform, normalization of Cuban relations, the war against ISIS, and the Paris Climate Agreement.

So how does Obama stack up against our attributes of leadership? Let's take stock. I have already mentioned trust – the necessary ingredient for Obama's notable achievements in foreign policy. Without a doubt, his compassion has also been prominently featured in his policies toward the middle class, veterans, immigrants, gay people, and the uninsured.

How about atonement? Indeed, one of the most consistent criticisms of Obama has been his tendency to apologize for U.S. behavior. Here is one example in a speech delivered in France, early in his presidency.[8]

> So we must be honest with ourselves... In America, there's a failure to appreciate Europe's leading role in the world. Instead of celebrating your dynamic union and seeking to partner with you to meet common challenges, there have been times where America has shown arrogance and been dismissive, even derisive.

Although not actually apologizing, Obama demonstrated a remarkable willingness to acknowledge shortfalls in U.S. policy toward other nations, a rare attribute for a leader in the political arena. While I have included this brand of honesty as a crucial attribute of a great leader, I must admit we are far from consensus on this as a desirable approach.

And what shall we say about coalescence? After all, this was one of Obama's signature goals and a dominant theme in all his speeches – his aim to cross political boundaries, his ambition to bind us together as one nation, his aspiration to unite us in a common cause. Did Obama attain the change he sought? Did he narrow the blue and red state gap to bring about national harmony? Did he bridge the divide? Even Obama would have to admit this was one of the disappointments of his presidency.

Despite Obama's persistent efforts to find common ground, Americans remained at odds – as evidenced by their votes. While Reagan's initial popular vote margin of 10% expanded to an astonishing 18% by his second term, Obama's narrowed – from 7% to 4%. By no means did he succeed in bringing the greater part of America into a single camp, as Reagan did.

Ironically, despite his impressive eloquence in rousing speeches during his campaigns, notwithstanding his soaring oratory, which could move vast crowds of enraptured followers, Obama was, oddly enough, *not* considered to be a great communicator. In this sense, his braid was not complete.

Indeed, during the rough and tumble of legislative battles, he was not as adept as Reagan at packaging his policies into compelling simple truths that could win broad support, not as skilled at closing the deal. In fact, Obama's demeanor was often described as "cool" and "aloof." Reagan, by comparison, with his simple, warm, folksy style, spiked with wit, charm, and humor, had an unearthly ability to win the support of every day Americans.

But then, again, Reagan was *White*. As America's first *Black* president, Obama had a major headwind to surmount: the deeply imbedded group bias that led a large share of the electorate to view him with suspicion and mistrust, if not outright anger, for violating their sense of normalcy in politics. Perhaps it was not reasonable to hope that he might win the hearts and minds of the vast majority of Americans. Perhaps it was not fair to expect the impossible. Perhaps it was miracle enough for him merely to win victories in two successive elections – as America's *first* Black president.

But we should give Obama some serious credit for what he accomplished against this headwind. Reagan, Bush, and now, Trump, all expanded the economy the old-fashioned way: by increasing the deficit. By running up the credit card. Each cut taxes while increasing government spending, producing a classic fiscal stimulus on borrowed money. Smoke and mirrors.

Obama, on the other hand, conquered a brutal recession, set an all-time record for consecutive months of jobs growth, and added health coverage for 20 million Americans while *cutting* the deficit – by more than half. The presidential equivalent of solving Rubik's cube while pedaling a unicycle across a tightrope and whistling *The Battle Hymn of the Republic*.

What kind of physician would Obama have been? In my view, he would have been the consummate internist – *my* specialty. When presented with challenges, he reviewed the facts, interpreted the evidence, and considered all the possibilities. He completed an assessment, established a diagnosis, and then deliberated – thoughtfully, sensibly, and in measured strokes. His final decisions were the product of careful analysis and meticulous preparation. All planned. All implemented. All on purpose.

Thus, Obama perfected the *science* of the presidency. He effectively turned the gears of the executive branch without the support of a Republican Congress. He successfully pulled the levers of government in the face of implacable opposition from the politically potent Tea Party. And he somehow found the way forward despite blatant institutional racism embodied in the hateful lie of Birtherism – yet never lost his cool.

Indeed, in the face of constant political flak, Obama systematically moved the needle on economic recovery, universal health care, and civil rights, and shored up our defense against terrorism, nuclear proliferation, and climate change. While he admittedly did not win over the electorate as Reagan did, Obama's presidency will be remembered for impressive policy achievements executed cleanly, without fraud, leaks, or scandal.

No-Drama Obama.

Trump:
Deny the Self

> One day we were in the playroom of our house, building with blocks... I asked Robert if I could borrow some of his, and he said, "Okay, but you have to give them back when you're done." I ended up using all my blocks, and then all of his, and when I was done, I'd created a beautiful building. I liked it so much that I glued the whole thing together. And that was the end of Robert's blocks.[1]
>
> From *Trump: The Art of the Deal,* Donald Trump, 1987

Donald John Trump was born in 1946 in Queens, New York. He was undeniably the child of immigrants as his mother and all four grandparents were born outside the U.S. Donald's father, Fred Trump, was the exception. Born in the Bronx, Fred became a prominent real estate developer, building thousands of homes for New York City residents.

As a teenager, Donald was a self-admitted handful – so much so that his parents enrolled him in the New York Military Academy at the age of 13. In the fall of 1964, he entered Fordham University, only to transfer to Wharton School of Business two years later to study real estate. Shortly afterward, Trump joined his father's business – developing middle-class housing in Brooklyn and Queens.

By 1971, Trump had become president of his father's company, now named The Trump Organization, and his father remained chairman of the board. Two years later, the U.S. Department of Justice brought suit for discrimination against minorities.

Federal agents, disguised as applicants looking for housing, found that The Trump Organization steered Black applicants away from predominantly White apartment buildings, while those same buildings were marketed to White applicants. In a settlement, the Trumps made no admission of guilt but promised to revise their policies to end the practice of discrimination.

In 1978, the younger Trump made his first move into Manhattan. He spied an opening in the aging Commodore Hotel adjacent to Grand Central Terminal in Midtown. He purchased a half-share, remodeled the hotel from top to bottom, and re-opened it as the gleaming all-glass Grand Hyatt Hotel. By all accounts, the project was a resounding success. A star was born.

At about the same time, Trump purchased the Fifth Avenue site on which he was to build Trump Tower, his signature Manhattan property that would eventually become a luxury apartment building, his primary residence, and the future site of the filming studio for *The Apprentice*.

By the late 1980s, Trump was flying high – a respected developer with a national reputation, and owner of several Manhattan hotels, including the Plaza. For personal use, he had purchased the historic Mar-a-Lago estate, former residence of Marjorie Merriweather Post, in Palm Beach, Florida.

No project was too big, no jewel beyond reach for this brash, self-confident maven of real estate fame. Not even Atlantic City, the Las Vegas of the eastern seaboard. In this oceanside gambling mecca, however, Trump would finally meet his match. The story of this misadventure offers deep revelations about Trump and is worth exploring.

Trump's first two projects in Atlantic City were Harrah's at Trump Plaza and Trump's Castle. A joint venture between Trump and the Holiday Corporation, Harrah's was his first foray into the casino-hotel business. As he agreed to the deal, Trump could hardly believe his good fortune. "This was almost too good to believe. Several times, I looked over at Robert and Harvey just to see if perhaps I was missing something."[2]

He was. Soon after it opened in 1984, the boardwalk casino-hotel hit financial trouble. As disputes developed over the results, Trump bought out his partner's stake and took complete ownership. Yet he continued to be unaware of the trouble that was brewing in Atlantic City, even as late as 1987. "Suffice it to say that my ultimate buyout of Holiday Inns' share of our casino-hotel in February 1986 was one of my most savored transactions."[3]

As for Trump's Castle, Trump purchased the partially completed building and property from the Hilton Corporation for $320 million. One aspect of the deal was unusual for Trump. In retrospect, it revealed a reckless streak that would haunt his Atlantic City misadventures.

By Trump's own admission, he purchased the casino-hotel *sight-unseen*, a breathtaking display of unchecked impulsivity and unbridled hubris. A year later, as the project began to falter, visions of grandeur still danced in his head. "We are projecting revenues of $310 million and a gross operating profit well in excess of $70 million. *It pays to trust your instincts*."[4]

Thus, by the late-1980s, Trump had seized ownership of a pair of large casino-hotels soon to become albatrosses in his real estate portfolio, a debt-laden duo that would bring the high-flying mogul back to earth. But these mishaps, as bad as they were, would soon be eclipsed by a much more regrettable adventure.

The premiere event in Donald Trump's business career – the rise and fall of the Taj Mahal casino – was a saga that began in the early 1980s. The Taj was initially conceived and launched by Resorts International, a major player in the Atlantic City casino industry. Construction began in 1983 with an initial budget of $250 million. By 1986, the mammoth project was in deep financial trouble, and the parent company became an attractive takeover target. Enter Donald Trump – the irrepressible opportunist.[5]

In 1988, after a high stakes battle for control of the company, Trump purchased the Taj – for $273 million. But the casino was only partly finished. Trump would need to raise an additional $675 million to complete it, and here is where he hit rough sledding. In 1988, just one year after Black Friday – the precipitous October, 1987 drop in the stock market that ushered in a collapse in real estate prices – the well was dry.

But Trump had already committed himself with his big purchase. Unless the casino opened, he would lose his entire stake. So he made an ill-fated decision that would ultimately doom the project, a pact with the devil that would smother the baby in its crib. A dubious strategy that he had explicitly promised the gaming commission he would not pursue, and that any junior accountant would recognize as a colossal misjudgment.[6]

He financed the remaining construction with junk bonds. Junk bonds were financial instruments tied up in shaky projects at excessive interest rates. Potentially lucrative but at high risk for lenders and abusively expensive for borrowers. The legal equivalent of owing to the mob.

Trump, the borrower, agreed to pay an annual interest rate of 14%![7] There was no chance that an Atlantic City casino-hotel could earn enough revenue to cover that expense, especially considering Trump would be in competition with *himself*, cannibalizing customers from his own casino across the street.

The project was completed within two years, and the Taj Mahal colossus opened to great fanfare in April, 1990 – billed as the eighth wonder of the world. And, as any first-year business school student could easily have predicted, the ill-conceived project immediately went under. The fledgling bird inched out of the nest and dropped like a stone.

At the close of construction, Trump could not even afford to pay contractors for work they had done, forcing several bankruptcies in local construction firms.[8] Then, within ten weeks of opening the Taj, Trump missed a monthly payment on Trump's Castle – a first for him. He soon had enormous cash flow problems leading to bankruptcies for each of his three casinos.

In late 1990, Trump renegotiated with bondholders by yielding a 50% stake in his company in exchange for reduced interest rates and a more favorable payoff schedule. On the verge of financial collapse, he was in a terribly weak negotiating position. One has to admire his determination, hanging on by his fingertips to extract crucial concessions from his lenders.

As always, Trump's most valuable asset was his sheer bravado – threatening bankers with the loss of their entire stake if they forced him out. What would the Trump-branded casinos be without Trump? In the end, he still held all the cards.

Nonetheless, his businesses were deep under water and his bankers forced him to sell his prized assets: Trump Shuttle, his ill-fated airline, Trump Princess, his luxury yacht, and the Plaza Hotel, his treasured property in mid-town Manhattan. In 1988, Trump had bought the Plaza for the stratospheric price of $407 million, another example of his reckless tendency to overreach on vanity projects.[9] In 1992, the Plaza became his fourth bankruptcy.

By 1995, Trump was limping along – still struggling under the burden of huge debts. Then, he had an inspiration. Once again, he would bank on his brand. He started a new publicly traded stock company, Trump Hotels & Casino Resorts, with the ticker symbol DJT, which would offer investors a stake in the Trump name and a chance to share in his alleged success.

Oddly enough, after four corporate bankruptcies, after reneging on payments to bankers, investors, and contractors at will, Trump had no difficulty wooing a pool of new investors eager to profit from his business savvy, and he raised a quick $140 million – a testament to his incomparable salesmanship and the lure of his brand.[10]

Soon after, Trump pulled off the signature transaction of his career. The most brazen, self-centered, underhanded feat of a lifetime. His *Opus Horribilis.* As executive in control, he forced his new public company to buy his failing casinos from *himself,* at premium prices, using the money he had raised from his new investors, reinforced by the sale of yet more junk bonds.

In other words, Trump, the failed real estate tycoon, threw his new investor-partners under the bus to save his own skin, by dumping his debt-laden casino dogs onto *their* balance sheets, putting himself into the clear. It was an outrageous transaction that completely wiped out the value of their investments. One wonders how this can even be *legal.*

Not surprisingly, over the next ten years, saddled with these boondoggles, DJT stock lost 96% of its value.[11] In 2004, Trump Hotels & Casino Resorts filed for bankruptcy. Trump's fifth. Small wonder. Trump's Castle, which Trump had dumped onto his stock company in 1996 for $525 million, was eventually sold in 2011 for $38 million – 7 cents on the dollar.[12]

Meanwhile, Donald Trump, private citizen, escaped unscathed. The modern-day Houdini had loosened the handcuffs, unshackled the chains, and picked the locks, thus escaping from his underwater coffin to emerge on shore, dripping wet but free and alive.

Let me close this story with an echo of Trump's own words – eerily prescient from his childhood. *In building the Taj, he ended up using his own blocks, and then all of his bankers', investors', and contractors' blocks. When he was done he had created a beautiful building. He liked it so much that he glued the whole thing together. And that was the end of everyone's blocks.*

It would have been most fitting if this account had followed Chapter 10. Although Trump never personally filed for bankruptcy, his businesses repeatedly did so under Chapter 11. Because of federal regulations, however, his businesses continued to operate under bankruptcy protection even when he failed to meet obligations on his debts. Those same rules, by the way, do not permit a middle-class American to remain in her home when unable to meet mortgage obligations in a *personal* bankruptcy.

Of course, every time Trump declared bankruptcy, he stiffed his creditors. He forced them to forgive part of his debt, cut his payments, or reduce his obligations so that he could revive his properties as going concerns. And he was neither defensive nor apologetic about this behavior. On the contrary, Trump's prolific use of bankruptcies was integral to his business model, and a matter of personal pride. "I do play with the bankruptcy laws. They're very good for me."[13]

Indeed, if such laws were ever created to protect a businessman from the consequences of poor judgment and gross mismanagement, they were fashioned to shelter Trump. Few individuals in American history have lost greater amounts of other people's money without paying the price.

The remainder of the Trump story is pretty well known by now. In 2003, he became executive producer and host of NBC's *The Apprentice*, a reality show in which contestants vied for the opportunity to work for Trump or be "fired" by Trump himself.

The show was a hit and aired with Trump in his starring role until 2015, when he parted ways to pursue political ambitions. In the meantime, he continued to acquire and build hotel properties. In subsequent years, he also took ownership or management responsibilities for a number of golf courses around the world.

In late 2015, Trump declared his candidacy for the presidency. In July, 2016, he officially won the nomination of the Republican party, and in November, he won the national election. Donald J. Trump – 45th president of the United States. What happened since then could fill an encyclopedia, so I will end my story here and take a few moments to reflect upon what we knew *before* the election.

It is not easy to pretend to forget what we have learned about events that followed, but I would like to focus for a moment on Donald Trump, the *candidate*. Only then can we render a pure judgment about the fateful decision to elect him without lacing it with the prejudicial knowledge of its eventual consequences. So how can we sum up his resumé?

In short, Trump has royally succeeded in life by almost any standard measure. He has repeatedly set a compass heading toward an ambitious destination and maneuvered his way to goal displaying a variety of formidable attributes: inventive problem-solving, uncanny timing, and dogged persistence, as well as seduction, coercion, and frank duplicity.

Most impressive of these is his phenomenal persistence – a man not to be denied. And if a leader is someone who takes people to a new place, Trump has at least one essential skill: persuasion. He knows where he wants to go, divines how to get there, and inspires others to join him – bankers, investors, and customers – in droves.

This singular trait – his salesmanship – is probably the greatest key to Trump's success. After repeated bankruptcies in which he lost obscene amounts of other people's money, he never stopped convincing yet new potential partners that he could be trusted to make them rich.

And, in the greatest test of all, he won the American presidency in the wake of several scandalous revelations, any single one of which would have been sufficient to bring down a less resilient candidate. It would be dangerous for his opponents to underestimate Trump's talent for getting to goal.

At the same time, we must acknowledge some dark truths. First and foremost, Trump is a bully. He strokes his fragile ego by dominating others. He teases, belittles, and threatens. As presidential candidate, Trump continued to bully. He insulted his opponents with petty nicknames, kicked sand in the faces of our allies, and repeatedly humiliated Mexico over the border wall. Classic bullying behavior.

In this vein, Trump's life story includes an amazing coincidence. Beginning with his staunch resistance against government charges of racial discrimination and throughout his early career, Trump employed the services of a notable attorney, a well-known public figure of dubious ethical principles, an experienced attack dog who took no prisoners in any dispute.

This attorney was none other than Roy Cohn, the egregious mouthpiece of Joseph McCarthy, prize bully of the Red Scare era – one and the same. It is not difficult to draw a straight line from McCarthy to Trump through Roy Cohn, master of the public smear.

Second, Trump is allergic to the truth – a serial confabulator. Like a Munchausen patient, his propensity to tell tall tales has completely obliterated the margin between fact and fiction. Perhaps a lifetime of enthusiastic salesmanship has left him unable to tell the difference.

Of course, one of the most shameful lies that Trump ever propagated was the racist claim that President Obama was not born in the United States – that he was not an authentic American. Despite eliciting a bona fide birth certificate, which no *White* president has ever been asked to produce, Trump continued to foster McCarthyesque doubts about Obama's heritage for the better part of his two terms with bogus claims. "I have people that actually have been studying it...and they cannot *believe* what they're finding."[14]

Third, Trump is a narcissist. In my world, this is a highly destructive personality trait. Narcissists demonstrate exaggerated feelings of self-importance and an obsessive need for admiration. Each becomes a black hole of psychopathology, relentlessly drawing every particle of attention into his or her gravitational field. Does this sound like anyone you know?

As narcissism is Trump's most prominent attribute, I am not surprised by the turbulence of his presidency – the chaotic cloud of constant combat, media skirmishes, and foreign policy confusion. The endless speculation about his motives, the monumental conflict that instantly appeared within hours of his inauguration, the near-fatal overdose of palace intrigue. These are the classic calling cards of an attention-seeking narcissist, the ultimate destructive force in any organization – hospital, business, or government.

For this reason alone, I am also not surprised by Trump's failure to win re-election despite his remarkable gifts of persuasion and salesmanship. His inability to "deny the self" betrayed his lack of concern for anyone other than himself and his family, much less the working class Americans who elected him in the first place.

How does Trump measure up against our great leader phenotype? Let's use the COVID-19 pandemic as our yardstick. This leadership challenge is fresh in everyone's mind and has had measurable consequences. Even better, it has objective metrics that lend themselves to comparisons across nations and their leaders. Above all, this report card will be evidence-based.

To put this challenge into context, it is useful to note that the response to a pandemic is not exactly rocket science; the algorithm is well-established. As soon as it is clear that the nation is at risk, the first step is to secure ports of entry and to "identify and isolate" individual cases. Ideally, authorities will identify cases through symptom tracking and comprehensive testing. Cases must then be isolated, as well as their contacts.

If this is done well, a single case does not become a large cluster of cases. If this is done rigorously across the nation, the pandemic can be nipped in the bud. South Korea and Taiwan did this extremely well under strong national leadership – and effectively shut down the pandemic within their borders. This is why South Korea had only 11,000 cases by the time the US had a 1.5 million.[15] This is Plan A: an ounce of prevention.

If the nation does not activate Plan A, then it must turn to plan B: a pound of cure. The U.S. is a case in point. For the first two months after receiving advance notice, the federal government effectively did nothing to prevent the pandemic from settling in.[16] Once it took root, we had no choice but to shut it down with "shelter in place" policies that closed schools, businesses, and social interactions. This was painful and costly but absolutely necessary, and much preferable to plan C. let the virus run its course.

Plan C, which would result in upwards of 200 million Americans becoming infected, would be unthinkable. The New York City experience, which I have saved for the next chapter, gave us a small taste of what plan C would look like. Only 25% of city residents became infected yet completely overran the health system.[17] Two million lives lost would create a sea of death that would quintuple American fatalities in World War II.[18] Not to be considered. Once we passed on Plan A, Plan B was the only viable option.

So, what is an ounce of prevention worth? We actually know the answer to this question: more than 5 trillion dollars, 8 million jobs, and 560,000 lives - as of this writing.[19] By the time these words are read, the total number of deaths will be even higher. That is the price of denying the truth, of ignoring the facts, of persisting in magical thinking that we were somehow immune to a virus that ran rampant in China and Europe before coming to America. It is the price of the lack of leadership. Let's now assess our commander-in-chief against our nine attributes of leadership, one at a time.

Was Trump able to admit his mistakes in the delayed ramp-up? Not in the least. To this day, he continues to falsely assert that he saw the epidemic coming before anyone else and jumped on it early, yet video evidence proves otherwise.[20,21] Was Trump able to forgive others in *their* responses? Apparently not, as Trump supported the firings of a Navy captain who called for a COVID-19 rescue for his ship,[22] a public health authority who contradicted Trump's promotion of an unproven treatment,[23] and an inspector general who had pointed out the national shortage of testing supplies and PPE.[24]

Did Trump instill trust in his leadership? Not in his daily ramblings that emphasized politics at the expense of science. Trump's lack of integrity undermined his credibility, and his false pronouncements eroded the public trust. Did Trump gather information before making decisions? Again, no. His marginalization of scientists has befuddled public health experts, and his impulsive pronouncements have dismayed even his closest supporters.[25]

Did Trump take decisive action when called for? Clearly this was not the case as two crucial months passed before he took the helm. Instead, he made matters worse by repeatedly downplaying the implications of a national pandemic.[21] Did Trump base his decisions on evidence? On the contrary. His recommendations ran counter to the facts: excessive promotion of the unproven medication hydroxychloroquine and a bizarre suggestion for patients to ingest cleansing agents.

We should not have been surprised. Any doubts about Trump's affiliation with evidence evaporated in an instant when the Centers for Disease Control and Prevention (CDC) announced in December, 2017 that they were forbidden by the Trump administration to use the term "evidence-based" in any of their scientific recommendations. He might as well have put a stake in my heart. What an astonishing blow against modern science and the systematic approach to leadership!

Did Trump show compassion? Unfortunately, one of the conspicuous elements of Trump's daily news conferences was the dearth of empathy and his seeming lack of concern for the human devastation of COVID-19.[26] Did Trump bridge the divide? Regrettably, Trump never passed up an opportunity to drive a wedge. His persistent use of the term "Chinese virus" and repeated finger-pointing at the Chinese government betrayed his signature response to any crisis: find a scapegoat and hammer away.

Finally...coalescence. Indeed, Trump passed on far too many opportunities to draw our nation together or to cross international boundaries to lead a cohesive global response to the epidemic. As a result, the states fought the war on a local basis, even competing with each other for staff and supplies. And the global community lost a ripe opportunity to collaborate in battle against a common foe. Lack of coalescence was the fatal flaw in our response.

Reviewing the nine-point leadership checklist leads to a shocking conclusion. Trump lacks a single positive attribute. He is the photographic negative of a successful leader – the *anti*-president. In the final analysis, I must sum up Trump's performance with a simple, devastating truth.

The emperor was wearing no clothes.

So, what type of physician would Trump be? I can say with relief that Trump could not ever be a physician. He has landed the remarkable trifecta of narcissism, dishonesty, and bullying behavior. His narcissism would be red-flagged at the interview stage, which would prevent his acceptance to medical school. If not, his dishonesty would be seen as an ethical lapse that would thwart his successful completion of residency training.

If he somehow miraculously were to advance to the role of attending physician, Trump's bullying would be seen as disruptive behavior that would result in his removal from the medical staff. Indeed, most hospitals nowadays, including mine, will not maintain admitting privileges for a physician who humiliates, degrades, and disrespects staff members, let alone patients. Thank goodness for that!

And what nickname shall we ascribe to our 45th president? I suggest the best choice would be "Bankrupt Donald." It is a relevant descriptor that has the added advantage of being true. True seven times over. We can start with the Plaza Hotel. That's one. Three casino-hotel lemons get us to four. Two more failed Atlantic City ventures make an even half-dozen.

The seventh and most spectacular bankruptcy is, of course, Trump's presidency. Bankrupt of vision. Bankrupt of strategy. Bankrupt of integrity. A steady flow of red ink. A daily tweetstorm of small-minded barbs and vulgar insults. A relentless parade of shady appointees ushered out the back door. Tens of millions of American voters betrayed by Trump's myopic goals: tax cuts for the rich, health cuts for the middle class, and pay cuts for NATO. Instead of making America great again, Trump made America small for the first time. *Bankrupt Donald*.

But enough about Trump. I have bigger fish to fry. Trump was our president for just four years, yet America's chronic illness has been brewing for four decades! So let's not forget that while Trump was an impressive manifestation of the pathology in our political system, *he was merely a symptom.*

After all, Trump did not pull the wool over our eyes. He was the free choice of an engaged electorate that was fully aware of his florid faults. The deeper question is *why*. Why did so many American voters make this selection? How could they ignore this candidate's evident, disqualifying flaws? What is the truth that lies beneath? If we focus too much on Trump, we will miss the diagnosis – the surest way to the podium at the M&M.

But if we get the diagnosis and treatment right, the symptoms will simply melt away, and we will restore our health and sanity. The voters will move on, and Donald Trump, our modern-day McCarthy, too bad to be true, will fade into irrelevance just like the first one – one more discredited demagogue consigned to the ash heap of history.

This, then, may be the most important conclusion of this lesson: our fanatical obsession with Donald Trump is overblown and misdirected. He is a tantalizing distraction. A false prophet. Just another cheap parlor trick to draw our attention away from the truth. To cure the disease, we must go much deeper than the 45th president. We must get to the very root. That will be the objective of the next three chapters.

Mission:
Set the Compass

> And the disease, by being communicated from the sick to the well, seemed daily to get ahead, and to rage the more, as fire will do by laying on fresh combustibles...such, I say was the quality of the pestilential matter, as to pass not only from man to man, but, what is more strange...that anything belonging to the infected, if touched by any other creature would certainly infect, and even kill that creature in a short space of time.
>
> From a description of the Plague in *The Decameron*,
> Giovanni Boccaccio, c. 1353

"So, what's the problem?"

"We have COVID-19 patients coming out our ears! Nearly three hundred on Medicine and a hundred in the ICUs – pretty much all on vents."

"How did you get to a hundred?"

"We have 56 in the main ICUs, 10 in the Endoscopy Suite, and 12 in the Amb Surg suite. And now we have 25 in the ED. That makes a hundred."

"Okay, so what's the problem?"

"We're out of space. Where do we put the next ventilator patient? And the one after that? What if we get a dozen more tonight?"

"We go to Plan B. Just like we agreed. Four ventilator patients in each operating room."

"We've been through this before. The nurses hate that idea. Each OR will be a hot zone. They'll be wearing N95s all day long without a break."

The Webex is abruptly overtaken by traffic noise. "Mute your mikes!" someone shouts in frustration and the background is suddenly silenced.

"So, what do the nurses prefer?"

"Double up."

"Double up? What's that supposed to mean?"

"You know how we have a COVID patient in each ICU cubicle?"

"Sure. That's the perfect space for a vent patient."

"Each one gets a roommate. Double up."

On January, 8, 2020, the Centers for Disease Control and Prevention (CDC) circulated a report about 59 patients with a respiratory illness of unknown origin in Wuhan province – our first public alert about coronavirus. Two days later, our special pathogens team began planning Bellevue's response.[1] Although the CDC alert was short on details, our hospital leaders were already sensitized to the risk of a highly lethal communicable disease. Just six years earlier we had confronted a deadly pathogen of our own.

In late summer 2014, when Ebola was raging in West Africa, we realized that any case appearing in New York City would likely find its way to Bellevue, so we spent ten weeks preparing a 2-bed isolation unit, building a dedicated laboratory, purchasing personal protective equipment (PPE), and training staff how to take care of an Ebola patient – just in case.

At the end of our preparatory period, almost on cue, a real patient appeared in the city, landed in our unit (as expected), and was cured of his disease over a three-week period. Thus, we became the first and only general hospital in the U.S. to safely and successfully treat an Ebola patient.

Following that success, Bellevue joined University of Nebraska Medical Center and Emory University to form NETEC: the National Emerging Special Pathogen Training and Education Center, a federally-funded program to prepare American hospitals for an outbreak of a lethal infectious agent.[2] This ongoing participation in national preparedness enhanced our sensitivity to a potential epidemic and fostered our hair-trigger response to the Wuhan virus.

We felt our Ebola unit would be the perfect venue in which to treat a coronavirus case, so we set aside two rooms in the unlikely event that a patient or two would show up in our ED. Three months later we would see this 2-bed allotment exceeded 200-fold by a deluge of infected patients.

In late January, the pandemic reached the US, and the Pacific Northwest soon became a focus of coronavirus disease, by then known as COVID-19. As coronavirus patients overwhelmed Seattle-area hospitals, we began to think about designating an entire 30-bed unit for cases of our own.

In early March, the first COVID-19 case was identified in the New York City area. With an extreme limitation on available testing, it was impossible to know how many city residents were silent carriers, but we sensed there was a huge number of invisible cases right on our doorstep.

"We should presume that every respiratory infection is COVID-19 until proven otherwise," Kerry cautioned us. Dr. Kerry Dierberg is our Hospital Epidemiologist and Chief of Infectious Disease. She speaks with authority about special pathogens. In 2014, while our hospital treated a single Ebola patient under impeccable conditions, Kerry treated many dozens of such patients in West Africa inside a tent. Now, she had a bad feeling. "We shouldn't drop our guard over lack of testing. Let's assume the worst."

By Thursday, March 12, we had taken in a number of patients with suspected COVID-19 infections, and we were still in the dark. The public health system had inadequate testing capacity, and the private labs took as long as a week to return results. Nonetheless, we realized we were about to be caught up in a major outbreak and would need to rapidly expand our capacity to accommodate as many as a hundred inpatient cases.

On this date, we were still functioning as a normal hospital, full of our usual non-COVID patients. But knowing this was about to change, we cancelled all elective surgeries for the following week to free up rooms and resources. We then began two daily one-hour meetings: an operations meeting at 8:30 am for hospital leaders, and a clinical response meeting at 4:30 pm for service chiefs. These meetings would continue daily through May, well after the COVID-19 surge had passed.

From the start, we obsessed about flow through the Emergency Department (ED). We knew that if a flood of patients cascaded into the ED with nowhere to go, we would drown in a sea of COVID-19. To prevent this, we would have to swiftly open up new hospital units with empty beds, ready to accept fresh patients, and we would have to correct the longstanding culture of an institution that normally tolerated as many as 30 patients backed up in the ED waiting for an inpatient bed to materialize. This culture change would need help from the top.

Bill Hicks is our Chief Executive Officer (CEO), my direct boss. Bill is a flow master. He has a platinum belt in "Lean" methodology and had once directed the Lean performance improvement program at one of our sister public hospitals. When Bill came to Bellevue seven years ago, he masterminded the rapid improvement event that reduced the outpatient pharmacy wait from 3 hours to 15 minutes. When Bill talks about flow, I listen.

Bill is also the prototype manager I described earlier from the book, "Good to Great." A humble leader who puts the institution first. As we began our daily meetings, Bill pulled me aside. "Nate, our COVID-19 strategy is going to be a clinical one, so I need the service chiefs to be actively engaged. I guarantee that you and the team will have everything you need – staff, space, equipment, and supplies. Just make sure our physician leaders are fully involved in all the planning."

On March 16, we began to carry out our COVID-19 response. To create ICU space for our new admissions, we decided to move all current *non*-COVID patients out of our 56-bed ICU floor and into the Post-Anesthesia Care Unit (PACU), the recovery room for patients after surgery. Since we were cutting down on surgeries, the PACU was the perfect place to put these patients. But, because the PACU was less than half the size of our combined ICUs, we would have to shoehorn 56 patients into 25 beds.[3]

We started with the west wing of the ICU floor. Over the course of a week, we moved equipment, supplies, IV pumps, medication dispensers, and then patients themselves to the PACU. This simple maneuver was confounded by every conceivable obstacle, including nurse staffing constraints. Meanwhile, our facilities staff began working on the ICU units under the direction of Michael Rawlings, our Chief Operating Officer.

Before becoming COO, Michael had been Director of Facilities, which meant he was completely familiar with the architecture of our 50 year-old building and had worked closely with all our tradespeople: the electricians, plumbers, and carpenters who were to become unlikely partners in our COVID-19 response.[4] Michael suggested that we redesign the entire ICU floor.

"I can have my guys replace an exterior window in each cubicle with a customized cutout for an exhaust duct. Then we can install a HEPA filter with a fan and turn each cubicle into a negative pressure room. Fresh air will be drawn into the cubicle from the hallway and then exhausted out the window after filtration. Perfect for staff safety."

"That sounds great. How long will that take?"

"We can knock out five or six in a day. I just need to order some more HEPA filters. Hold off the patients to give us time to do the work."

Hold off the patients? They were now flying in through the ED front door in daily waves. Dr. Rajneesh Gulati, Chief of the Emergency Department, had never seen anything like this before. "The ILIs have taken over. We need to separate them out from everyone else."

ILI stood for "influenza-like illness," which implied COVID-19 infection. Although it was not clear at the time, nearly all the ILIs would eventually be confirmed as COVID-19 cases. Because of the high volume, Raj decided to cordon off part of the ED for patients like these. In this "hot zone," the staff would continuously wear PPE, including an N95 mask, throughout their shift.

One striking feature of the ILIs was their propensity to decompensate rapidly into respiratory failure, requiring emergency intubation in the ED. In this procedure, a physician sedates the patient and then passes a plastic tube through the mouth into the windpipe to connect the patient to a ventilator.

Intubation is a significant rite of passage, from a patient who is awake and can breathe for herself, to a heavily sedated patient connected to life support. For too many COVID-19 fatalities, the moment before intubation would be their final moment of awareness. In the space of a few hours one day, Raj's team had intubated four patients and sent them to the ICU.

Meanwhile, the ICU floor was being rapidly emptied of all non-COVID patients, who were relocated to the PACU as quickly as nurses could organize the exodus. As each room emptied out, the facilities staff quickly moved in to convert the air flow. Practically as soon as each room was converted, Raj sent up a COVID-19 patient to fill the bed.

It was a desperate race between the engineers and the patients around the perimeter of the ICU floor, an acre of space being rapidly transformed into a full-scale COVID-19 unit. The engineers won. Over the course of ten days, they always kept one or two rooms ahead of the new occupants.

Finally, the transformation was complete. Every one of the 56 cubicles was emptied of a non-COVID patient. Every cubicle was converted to negative pressure airflow. And every cubicle was now filled with a COVID-19 patient. At no time did we fall behind. At no point did the ED back up with patients.

While this was going on, the non-ICU rooms filled up even more rapidly than the ICUs, as our flood of new patients had a ravenous appetite for space. First, we filled a Rehab unit with 22 COVID-19 patients. Then we opened up an empty unit on 17 East for 26 more. Then we converted the World Trade Center (WTC) Clinic back into a 30-bed inpatient unit, which it had once been decades earlier.[5]

The WTC Clinic, which treats first responders for chronic diseases acquired through their environmental exposures on 9/11, had shut down operations and begun doing telephone visits for their patients from offsite locations. And Dr. Joan Reibman, their director, had already anticipated this need. "I see what's happening here. You are welcome to use our space for inpatient care. Just remember to give it back when you're done."

Michael's team was just getting started. Next, they relocated Employee Health, Pre-Op Testing, and Trauma team offices so that another unit, 15 East, could be taken out of mothballs. And then onto 7 North, where an old tuberculosis (TB) ward was re-activated by displacing even more programs.

The 7 North unit had the advantage of built-in negative pressure airflow in each room, a holdover from TB treatments in the 1980s. This was the very unit from which I had discharged Alec Secceño with the incorrect prescriptions in my opening Bellevue story. By restoring these old inpatient units, it seemed that we were running the Bellevue clock in reverse, bringing our history back to life. In practically no time, our facilities staff had created 240 extra spaces for COVID-19 patients – 112 ICU and 128 floor beds.

All this work was completed, just like the main ICU floor, barely one step ahead of the patients pouring into the ED. The stakes could not have been higher. We were paddling furiously to stay ahead of a tidal wave. If we hesitated for a moment, we would be overtaken by the tsunami of patients coming in through the front door. If we slowed for a second, we would drown. Yet, we never did. The five units that Michael's staff opened up kept us paddling ahead of the wave. Even at the peak of our COVID-19 deluge, the ED never backed up with respiratory cases.[6]

By the end of the two-week surge, our ICU floor was full of COVID-19 and we were having trouble finding open rooms for new admissions. Yet, when we looked around our system, the situation was much worse. In the outer boroughs, five of our sister hospitals had been buried in a complete avalanche of patients. Queens and Elmhurst Hospitals in Queens, Woodhull and Coney Island Hospitals in Brooklyn, and Lincoln Hospital in the Bronx were devastated by a crushing wave of COVID-19, and their EDs were packed with patients on stretchers, a hundred deep, seeking inpatient beds.

At this point, I began receiving calls from Dr. Eric Wei, Chief Quality Officer for our system. Eric reports to Mitchell Katz, our system CEO,[7] who, in turn, reports to the mayor.[8] In my role, I am accountable to Eric as well as to Machelle Allen, system CMO (Chief Medical Officer).[9] When Eric first joined our system in 2018, he held a webinar for all the staff at our eleven hospitals. We signed on expecting to hear a cogent description of how he expected us to improve quality of care throughout our hospital system.

Instead, Eric told of a mistake he had once made as an ED physician, an error that resulted in the death of a patient and personally traumatized him. The purpose of the story was to acknowledge that everyone makes mistakes, that those who make mistakes suffer personal consequences, and that the system needed to recognize *their* needs as well as those of patients.

It was his introduction of a new program called "Helping Healers Heal (H3)" that would provide emotional support for any staff who experienced psychological trauma from an adverse outcome. H3 was to become the cornerstone of staff support during the COVID-19 crisis. The reader will recognize this as an affirmation of the Just Culture. It was a sentinel moment in our system, a cultural turning point for the enterprise.

Through his calls, Eric had a simple purpose – to transfer patients from the afflicted hospitals in the outer boroughs to their less overrun siblings, such as Bellevue. As much as we had felt swamped by the COVID-19 wave, it was far worse elsewhere. Could we find the capacity to take a couple of ICU patient transfers and perhaps six non-ICU (floor) transfers? From this vantage point, we knew there was only one correct answer. We took the transfers.

By now, our most pressing issue was nurse staffing. While the national standard for the nurse:patient ratio in an ICU setting was 1:2, our swelling ICU census, coupled with growing nurse callouts for COVID-like symptoms, had stretched our ratio to 1:4. In pre-COVID days, this ratio would be considered a never event, according to Omar.

Omar Abedalrhman is our Chief Nursing Officer. Omar grew up in northern Israel, not far from the Lebanese border. I have always felt the setting of Omar's upbringing made him tough as a leader: fair but firm. His decisiveness would prove to be a huge asset in the crisis. And in this situation, he did not mince words.

"The ICU nurses are overwhelmed. These are very complicated patients. Some of them are on six or seven titratable IV drips. They have to be proned. Everyone has to wear PPE, so every step is as slow as molasses. Without outside help, we can't possibly cope with the volume."

Indeed, in the absence of reinforcements, we had advised our nurses to prioritize their responsibilities. Skip the paper work, we said. Forego documentation of the care plan, patient education, and nurse assessments that can dominate a nurse's attention. Focus instead on giving meds, controlling the IV drips, and paying attention to the patient. The important stuff.

Nonetheless, the ICU nurses struggled to stay afloat and had no choice but to improvise. They attached extra-long intravenous (IV) tubing so that the IV poles with medication pumps could stand outside the cubicle's glass doors, while the IV tubing ran through a crack between the doors to the patient. In this way, nurses could respond to alarms and adjust the flow of fluids and medications without completely suiting up to enter the room.[10]

Finally, our Central Office began to supply extra nurses through private agencies. Since operating rooms across the nation had gone on hiatus, and nurses at those hospitals had been furloughed, some private companies were snapping up the available nurses by the hundreds, shipping them to New York City, putting them up at a midtown hotel, and busing them daily to our public hospitals to supplement the shrinking complement of our own staff nurses.

For physician staffing, we had a similar challenge. With a growing census, we needed reinforcements for the front lines. Our primary source was physicians, nurse practitioners (NPs), and physician assistants (PAs) who were freed up from the cancellation of surgeries. It was gratifying that each department found a way to help without being asked.

For example, our surgeons, who had voluntarily cancelled their elective cases, were eager to contribute. Shortly after their non-COVID ICU patients were moved to the PACU, Dr. Spiros Frangos, Chief of Surgery, reached out to the Medicine Department with a generous offer.

"Since your folks are taking care of all the COVID ICU patients on the main ICU floor, my team will manage all the *non*-COVID ICU patients in the PACU – even the Medicine cases. And our department will be happy to staff one of the eight COVID ICU teams."

The Anesthesiology Department quickly followed suit. On one of the afternoon calls early on, their chief, Dr. Sudheer Jain, announced, "I've put my physicians on day and night schedules to join the ICU teams. We'll be doing all the procedures on COVID-19 patients: intubations, central lines, even simple blood drawing – 24/7. Just let us know what you need." By late March, the anesthesiologists were staffing *all* the hospital wards to help out with every routine procedure and every life-threatening emergency – a reassuring presence for the nurses.

Not to be outdone, the orthopedic surgeons formed a proning team. A well-proven technique to improve lung function is to turn patients face down for up to 16 hours per day. Repositioning a patient in this way is labor-intensive, so the orthopedic residents came through the ICUs twice daily, turning all the designated patients on each pass. As Dr. Toni McLaurin, Chief of Orthopedics put it, "Ortho surgeons are good at positioning patients. We do it all the time in the OR."

Likewise, our Cardiology Service, led by Dr. Norma Keller, was fully occupied in the cath lab. I was pleased to see that during the peak month of COVID-19, we accepted the usual number of transfers from other hospitals for treatment of heart attacks and other cardiac emergencies.

In fact, on one busy overnight, the service treated three consecutive patients with myocardial infarctions (MIs) in the cath lab, one of their busiest nights ever. I was relieved. "Norma, it's nice to hear that our non-COVID patients haven't completely disappeared." She looked at me askance.

"I hope you're not surprised to hear this, Nate, but all three MIs were COVID positive. Pretty much everyone we see these days is COVID positive." Norma was correct. In just a few weeks we had replaced all our non-COVID patients with COVID-19 patients. We were now living in a COVID world.

Fortunately, every department had figured out a way to help. Each service chief and nurse leader was anticipating every need and pivoting resources to meet it. Usually without even asking. At times, it seemed the hospital was just running itself. Even still, there were innumerable gaps to fill as the number of critical care teams swelled from one to eight, and the floor teams expanded from 12 to 22. All available staff needed to be redeployed in a massive shift of human resources. We were only halfway there.

One morning I received a call from Ann Ostrovsky, our Chief of Ophthalmology. Ann is a talented clinician with formidable administrative skills. "How can I help?" were Ann's welcome first words. "I have assigned my staff to the ICU teams and now I have time on my hands. I'll be happy to suit up and see COVID patients in the ED."

"Ann, your timing is perfect. How would you like to organize the redeployment of our physicians? You can collect names of staff the services are able to donate and match them to the needs of the chiefs who are overseeing COVID-19 care. I'm warning you, though. This is a massive task."

Ann was undaunted. With the assistance of an administrator, she matched all physician "donations" to the many clinical needs. She also organized the incoming volunteers, many of whom were former Bellevue attendings and residents who were now practicing in another state but flocking back to their alma mater to join the cause.

One day, late in the evening, I contacted Ann to discuss the deployment. "Why do you sound so far away?" I asked.

"I'm wearing a mask."

"Are you with a patient?"

"No, I'm with my kids."

"I don't get it. Where *are* you?"

"I have been living apart from my family while I continue working in the hospital. I'm seeing them for the first time in three weeks and I just want them to be safe."

I pictured Ann, wearing a mask, together with her family. "Well, you better stay safe as well. I need you to keep handling the redeployment."

"Not to worry. My kids made magical PPE for me to wear. A necklace and bracelet. Wearing these, I am pretty much indestructible."

This was all I needed to hear. Within a few short days, I had commissioned Ann's children to make a bracelet for me as well. As far as I could tell, the magical PPE never failed to protect me.

Nonetheless, our hospital staff remained at risk, commuting to work, interacting with colleagues, and caring for patients. Not surprisingly, there was a flurry of call-outs for COVID-like symptoms, which required a minimum medical leave of seven days. Over two months, 1,300 employees temporarily disappeared from our workforce. We would later learn through antibody testing that 20% of our employees had sustained COVID-19 infections.[11]

In our daily conference calls, one of our standing reports always came from Dr. Mary Anne Badaracco, Chief of Psychiatry, who oversees nine inpatient units, a large outpatient program, and multiple services to treat addictions. One of Mary Anne's best attributes is her self-sufficiency. She considers herself responsible for every outcome in her enormous department and expects to be held accountable for the same.

From the very start, we worried about the impact of COVID 19 on the nearly 200 Psychiatry inpatients. This communal setting, where patients reside for two weeks or more, interact socially in group settings, and congregate for meals in a common space, is not unlike a cruise ship in those respects. In other words, the perfect place for coronavirus to spread.

Shortly after COVID-19 cases began to appear in our ED, Mary Anne reported the first possible case on one of her inpatient units during our morning call. "We have a patient with fever and cough. Because of the risk to the other patients, we have isolated him in a separate room, and our staff will continue to treat him while wearing PPE.

This was a bold move. Mary Anne was proposing to keep this and subsequent cases on the cruise ship, using classic principles of identification and isolation to keep the other patients safe. Over the course of a month, the Psychiatry units identified 90 patients with symptoms who were temporarily isolated and tested. In the end, nearly 40 tested positive for coronavirus. All remained on Psychiatry. None were transferred to Medicine.

Meanwhile, our census continued to grow and we furthered our expansion. Michael's team converted the Endoscopy suite into a 10-bed ICU and transformed the Ambulatory Surgery Suite into a 12-bed ICU. As we continued to take in more transfers, five or six per day, we quickly filled up these ICUs as well. Amazingly, the ED was *still* not backed up. On most mornings there were zero patients waiting for beds – our target state.

To explain the rationale for taking in transfers from other hospitals despite our growing patient burden, we held an online conference for all our physicians. This was basically a pep talk. Among the physician leaders I invited to the stage was Dr. Amit Uppal, Director of Critical Care.

Amit was responsible for the ICUs, and he offered his crucial endorsement of the policy to bring in transfers. Since he had personally visited some of our sister facilities, he could attest to the harsh situation there. His essential point was that we were accepting transfers in order to save lives.

Near the end of the conference, as I shared the story of my protective bracelet to the audience, Amit caught my eye and smiled sheepishly as he pulled a beaded necklace out from under his collar. Apparently, I was not the only one who had commissioned Ann's kids for magical PPE.

When Eric called me the next time to send more transfers, I finally balked. "Eric, we have filled our 25-bed PACU, our 56-bed main ICU floor, and two more ICUs totaling 22 beds. If you give me any more patients, they will just pile up in the ED like the other hospitals. I don't see the point."

Eric hesitated for a moment and then chose his words carefully. "Well, Nate, think about this: Woodhull has 14 ventilator patients planted in their ED. Wouldn't two of those patients be better off in the Bellevue ED, which is completely clear, then the Woodhull ED, which is still packed with patients?" When the request was framed this way, I had to say yes. But I wasn't happy.

From the very start, we had kept our ED pristine. Our facilities team had created more than 200 beds for us to maintain the capacity that preserved the patient flow that kept the ED surprisingly empty. It was a simple metric that had worked perfectly well. No patient was allowed to wait for a bed. No COVID-19 patients were permitted to pile up anywhere. The ED needed to be clear at all costs – and it was. Our dwell time was *zero*.

Because of that principle, ironically, the ED was now the one place in the hospital that had unused capacity. The ED actually had space, nurses, and doctors available for additional patients. Eric was proposing to tap into that capacity to help out another hospital, and I was ashamed to admit that I was holding back this gift to the system. So, we took those two patients.

The next day, we took five more. The day after that, we took 10, at *our* request. To those 10 ICU patients we added 30 *non*-ICU patients because the floor teams could handle a higher workload, and because Michael's staff had created so much extra bed capacity, it would have been a shame not to use it.

For five consecutive days we took 40 transfers per day: 10 ICU/ 30 floor – 200 in all. As much as this helped, I am sure it was not enough. One of the staff at a sister hospital told us that the most important part of their day was when they learned how many patients they could transfer out to Bellevue.

Thus, we filled our new floor beds, we filled our old ICU beds, we filled our new ICU beds, and we found spaces in the ED to park 25 additional patients on ventilators. After we filled the ED, we returned to the ICU floor and began doubling up – two patients per cubicle, labelled A and Z. At one point, 24 ICU patients had a roomate.

By mid April our hospital census of COVID-related illness peaked at 400 inpatients, 110 in ICU spaces and 290 on the floors. Our COVID machine was now running at full tilt. Nurses and doctors had been adequately supplemented and there was plenty of PPE to go around. This was the new normal.

As I rounded daily on the ICU floor, I would often encounter staff members standing outside ICU cubicles, peering through the glass doors and holding their cell phones up to the glass. These were social workers with a crucial function: communication bridge between patient and family.

Regrettably, visitation was not allowed. Yet, via her cell phone, a social worker could maintain a vital conversation between patients and their families, both audio and video, in real time. Even if the patient was unconscious, she could offer the family a video view of their loved one, perhaps a final remembrance. These communications were heartbreaking. During one of my visits, I found this note taped to the glass door of an ICU cubicle.

> Dear compassionate nurse,
>
> Firstly, thank you for your dedication + care...We hope you may be able to fulfill our request. It is in our culture that he is in certain clothing when the time comes. Please have dad wear his fleece jacket + socks. If he cannot wear the jacket, please have it draped or covering his shoulders... We appreciate your help infinitely.
>
> With gratitude...

As we approached our peak census, Amit began to get nervous. He has impeccably high standards of quality and they were getting violated every day. "I have to tell you our doctors and nurses are making mistakes that would normally never happen. Yesterday, one of the nurses pushed a med on the wrong patient because she had two patients side-by-side in one cubicle."

Indeed, since we had started doubling up patients in the cubicles, it was far too easy to mix them up. So the staff put large signs with "A" or "Z" on the beds, the monitors, and the IV pumps to eliminate any confusion. Even still, with all the wires and tubes emanating from each patient, it was quite a dance to move about in the crowded cubicle.

And Amit was clearly unhappy. Despite the rapid transformation of space, staff, and medical care, the ICU had maintained a semblance of normalcy, upholding the usual high standards of care through eight clinical teams, each directed by a critical care specialist: tweaking ventilator settings, managing titratable IV drips, even proning the patients on a daily schedule. Despite our permissions, the staff were actually *not* cutting any corners.

Now here we were tolerating mistakes that would never be considered acceptable under normal conditions. And we were being pushed to the limit on supplies. One night we were down to our very last dialysis filter until an emergency supply arrived late in the evening.

"I'm not sure what the point is of bringing these patients in," Amit continued, "if we are not giving them what they need. We are just transferring them from one overrun hospital to another." His position was echoed by Doug and Verity, who were struck by the impact on morale.

Dr. Douglas Bails is the Chief of Medicine and Dr. Verity Schaye oversees the inpatient Medicine teams. Doug and Verity had organized 22 attending-led housestaff teams to care for 290 patients outside the ICU, an organizational triumph that insured we never fell short in COVID-19 care.[13]

"The residents are doing an absolutely amazing job but we have put them in a maximally stressful situation," reported Doug. "We are monitoring 40 patients on the highest levels of oxygen. They are on the verge of decompensation at any minute, and..."

Verity finished his thought. "They are sitting ducks for a respiratory event and we are running around all day responding to emergencies."

Their point was well taken. We were experiencing 25-30 overhead calls per day for airway teams and rapid response calls, compared to less than one per day in our pre-COVID era. We couldn't possibly claim that this was a desirable situation. Yet, when I contacted the other hospitals, it was even worse. Elmhurst had 160 patients on ventilators, and Queens had over 100 patients packed in their ED. We had only 25 – by design.

We were at a crucial decision point. Taking transfers was exhausting our staff, compromising our care, and jeopardizing our organization. Perhaps even risking our reputation. Didn't we have a responsibility to protect the integrity of our hospital? How could we say yes? But, when we looked across the city, we were stunned by the devastation. How could we say no?

I was imagining we were on a lifeboat, packed with survivors, while a sailor floundering in the sea petitions to come aboard. If we take him on, we might sink the boat. If we turn him away, he will surely drown. What should we do? Upon reflection, Amit, Doug, and Verity all agreed we should keep taking transfers, regardless of the risk. In the end, we brought more than 600 drowning sailors into our lifeboat.[14] It sprang a few leaks but it never sank.

Yet COVID-19 continued in its brutal course. So often, there was simply a relentless progression: from nasal oxygen to face mask, from nonrebreather mask to intubation, from life support to organ failure, and then to death. We were saving lives at the margin but we were also seeing more deaths than ever before. In just a month, we had experienced a year's worth of fatalities.

The worst one for me was one of our star employees who died after a lengthy stay. I came to the area of the ICU where he had just died and found it packed with several dozen physicians and nurses, milling about in the hallway. Everyone was wearing a mask. Many were in tears. One at a time they approached his cubicle, touched the glass door, and peered inside.

He was lying in repose on his hospital bed, much like he might have been in a coffin at a viewing. Prayers were offered through masks. Bible passages were read under face shields. A few hugs were awkwardly extended around hospital gowns. This was a COVID era wake, where expressions of grief were inhibited by PPE and social distancing.

As the crowd dispersed, I realized this was a watershed moment. Until then, we had shielded ourselves through *psychological* distancing, had curbed our emotional responses by thinking of COVID-19 victims as statistics. But this particular death humanized the losses, put a face to the suffering.

In subsequent days we would hear his story, meet his family, and share tears in publicly mourning this incomprehensible tragedy. Combining the full extent of this specific loss with the two hundred COVID-19 patients who died over six weeks at our hospital exposed an unfathomable burden of sorrow.

By late April, our COVID-19 census was finally in decline, and we had addressed every challenge: the initial COVID surge, the subsequent flood of transfers, daily reconfigurations of space, redeployment of staff, dialysis needs, PPE distribution, procurement of scarce supplies, and, sadly, the loss of seven staff members to coronavirus infections.

Although our new COVID world would present many complex challenges, it was clear that we had climbed a mountain. Over four weeks, we had absorbed a massive wave of 700 COVID-19 inpatients entering through the ED and then voluntarily accepted a second wave of 600 incoming transfers, yet maintained our integrity as a hospital. We were still standing.

And by this point, we had much to savor: a rapid transformation of our hospital, more than 100 patients weaned from life support, and more than 800 patients successfully discharged. Our COVID-19 hospital mortality rate was an astonishingly high 19.5%, yet well below the city average of 27.8%.[15]

In the end, we had measured up to the greatest challenge of our time. Thus, it is worthwhile, in retrospect, to understand the contributors to our success.

First: Process. We prepared for the pandemic by the same systematic process that we had used in every other realm of the institution: Target State, Gap Analysis, Solution Approach. We did this through our daily leadership meetings, which achieved full transparency in identifying and solving problems from one day to the next. Every gap was exposed, discussed publicly, and solved through open collaboration. ED flow was our North Star metric, our compass heading for two solid months, to guide this work.

Second: Coalescence. Our success was remarkably cooperative as everyone contributed toward the common goal. I will never forget the images of selfless commitment: Surgeons giving up surgery to care for patients in other departments. Anesthesiologists volunteering to perform procedures for Critical Care colleagues. Ophthalmologists agreeing to join the ICU teams. Orthopedic surgeons offering to prone vent patients. Cardiologists treating MIs in the cath lab all night in full PPE. Psychiatrists managing their *own* patients in full PPE. Volunteers flocking back to New York to serve in their former training site for no pay. Social workers bridging patients and families in their final conversations. Housekeepers tirelessly scrubbing rooms. Nurses bending but never breaking. And carpenters, plumbers, and electricians transforming our hospital, one room at a time, always one step ahead of the patients. Everyone leaned in. All contributed freely. No one had to be asked.

Likewise, our administrative and nursing leaders joined in a hospital-wide effort to meet every challenge in real time. We made plans in the morning and carried them out in the afternoon. We identified gaps in the afternoon and closed them by evening. We encountered obstacles in the evening and solved them overnight. The impact of the alignment was astounding. Never before have I seen so many people lifting so hard in the same direction, all together. It felt as though we had lifted our building right out of its foundation.

And let's not forget our collaboration with NYU, faithful partner for nearly 200 years. While Bellevue coped with the COVID challenge on *our* side of the street, NYU-Langone Medical Center was doing the same one block north. And well. More to the point, we had to find a way to share our faculty, residents, and interns across both our institutions without disintegrating into a free-for-all. That we did so without conflict is a tribute to our shared values and the professional standards that prevail at both institutions.

Finally, and most important: *Mission.* For three centuries, Bellevue's mission has been to treat all New Yorkers without exception. No questions asked. An essential element of this mission has always been to serve as the frontline of defense against highly fatal infectious diseases. No matter the pathogen, Bellevue has always been the preferred destination.

In the 1700s, Bellevue was the hospital of choice for patients dying from yellow fever and smallpox. In the mid-1800s, smallpox was superseded by typhus. In the late 1800s, Bellevue became a center for tuberculosis, maintaining a sanitorium on a barge in the East River. In the 1980s, it was dominated by AIDS. In 2014, it was Ebola. In 2020, COVID-19.

By having an explicit mission baked into our DNA, we have never been doubtful of the objective, unsure of our direction, or at loss for a plan. We always know where we are headed. So, while most hospitals in the nation were wondering if they could, would, or *should* be preparing for Ebola, and many vacillated about next steps, we had no doubt we would be the one.

And while many hospitals might have felt ambivalent about *importing* COVID-19 patients in the midst of their *own* deluge, we sensed a calling to open our doors to patients in need. It has, after all, always been our place to do so.

Thus, when our turn came, there was no confusion about our role. No bickering about our goal. Not a single physician, nurse, or hospital leader questioned our mission to be the designated hospital for special pathogens, a vital backstop for the city. No one balked. No one faltered. No one asked, "Why us?" It is so much easier to overcome insurmountable odds when you have consensus on the target state.

Does *every* hospital have a mission? A compass heading? A target state? In short, yes. *We* certainly do. Our mission statement perfectly defines us with this exact phrase: "treat every patient without exception." Irrespective of origin. Regardless of ability to pay. Notwithstanding the risk.

That phrase would not necessarily be in the mission statement of a prestigious academic medical center seeking financial stability to achieve its more pressing aims: exceptional patient care, elite education, ground-breaking research. And it was not always in ours.

Funny story: Some years ago, and several generations of executives back in our past, our hospital had a leadership retreat to review our strategic plan. At this event, our executive director at the time publicly complained that our mission was interfering with our *financial* plan. All those uninsured patients were making it impossible to balance the books.

It was a ridiculous thing to say. As a safety net hospital, our mission was the reason we existed. Giving that up would take away our super power. Would make us like any other hospital. Without our mission, we might as well just close our doors. The financial plan was there to serve the mission, not the other way around.

Yet, to my surprise, our mission statement *was* revised to exclude the phrase, "regardless of the ability to pay." It remained so for nearly a year – until we finally returned to our senses. And our purpose. My point here is that the mission is the immutable anchor that keeps us grounded, the basis for all our planning, and the touchstone for everything we do. The indispensable role of the mission in all decision-making has been reinforced repeatedly in my hospital career – yet another lesson from the bedside.

Now, what does mission have to do with *national* leadership?

Bivouac

Why do I feel we have been climbing Mount Everest? It seems that we have been slogging through a thick carpet of snow and scampering across treacherous patches of ice while barely dodging deep and dark crevasses. Yet we continue to make progress, trudging up a steep slope in the rarified air of the upper atmosphere. The wind is picking up, so let's make this our final bivouac before we assault the summit.

To review once more: We started with the concept of a golden braid – the intertwined marriage of art and science. We defined the individual strands of the braid as nine lessons in leadership. Then we tested our lessons against contentious issues facing our nation. It appears that three additional chapters added even more strands to our braid – supplemental lessons in curiosity, courage, and compromise.

Finally, we tested our lessons against real life presidents: Reagan, Obama, and Trump. In these brief reviews, we came to realize how complicated is the task of governance, how crucial are the attributes of great leadership, and how difficult it is to master them all.

Is there no end to the complexity of this braid? Evidently not. As much as we have covered already, we have barely touched upon essential skills in communication, persuasion, and motivation. Not to mention knowledge, determination, and consistency. The list goes on.

Nonetheless, I am struck by how perfectly the lessons of *my* world – patient care and hospital governance – transcend natural boundaries to inform the leaders of our nation. The central conceit of this book, if you will, is that these collective attributes may serve as a Rosetta Stone of sorts for those who choose our leaders, a decryption key for those of us who vote.

But now, finally, the time has come. We are ready to return to the nearly-forgotten patient, our nation, who is lying moribund on the operating table. Like Seth Feyland, she is suffering. Like Juan Verdad, she is barely breathing. Like Candice Staner, she ails from total body malfunction, an incestuous collaboration between all her failing organs to do her in. Solving this case is our calling.

This is why we are here.

Revelation:
Expose the Gap

'Twas brillig, and the slithy toves
Did gyre and gimble in the wabe:
All mimsy were the borogoves,
And the mome raths outgrabe.
'Beware the Jabberwock, my son!
The jaws that bite, the claws that catch!
Beware the Jubjub bird, and shun
The frumious Bandersnatch!...
One two! One two! And through and through
The vorpal blade went snicker-snack!
He left it dead, and with its head
He went galumphing back.

From *The Jabberwocky*, in Through the Looking-Glass
and What Alice Found There, Lewis Carroll, 1872

March is the cruelest month. Winter's icy traces linger while Spring is but a promise. The words are still flowing, and I have a recurring dream. Ted Cruz, Paul Ryan, and Marco Rubio are relaxing on a rubber dinghy floating in a vast sea. Donald Trump is the confident captain, reclining on a satin pillow, smoking a cigar. They do not seem to hear the low hissing noise from a leak in the raft. Pfffft.

What makes this sound? Atlantic seawater gently lapping over asphalt Florida roadways? Flowing sheets of ice crisply snapping free from majestic Alaskan glaciers? The crackling burn of ancient Oregon forests? It does not matter. No one is listening. Nobody seems to care.

Trump pops the cork. He is self-assured. The alpha male. Commander of the seas. Only he is not alone. There are seven billion people on this raft. For this mass of humanity, the raft is life-sustaining. But not for long. As he slowly sinks into the unforgiving sea, the captain's false assurances fade into a faint, gurgly lub-dub while the frigid ocean waters embrace his craft. No one is there to notice a bright orange tuft of hair disappearing beneath the waves. I wonder to myself: how could it possibly have come to this?

Does our *nation* have a mission? A compass heading? A *target* state? Not exactly. I suggest the closest we have to a mission statement is the *Declaration of Independence*, which laid out the case for our nation's birth. But a careful review of this venerable document reveals it is primarily a list of grievances justifying our independence. We need the modern version of a mission statement for America – which should align with our target state.

Is that even possible? I must be in *La La Land*. On what planet could we, America, even *begin* to agree on our target state, the place we are all trying to get to. We can't even agree on who we *are*.

My first answer to that question is that we have no choice. Without a compass setting, it is truly impossible to govern. There is no way to move forward if we cannot agree on a direction. We would not even know how to start. The mission is the essential beginning of the systematic approach.

My second answer is that I *do* think it is possible to agree on simple goals. From this perspective, it will be clear that coming to consensus on a target state is not so difficult as agreeing on how to get there. We learned this lesson in our Year of Ebola, and we learned it again in the Year of COVID-19.

I will preface this exercise in grandiosity by admitting that the setting of a national target state is way above my pay grade. Nonetheless, I don't know how else to proceed. So think of this as an example. And let's keep it simple. Here are my suggested nine elements of the target state for America:

1. We will be free.
2. We will be safe.
3. We will be healthy.
4. We will have opportunity.
5. We will prosper.
6. We will protect our planet.
7. We will expand knowledge.
8. We will live in harmony.
9. We will lead the world.

Okay, that is the *short* version. That sounds pretty straightforward and came more easily than I expected, but the challenge is in the details. Here is the longer, more complex, version.

1. **We will be free to live our lives as we choose so long as we do not hurt others. We may believe and say what we wish. We may practice our religion without restriction. We may decide for ourselves how to live our lives without outside interference unless our behavior infringes on the rights of others.** *I started with freedom for a reason. I think it best captures the essence of the Bill of Rights and explains why our nation was born in the first place. The problem arises only when there are competing rights which, unfortunately, is usually the case – see Chapter 12.*

2. **We will be safe from bodily harm by internal and external threats.** *This statement covers a lot of ground: national security, anti-terrorism activities, local policing – even programs to inspect our food, maintain our highways, and promote safety in the workplace. This, too, is relatively non-controversial until you get to the details, especially when security competes with liberty or prosperity. How much should we spend on the military? Who should serve? When should we go to war? How closely should we surveil our citizens? How should our police behave? To what degree should we regulate the workplace?*

3. **We will all have access to affordable health care.** *Of course, no one would argue that people should not be healthy, but good health cannot actually be guaranteed. The best we can do is offer affordable health care to everyone, and the nature of how we do that is one of the most controversial topics in our nation right now. I am not even sure that everyone would agree with this element. Nonetheless, I would argue that it is untenable to defend a target state in which some American citizens do not have access to affordable health care.*

Freedom, Safety, and Good Health. Our foundation. What could be more basic than that? Now let's kick it up a notch.

4. **We will have the opportunity to achieve our personal aspirations.** *This one gets to the "pursuit of happiness" clause of the Declaration of Independence. Most Americans believe that everyone should be able to pursue their heart's desire, provided they are motivated, capable, and committed. Ideally, there should be no roadblocks of race, gender, or circumstance of birth standing in the way of "self-actualization," becoming the complete person we aim to be.*

5. **We will achieve broad based prosperity. The opportunity to earn a decent income that can support an acceptable quality of life will be within reach of all Americans.** *Note that this plank does not guarantee prosperity for everyone. Nor does it promote equality of wealth or income. And what do we mean exactly by "acceptable quality of life?" But we need a way to address everyone's recognized needs: food, shelter, clothing, education, and personal aspirations. And few will argue that prosperity being concentrated in a small segment of the electorate represents anything remotely resembling a target state.*

6. **We will preserve our local environment and protect our planet. We will keep our air, water, and land free of pollution and maintain climatic conditions that are friendly to humans.** *It is hard to argue with this goal but again the details are important. Are we willing to pay a significant price to achieve this target state? I think so, especially when you ask the question in reverse. Are we willing to pollute our air, water, and land and make the earth uninhabitable in order to promote economic advancement? Who would say yes to that?*

Opportunity, Prosperity, and a Habitable Environment. We seem to be ascending Maslow's Hierarchy of basic human needs.[1] Is there yet a higher level in our target state? Indeed, there is.

7. **We will expand our sphere of knowledge. We will continuously enlarge our understanding of the universe and impart that knowledge to each other and our children.** *The pursuit of knowledge, the drive to learn, is one of the great traditions of humankind in general and America in particular. This plank captures our restless spirit, our rampant curiosity, and our fervid imagination. Science, discovery, and exploration. They are all integral to knowledge. It is the only element of our mission that knows no bounds. And knowledge is, of course, essential to evidence-based leadership.*

8. **We will live in harmony. We will overcome our differences to work on common goals together.** *There it is again: coalescence. Is this an end in itself or merely the means to freedom, opportunity, and prosperity? I contend that harmony is an end in itself. If all our*

interactions are marked by continuous conflict, if safety comes only through constant combat, if peaceful coexistence persistently eludes us, we will not be at our target state even if we achieve our other goals.

9. **We will lead the world as an exemplar of democratic values, economic principles, and human rights.** *Is leadership of the world a core part of our mission? I believe the answer is clearly yes. Our model of democracy, with all its blemishes, cleared the path for the downfall of tyranny in the modern world. Our version of capitalism, despite its inherent flaws, pointed the way toward prosperity around the globe. And our focus on human rights, notwithstanding many egregious missteps of our own, has illuminated the path toward racial, religious, and gender equality for all nations. We cannot evade our historical legacy or shirk our modern role as international leader.*

Knowledge, Harmony, and Global Leadership. In this top tier, we find aspirational goals that uniquely define us. The holiest of grails. While they stand on the shoulders of the first six elements, they undeniably take us to a higher level. To our ultimate target state.

The long version of our goals makes it clear that our target state is not so controversial as the means to getting there. And when one element competes with another (security vs. freedom, health care vs. prosperity), we must find a proper balance. It makes no sense to blindly pursue one goal at the complete disregard of another when both are essential to our mission.

At this point, it is advisable to distill our objectives into a mission statement.[2] A well-crafted mission statement will provide a compass heading for everything we do in a pithy and concise construction. Here is an example that captures all the above elements:

As the first modern democracy, America aims to defend the freedom of its citizens, keep everyone safe, provide access to health care, foster individual opportunity, achieve broad-based prosperity, protect our planet, expand knowledge, and work harmoniously to lead the world as a positive example of democratic values, economic principles, and human rights.

Why not?

Our 52 word mission statement is quite a mouthful, but we should not be surprised. We are nation, not a hospital or a business. In fact, we are a vastly powerful, highly diverse, and exceedingly complex nation-state with many competing priorities and a multi-dimensional target state. If anything, this mission is an *under*statement of our aspirations.

Why did we do this? Why did we take this unexpected detour to summarize our mission? Quite simply, I could not proceed otherwise. Without a mission, there is no target state. Without a target state, there is no gap to analyze. Without a gap to analyze, there is no solution approach.

In other words, without a description of healthiness, we cannot tell if we are sick. The mission tells us what we are *missing*. The hole we must fill. The gap we must close. The mission statement is the first axiom, the essential beginning, the absolute starting point for the systematic approach.

Now, with the target state well-defined, the obvious question that follows will determine our work at hand: "Why are we not there yet?"

With our nine-point mission under our belt, we are ready to continue to the next step of the systematic approach. The work at hand is to identify the root causes of our national symptoms. Borrowing again from *my* world, we will do this through a gap analysis, which seeks to explain why things are the way they are and not the way we wish them to be – the reason we are not at the target state. We will begin the analysis by identifying our *current state* for the nine elements of our mission statement.

As you may have noticed, aspects of all these elements have been sprinkled throughout the preceding chapters in preparation for this moment. I have brought them forward here so that we may grade them one by one – on a ten-point scale. Again, I do not claim the last word in this analysis. I am just trying to illustrate a logical approach.

1. **Defend Our Freedom** – Overall, America has done a great job in guaranteeing personal freedom and human rights compared to other countries but continues to have a gap in solving flash points when rights overlap, as seen in our struggles with abortion and gun ownership. Recently, there has been a disturbing trend to equate Islam with terrorism, which may threaten freedom of religion for

some of our citizens. An additional point off for that current trend. Score 8/10.

2. **Keep Everyone Safe** – This is also one of our strengths. We have the strongest military in the world, our counter-terrorism program is robust, and we maintain ample oversight to protect citizens from harm. Some would say too much so. Yet we are still struggling with issues of personal surveillance, community policing, and international alliances. Nuclear proliferation is a huge threat without a sensible solution. Americans are anxious. Score 7/10.

3. **Provide Access to Health Care** – We took a big step forward with the Affordable Care Act, but we still have a gap to close, and the rapidly increasing expense of health care is threatening the viability of our entire system. Score 6/10 – mainly because of future risk.

4. **Foster Opportunity** – As noted above, we still have huge challenges with racism and paradigms of group behavior. Access to higher education is uneven, and it is still not the case that everyone can be whoever they want to be, despite their best effort. Score 5/10.

5. **Achieve Broad-Based Prosperity** – This is clearly a problem in search of a solution. Not only has economic advancement fallen off its trajectory, increasing income inequality is challenging the middle-class like never before in our lifetime. See Chapter 10. Score 4/10.

6. **Protect the Planet** – At the end of the Obama administration, I would have scored this an 8/10. Now I will give it a 3. For the past four years, no one in the U.S. government showed the least bit of concern about the future of the environment. Score 3/10.

As for the upper tier of the target state: knowledge, harmony, and leadership, I will leave scoring to the reader. But it doesn't take a genius to see we are a long way from harmony. And though we excel at advancing knowledge, we lose credibility when we refuse to accept that knowledge (e.g., the truth about climate change), make silly rules, such as banning the term "evidence-based" from our lexicon, or fail to educate our children.

As for leadership? Suffice it to say that it is nigh impossible to model exemplary behavior when we ourselves are failing to advance unlimited opportunity, promote broad-based prosperity, or face facts about climate change. We can't even agree on immigration, one of the fundamental principles that built our nation. The world is watching – and waiting – for us to return to the helm.

If we think of our target state as 10/10, it is easy to identify the gaps between our current and target states. Simple math. Even if you did not exactly agree with my grades, the point is still clear. We have gaps. Big ones. Our next step is to analyze those gaps to get to the root cause. And, if we are to rank our goals by the size of the gap, we *have* to start with the environment.

There is certainly no greater symptom of illness in a representative democracy then the failure of the will of the people to be realized. In a Gallup poll in March, 2016, 90% of Americans stated their belief that global warming will actually occur, 65% believed it is due to human activity, and 64% were worried about it.[3] Yet our leaders are *not* responding to the concerns of the electorate. In a *democracy*, no less. Why not?

The answer to that question is exactly what the gap analysis is all about. Let's employ one of my favorite gap analysis tools – the Five Whys – which I introduced in Chapter 2. We will start with a simple Why question about climate change and then take it from there.

1. Why do our current national leaders *not* take the necessary steps toward addressing the danger of climate change? *Because the Republican Party shares control of our government, and their spokespeople deny that climate change is even happening, much less that it matters. If you have any doubts that this is a* <u>*partisan*</u> *topic, please reread Chapter 4.*

2. Why does the Republican Party deny climate change when scientists of the world so clearly agree it is true? *Because Republicans believe efforts to address the environment will be harmful to big business.*

3. Why do Republican leaders consider the business environment to be a higher priority than the natural environment, in opposition to the will of the American people? *Because they have a particular interest in the success of coal, oil, and gas industries, above all else.*

4. Why do Republican leaders put the interests of coal, oil, and gas industries above the expressed wishes of the American people? *Because coal, oil, and gas industries make campaign donations disproportionately to national Republican leaders.*

5. Why do these industries make donations disproportionately to Republican leaders? *Because it works. Campaign donations have successfully purchased votes in the House and the Senate, even when those votes defied the expressed wishes of the American people.*

Wow! That is a strong statement. Is it *evidence-based*? You can decide that for yourself. First, the total amount spent on lobbying and campaign financing by energy industries in 2016 was $117 million![4] The top three spenders were Exxon ($11.8 million), Koch Industries ($9.8 million), and Royal Dutch Shell ($9.0 million). In all, 175 industry clients employed 720 (!) lobbyists to influence government policy.

As far as *direct contributions to Congress*, the total was $29.5 million, of which *86%* went to Republicans. Incidentally, the vast majority of these dollars (83%) went to incumbents. Is it any surprise that Congress never votes for campaign finance reform? It is a system perfectly designed to help officeholders keep their jobs.

Who were the top three recipients of this largesse? Ted Cruz ($1.2 million), Paul Ryan ($650,000), and Marco Rubio ($630,000). Go back and read the Cruz, Ryan, and Rubio quotes in Chapter 4. What is the price of a prominent lie repeatedly told by an influential government leader? Apparently, about $600,000. Double that if you want your leader to say something completely absurd, such as, "Climate change is not science. It's religion."

Let's try another:

1. Why is there increasing income inequality in America? *Because American workers have lost the clout to advocate for better salaries and because federal tax policies have tilted toward the rich since 1980.*

2. Why have tax policies tilted toward the rich, even though most voters are in the middle class? *Because Republicans have consistently and successfully promoted the theory of Supply-Side Economics.*

3. Why have Republicans promoted Supply Side Economics when tax cuts for the rich are opposed by the American people? *Because the wealthy make campaign donations disproportionately to national Republican leaders.*

4. Why do the rich make donations disproportionately to Republican leaders? *Because it works. Campaign donations have successfully purchased votes in the House and the Senate, even when those votes were contrary to the expressed wishes of the American people.*

Hmm. This time we got to exactly the same place in one less step. Where's the beef? Is there proof to *this* claim? In May, 2015, a New York Times/CBS Poll surveyed a national sample of Americans on their views about income inequality.[5] When asked if "everyone has a fair chance to get ahead in the long run in today's economy," 61% answered that just a few people at the top have a chance to get ahead. About 2/3 of respondents felt "the gap between rich and poor is getting larger," and a similar number supported higher taxes on people with salaries exceeding $1 million.

Why does the will of the people not seem to influence their elected representatives? Let's take a closer look. A New York Times article in 2015 summarized the state of campaign financing by the wealthy.[6]

> They are overwhelmingly white, rich, older and male...they are deploying their vast wealth in the political arena, providing almost half the seed money raised to support Democratic and Republican candidates. Just 158 families...contributed $176 million in the first phase of the campaign.

The families investing the most were conservative donors looking for candidates who pledged to pare regulations and cut taxes on income, capital gains, and inheritances. Sounds a lot like Supply-Side Economics, no?

And who were these wealthy Americans supporting? Nearly all (138 families) were supporting Republican candidates. And their results were not in vain. Two years later, Republicans passed and Trump signed the *Tax Cuts and Jobs Act of 2017*, which followed the usual oddly symmetrical pattern of supply-side tax policy. The bottom 20% of American taxpayers received 1% of the cuts ($60 apiece), and the top 1% of Americans received 20% of the cuts ($51,000 apiece).[7] Astonishingly, the biggest windfall was for *corporations*, which saw their maximum tax rate drop from 35% to 21%.

Let's see who benefited most from this bounty. Workers, to be clear, experienced mixed results. While some businesses added employees, others made cuts.[8] For company *owners*, however, the news was all good. Shareholders got their payoff through increased dividends, a rising stock market, and a stock buyback binge that set new records in 2018.[8] Once again, the money went *up* the ladder. Once again, the owners won out.

How about the federal deficit? Did that melt away as predicted? Not a chance! In 2020, the annual deficit was projected to soar back up to a trillion dollars, not even counting the COVID-19 bailouts.[9] We seem to have added Exhibit 4 to our historical experiment – reasserting the utter failure of Supply-Side Economics to benefit everyday Americans while saddling them with future responsibility for huge federal deficits.

So, once again, *we borrowed money we didn't have and gave it to people who didn't need it.* Why would Republicans pass a tax cut that worked against the interest of the majority of voters? Take a wild guess.

> Republicans in Congress faced a near-mutiny last fall from some wealthy GOP donors frustrated with Washington's inability to get anything done. Then they passed the tax bill. Now the checkbooks are open again...just in time for a challenging midterm election cycle.[10]

The payoff started with big checks from conservative donor Charles Koch and his wife. Soon after, other GOP donors followed suit. Not surprisingly, the American people were not so thrilled with a tax cut that was concentrated in the upper tier, but the will of the voters yielded to the sway of the donors. In the end, it was clearer than ever who was really running the country when it came to tax policy.

> Republicans are struggling to make the $1.5 trillion Trump tax cuts a winning issue with voters in the [2018] midterm congressional elections, but the cuts are helping the party in another crucial way: unlocking tens of millions of dollars in campaign donations from the wealthy conservatives and corporate interests that benefited handsomely from it.[11]

When did we become an oligarchy, a great and powerful nation controlled by a small number of wealthy people?

Let's do one more in this vein: health care. Although 70% of all Americans support "Medicare for All," no progress has been made on expanding access to Medicare for anyone. Let me repeat my favorite line: There is no greater symptom of illness in a representative democracy then the failure of the will of the people...Oh, never mind!

1. Why do national leaders not allow Medicare to be one of the options on the health care exchanges even though it could save both consumers and the government at least 30% of the cost of care? *Because private health plans and the health care industry overall are opposed, and they make large campaign donations to national leaders.*

2. Why does the health care industry make so many campaign contributions to national leaders? *Because it works. Campaign donations have successfully purchased votes of both parties in the House and Senate, even when those votes were contrary to the expressed wishes of the American people.*

Now that's interesting. We wound up in *almost* the same place in just two Whys. This time, though, I did not single out Republicans. It appears the health care industry purchases votes from *both* major parties. Remember our binding contract? Let the chips fall where they may.

As per the Center for Responsive Politics, in 2016, "Health /HMOs" gave $14.6 million to Democrats and $9.9 million to Republicans, while "Hospitals/ Nursing Homes" gave $18.9 million to Democrats and $14.3 million to Republicans.[12] Not to be outgunned, "Health Professionals" gave about $45 million to each party. And why not? What is $90 million when tens of *billions* are up for grabs?

And let's not forget the crucial election cycle of 2008, when Democrats received large contributions from the health sector. This fact rankled many progressives who would have much preferred a national health plan based on "Medicare for everyone." It is important to remember that campaign contributions impact leaders in *both* parties.

It is rather striking that the same system defect – private campaign financing – is the roadblock to success on climate change, tax policy, and health care, three issues on which most Americans agree! If we don our "Lean" thinking caps, we might say the flow of influence from the electorate to their leaders has been obstructed by the overwhelming clout of dirty money. Like any other clogged pipe, this one needs a *"cloutbuster"* drug to clear the path and re-establish democratic control of our government.

Until we cure the *disease* by restoring the people's rule, we will be unable to durably treat our *symptoms* – our absurdly deficient responses to climate change, income inequality, and health care disparities – because any progress we make can be completely undone in the next election cycle. Every doctor knows you can't cure a disease just by relieving a symptom.

Let's change gears now. What about one of our gaps in freedom – the inability to come to consensus on social issues involving competing rights?

1. Why can't we agree on basic protections, and commensurate limits on those protections, for personal rights such as abortion and gun ownership? *Because national leaders have dug into extreme positions and are unable to budge.*

2. Why are they unable to budge? *Because any hint of compromise will cause them to lose electoral support.*

3. Why would a hint of compromise cause a national leader to lose electoral support? *Because leaders come from districts where voters hold homogenous and extreme views.*

4. Why do their voters hold homogenous and extreme views? *Because the boundaries of their districts have been gerrymandered to cater to one political party at the expense of the other.*

5. Why have the boundaries been gerrymandered? *So the representative will hold a safe seat, and no compromise will be necessary!*

Once again, pretty strong stuff. What's the evidence for *that* claim? I will start by explaining that gerrymandering is the term we use to describe the process to redraw a legislative district so that a given political party has an electoral advantage. The mimsical shape of some of these districts was once seen to resemble a "salamander," a modern-day jabberwocky.[13] How exactly does gerrymandering subvert democracy?

Imagine two congressional districts side by side. Each district has equal numbers of Democratic and Republican voters. Every election cycle, nominees of each party will gravitate to the center to attract votes of independents as well as some moderate voters of the opposite party in order to win a majority of votes overall. This moderation is essential to political survival. Thus, every election cycle becomes an exercise in coalition building.

Now imagine that the districts are redrawn (gerrymandered) so that nearly all Democrats wind up in one district and nearly all Republicans in the other. The smaller number of independent voters, such as myself, are split evenly between the two districts. In this way, the "outgroup" in each district finds itself completely marginalized, as each dissenting voter has now lost her electoral voice amidst the dominant rule of the majority group. In the general election, the Democratic candidate will clearly galumph to victory in the Democratic district while shunning independents and moderate Republicans. Same for the Republican nominee in the other gyre.

In fact, the *real* battle will be in the *primary* election, fighting to be the *nominee*. Here, the more extreme views of a "pure" liberal or conservative will outgrabe the nomination. Moreover, in the general election, there will be no reason to move to the center as the candidate has already bandersnatched her seat. Indeed, after winning their seats, neither Democratic nor Republican officeholders will have *any* incentive to work together.

Quite the opposite. A representative coming from a gerrymandered district will incur the rath of her electors – the jaws that bite, the claws that catch – for showing any hint of collaboration with members of the opposing party. As a result, coalescence will remain elusive. For that reason, the House will be unable to advance legislation even if it is clearly in the interest of the American people. At this point, the governing body becomes a limp piece of lettuce, incompetent to address any matter of national importance.

This, then, is the consequence of the fatal defect of gerrymandering, our second major root cause. The point is not that one party gets an advantage over another, which historically has gone both ways, but rather that neither party has any incentive to collaborate with the other. As a result, the House becomes utterly paralyzed, rendering federal government completely ineffectual. Not what our founding fathers had in mind.

The best example I know of the obstructionist impact of gerrymandering is the Republican party's failure to repeal and replace Obamacare even though it had control of all three branches of government. Why was the party unable to achieve consensus among its *own* members?

A big contributor was the House Freedom Caucus, a small band of highly conservative members who refused to compromise with their moderate colleagues. They held out for the most extreme version of legislation (repeal but *don't* replace) and refused to support a bill unless it conformed completely to their demands.

How could they get away with this frumious behavior? For starters, they didn't *have* to compromise. They came from safe districts, primarily through gerrymandering. In fact, any hint of compromise could have cost them their seat. This is how gerrymandering subverts democracy – by making it impossible to gimble in the wabe. It is certainly not what our founding fathers intended when they created a representational democracy, and it might prove to be *the* fatal flaw in our system.

How about a specific case? Up until 2010, North Carolina's Eleventh Congressional District was a fierce battleground between Democrats and Republicans. Between blue downtown Asheville and its red suburbs, and between the bluish counties to the south and the reddish counties to the north, there was real balance on the political spectrum. To win this seat, a candidate would have to appeal *across* party lines.

In 2011, North Carolina Republican leaders redrew the district by removing most of Asheville, creating a safe Republican seat. In the 2016 election, the Republican candidate won handily by a margin of 28 percent. His name? Mark Meadows, head of the Freedom Caucus.

Just for fun, take a look below at the shape of his district. See the hole in the middle? That is where blue Asheville, the beating heart of the district, was surgically excised by the vorpal sword – snickersnack. Brillig but slithy. One wonders how this can even be *legal.*

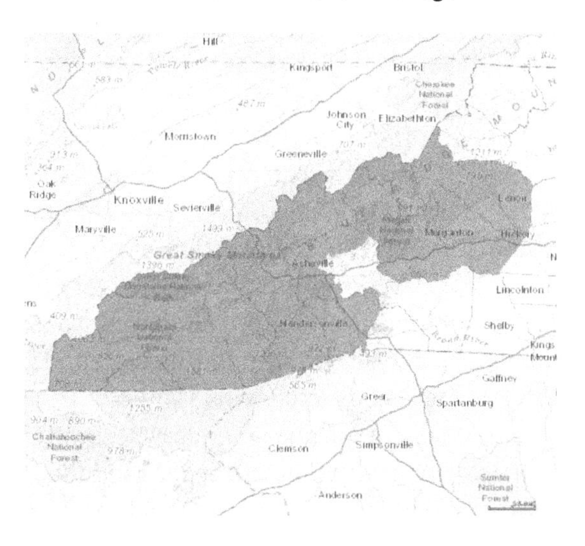

Nationwide, the increasing use of gerrymandering has chipped away at the competitiveness of district races over time. For example, in the 1976 national election, 62 of 435 House seats were competitive (i.e., won by a margin of 10% or less). By 2016, that number had dwindled to 32 (7%). Hence, 93% of representatives had no electoral incentive to work with the opposing party. Once again, the evidence speaks volumes.

And, while gerrymandering inhibits coalition-building, it also can enable a minority party to win the majority of seats. In a perverse manipulation of democratic principles, subtle and unsavory shifts in district lines may yield outsized differences in outcomes, the electoral butterfly effect, which further undermines our faith in the political process.

For example, in 2016, Republican candidates for the House earned 49% of the national vote and garnered 54% of the seats – granting them control. In 2012, in Pennsylvania, *my* state, Democratic candidates received 52% of the vote yet Republicans won 13 (72%) of 18 seats. At other times, Democrats have similarly benefited. Either way, the will of the people and the clout of the voter are diluted by manipulation of district lines.

While gerrymandering inhibits coalescence, it is not the only root cause of gridlock. Many have noted the increasing tendency of Americans to gravitate toward news sources that advance or amplify their personal positions. Unlike the pre-cable era, when Americans got most of their news from one of three politically moderate network news programs, citizens today can find a cable news outlet, radio talk show, or internet channel with extreme views that merely reinforce their current positions, unchallenged.

Over time, the electorate has broken up into blocs, each inside its own self-referential, politically-protected information bubble. Even worse, these factions are no longer situated in the center of the political spectrum. By some strange, invisible centripetal force, they have been drawn to the margins, far removed from any possibility of coalescence.

Factionalization, then, is our third major root cause. It naturally derives from our biological system defect, group bias, and gains invincible strength through current trends in information flow. The overall impact on government is that lack of collaboration has become the norm. And, with each passing year, it becomes more deeply imbedded in our political culture. By now, I fear that even if gerrymandering were to be eliminated, cooperation across party lines may still be considered practically an act of treason.

I could go through five more Whys on opportunity and harmony, but we will wind up in the same place. Gerrymandering and factionalization inhibit consensus on any sensitive matter touching on group dynamics, putting coalescence well beyond our reach.

Even our knowledge plank is impacted by these same roots. In our current state, those who hold extreme views may prevail simply by blocking evidence to the contrary. At that point we become, like Gerald Menard, unable to *learn*. Then, decision-making becomes anything *but* evidence-based. Although the sensory organs of our body politic are very well developed, it is unfortunately the case that we just can't handle the truth.

Oddly enough, in the target state on national safety, I detect a greater sense of unity. Yes, there is the perverse impact of the military-industrial complex. Yes, there is the subversive influence of extremist views. Nonetheless, Democrats and Republicans generally stand together on the danger of terrorism, the need for a strong military, and the importance of homeland security. Hence, disagreements are more likely to come up in discussions of strategy, not in the goals themselves. Political engagement is so much easier when there is bipartisan agreement on the target state.

Finally, we must recognize that our failure in global leadership is simply the result of gaps in the other domains. Private campaign financing, gerrymandering, and factionalization have so crippled our performance that we are too weak in our core to project confident leadership in the world.

Let me close this section by acknowledging some additional contributors to our disease state, mostly beyond our control. Rising global competition has certainly challenged our prosperity plank. We are now actively scrambling for market share in a highly competitive world.

The emergence of terrorism as a foreign policy focus has also challenged several of our goals – prosperity, freedom, and safety. Nonetheless, I would not describe terrorism as a root cause of our ailing nation. I believe our wounds are primarily self-inflicted.

Further, the aging of our population is exerting extreme pressure on our health system. Whatever we decide, the age demographic of America will continue to challenge our proposed solutions in health care delivery.

Of course, a final factor working against us is our inborn, genetically-predetermined tendency to factionalize, best illustrated by the minimal group paradigm. This is a major headwind we must overcome if we are ever going to collaborate on effective solutions. Forewarned is forearmed.

Let's sum up our gap analysis:

1. For some goals, we are unable to reach the target state because of *private campaign financing,* which offers wealthy groups and individuals the power to support their own positions at the expense of the will of the people, undermining democracy and preventing progress on income inequality, health care, and climate change.

2. For other goals, we are unable to achieve national consensus because of *gerrymandering*, which thwarts cooperation, collaboration, and coalition-building among elected officials across party lines.

3. The impact of gerrymandering is amplified by *factionalization* of the electorate, which derives from the way we assimilate information and position ourselves on the political spectrum. Factionalization inhibits consensus on issues that touch on group dynamics: civil rights, freedom, and opportunity, and stands firmly in the way of coalescence – our pathway to peaceful coexistence and a harmonious life.

Finally, the above three roots are strengthened by events beyond our control: growing global competition, rising forces of terrorism, aging of our population, and our natural inclinations to defend our "in-groups."

In this chapter, we have defined our current state and our target state, and we have analyzed the gap between them. The discerning reader will note that we have arrived at a *diagnosis*. Based on our analysis, the many symptoms of our disease have three main roots within our control: private campaign financing, gerrymandering, and factionalization of the electorate.

Let me take a step back to point out once again that the gap analysis, trying to understand why we are not at the destination, is an essential step in leadership of any organization, whether it be a hospital, a business, or a sovereign state. But a gap analysis is not even possible without a target state, so Step One is to figure out where this train should be heading. Only after we have identified our destination with a mission statement can we begin to understand why we are not there yet.

And now that we have completed the gap analysis, we must remember that it is merely a diagnostic exercise. From a proper diagnosis must emerge the correct remedy. Failure to address the roots of dysfunction will lead to treatment failure, a missed opportunity to cure the illness. In the case of a life-threatening disease, failure to administer the right therapy can lead to death of the patient. In the political world, an entire nation is at risk. Hence, in the next chapter we will look toward a viable solution – the proposed treatment of our ailing nation.

Solution:
Sever the Root

And would it have been worth it, after all,
After the cups, the marmalade, the tea,
Among the porcelain, among some talk of you and me...
To have squeezed the universe into a ball
To roll it towards some overwhelming question,
To say: "I am Lazarus, come from the dead,
Come back to tell you all, I shall tell you all"—
If one, settling a pillow by her head
Should say: "That is not what I meant at all;
That is not it, at all."

From *The Love Song of J. Alfred Prufrock*, T.S Eliot, 1920[1]

April brings verdant hope of renewal. I am healing. For six months I have been obsessed by an idea, driven by a force that I do not understand: a compulsion to channel fragments of distant memory toward a vital message. The ideas have taken shape, and the stories are complete, now linked in a grand procession toward an overarching theme: the phenotype of a great leader. This is the perfect conclusion to a life of lessons – a cogent message for America's leadership.

In these final three chapters I am bothered by a single loose thread that has bedeviled me since Chapter 4. I am struggling to understand why intelligent, well-educated, Republican officeholders continue to deny climate change, now an indisputable fact of science. Surely, they know the truth. If I didn't know better, I would say they are doing this on purpose.

This is a real head scratcher – an annoying fact that undermines my simplistic paradigm of an epidemic of misguided, incompetent leadership. In my gap analysis of the previous chapter, I am struck by an insight as I pore over the details of campaign contributions. This revelation does me in. It unravels my thesis and invalidates my original conclusions. I will have to rethink everything.

While composing these final chapters, I have been nagged by a mounting suspicion that I am slightly off-key somewhere in my conclusions about incompetent leadership. That happens to me sometimes as a physician – feeling an uneasy sense of foreboding as if I went ahead and assembled the puzzle without all the pieces locked into their proper places.

I *hate* this feeling. Sometimes it comes from a sense that a crucial fact is *missing*, like the Munchausen's diagnosis in Philip DeSare. The puzzle is nearly done, but a piece has been misplaced, lying on the shag carpet under the card table. A shortfall that makes me go back and hunt for more clues.

Sometimes it comes from an inconvenient *new* fact, like a faint whisper – the heart murmur I heard in Gerald Menard that did not fit into my working framework of a diagnosis. An extra puzzle piece in hand without a matching space. A troublesome detail that makes me go back and start all over again. Either way, I cannot relax until I have reconnected the dots.

And now I see it. The oversight. The cognitive deficit. The glaring blindspot of an experienced practitioner who surely should know better. How could I have failed to recognize what I so often preach in my daily work? The answer to the question that I always ask at every RCA but failed to raise in this book so far. The core principle of the Just Culture.

I am downright embarrassed to realize I have fallen into an age-old trap. I have assumed all along that our root cause was primarily a *people* problem. Hence, I have been blaming our elected leaders for their poor stewardship of our nation. For failing to apply the lessons of leadership.

But that is not what I meant at all. That is not it, at all.

Please recall from Chapter 2, that people problems are due to deliberate malfeasance committed by those rare individuals who display a wanton disregard for the rules. The outliers. The bad apples. But there is no malfeasance here. Our leaders are *not* bad apples. They are behaving exactly as one would expect given the dysfunctional political environment they work in.

Rich people buy off candidates because they can. Candidates take these bribes because they must. Voters accept this behavior because they see no other way. National leaders deny mistakes, ignore facts, and refuse to compromise because it is political suicide *not* to.

Of course! Just as in the case of Natalie and the nurses who ignored the alarms in the ICU, the universal pattern of misconduct that we see in our elected leaders is a sure sign that we have an *epidemic* of bad behavior. That is the lightning bolt insight that has just now struck me out of the blue – the missing puzzle piece that fits perfectly into the gap. I have said this exact phrase so many times, the words should just roll off my tongue.

What we have here is a *system* problem.

I truly believed all along that I was writing this book for our national leaders. I came to this point fully prepared to sum up our collected lessons, to squeeze them all up into a ball, and roll it toward the feet of our constitutionally-defined, democratically-elected office-holders. Now I have come to realize that I've completely missed the essence of the matter. Since *everyone* is misbehaving, it is most *obviously* a system problem.

I am already anticipating your response. How dare I condone all this bad behavior by excusing our leaders. Why should I let them off the hook? Where is the accountability? The justice? So, again, I return to Natalie and the ICU alarms – our most important lesson. There is *always* accountability. But in the case of a system problem, you must go one level *higher.*

You may now approach the porcelain elephant in the room to ask the obvious question: who *is* accountable for the system if not the president and members of Congress? These are the highest elected officials in the land. They run our country, don't they?

Again, the answer should be obvious by now. Accountability rests with the *leaders* of our leaders. Indeed! But who *are* the leaders of our leaders, the supreme commanders – the ultimate bosses? Who *can* we hold accountable for the advanced stage of illness in which we find the patient, our ailing nation? In other words, who are these lessons *really* for?

Now I believe you too must have a queasy feeling because you really *do* know the answer, and perhaps it has been creeping up on you like it has on me. Where *is* the seat of power from which our system emanates? Who *shall* we hold accountable for the system that brings out the worst in our national leaders. Who *is* it that these lessons from the bedside are truly meant for? And now I think you understand the very simple answer:

You. And me. The electorate. The American people. The true seat of power in any democracy. Like it or not, we are the board of directors, with absolute authority over our state – and complete control over our fate. We are "America's leaders" of this book's title, and all these lessons are for *us*. This final chapter, then, is the solution approach for the American people.

I realize I have shattered the glass to expose a shared responsibility between you, the reader, and me, the author – partners in crime. That happens sometimes when an issue turns out to be a system problem. In the end, we will find the accusatory finger pointing back at ourselves, ripe with responsibility for our predicament. And that is precisely the point. Our elected leaders aren't failing us. We are failing ourselves.

More important, we will learn that we have been holding the keys to the kingdom all along. Like Dorothy and her companions, we will finally realize that we have always had within our grasp what we have long been craving: the clout to mend our world. Let me explain.

When most folks talk about draining the swamp, they mean to purge it of the unsavory creatures – the eels, snakes, and alligators – that plumb its depths. Of course, we can cure the "people problem" in a single election cycle. But even if that purge were to be successful, the swamp would eventually fill up with the same foul fauna as before – the repugnant life forms that thrive in the murky, turbid waters of the marsh. It's just a matter of time.

When *I* say drain the swamp, I mean drain out the *water*. That's *system* change. Once dry, the new habitat will naturally favor the entry of desirable trees and plants, to be followed by our favorite forest creatures. In this way, draining the water is akin to the system change we need to permanently repopulate our national offices of leadership. This system change is remarkably simple and absolutely achievable. We can do this! In fact, it is much easier to change people's behavior by changing the environment than by changing the people!

We will begin with the principle causes of our affliction – private campaign financing, gerrymandering, and factionalization of the electorate. The central thrust of our solution approach will be to sever these three massive roots, starting with campaign financing.

At the heart of the current state is the unfortunate truth that a successful campaign for public office requires comprehensive media exposure. This calls for massive funding, of course, which is raised in the form of political contributions from the private sector. It follows that the better financed candidate has the upper hand in the campaign. Therefore, the number one priority of any candidate is to raise money.

Even worse, new electees become obsessed with financing the *next* campaign as soon as they win the first, and thus spend most of their time in office raising money – making cold calls, meeting with lobbyists, and holding fund raisers. In other words, shilling for dollars. Those who have too much integrity to adapt are culled from the herd through natural selection.

And what do the clients want in return for the billions they contribute? Access, clout, and "friendly" legislation, of course. Despite pious denials from our elected officials, there is otherwise no earthly reason why wealthy citizens would spend so much on political campaigns.

Why does everyone engage in such unseemly behavior? Because that is the way our system works. That is essentially the job description of our elected leaders, after all: peddle influence, raise money, get re-elected, and repeat as necessary. They are not bad people. It is a rotten *system*.

If we are going to excise this malignant root and restore the rule of the people, we need to change the system. We need a plan that renders fundraising unnecessary, that negates the need to make cold calls, meet with lobbyists, or serve tea and marmalade to fill the campaign coffers. That plan, that solution approach, that *cloutbuster* drug, is public campaign financing.

The idea of public campaign financing is not new, of course. In fact, there is a system in place to do just that for presidential elections. Unfortunately, recent candidates, including Bernie Sanders, Hillary Clinton, and Donald Trump, have not taken the offer, preferring to raise private funds. They quickly learned they could raise and spend much more on their own.

So why is public financing failing? Because we are too cheap. We have been outbid, outmanned, and outplanned by every wealthy benefactor, every rich politico, every well-funded organization truly serious about its own success. Everyone is behaving exactly as one would expect given the system defect that brings out their worst. So let's change the *system* and buy our government back. Let that be our next great order of business.

And here is why: throwing our current leaders out of office without addressing dirty money would be just like firing Natalie without fixing the alarm system, or clearing the swamp without draining the water. Highly satisfying, no doubt – but completely ineffectual. At the very next election, campaign funds will begin to flow again and a new generation of leaders will forget all about climate change, income inequality, and health care. Without system change, the swamp will repopulate with the same old same old.

Where shall we begin? For starters, we must extend public financing to include *all* candidates for national office: presidents, senators, and representatives. Why not? We paid for the government in the first place. We the American people put up nearly five trillion dollars to fund the federal budget, then stood back and watched as rich private citizens, corporations, and special interest groups purchased it right out from under our noses - for a song. It is as though we paid $50,000 for a fancy new car, only to see an interloper buy the keys for a mere $50 and drive our car right off the lot.

How much would it cost to win this epic battle? Based on current campaign spending figures, I generously estimate it would cost $5 billion per year to buy back our $5 *trillion* government.[2,3] Only then will we take over the reins of authority. Only then will our elected representatives actually work for *us*. Only then will we get to drive our own car off the lot.

Think about it. That is $1,000-worth of government for every dollar spent. Ten dollars-worth for a penny. One of the greatest deals of all time. That is why everyone *else* is doing it. Indeed, let's buy our government back!

The U.S. Supreme Court has upheld the constitutionality of public campaign financing, but has ruled that the decision to accept public funds in lieu of private contributions must be voluntary on the part of the candidates. Since we cannot mandate acceptance of the money, we will throw in an additional incentive to sweeten the pot. This is the clincher.

Whenever a candidate chooses *not* to accept public financing, his opponent will get *both* shares – double the money. Surely, no one will agree to funnel so much cash and media exposure to his opponent. How can I be so sure? I encourage you to read again the account of the UCLA experiment in Chapter 8. No one, but no one, *ever* wants to reward the "out-group." You can bank on that.

Who would resist such an obvious solution? Unfortunately, *everyone.* At least everyone now in charge. Current office holders (whose votes we obviously need) will be opposed because the present system strongly favors their re-election – as most private money goes to incumbents.

Undoubtedly, all *new* candidates for office would love to take public financing, until they win *their* seat. From that point forward, they will prefer to leave the system the way it is now. Even though the task of fundraising is a sheer misery, even though it makes them feel cheap and tawdry, even though it monopolizes their attention so they have no time to legislate, the current system delivers on the one thing most dear to their hearts – winning re-election. For that one reason, they will never willingly go along.

Who else will be opposed? All the private sources of current campaign financing, of course. No one wants to be outbid, outmanned, and outplanned. Certainly not by ordinary voters. Not when they have such a fantastic bargain. Not when they are getting complete control of the federal government for less than a tenth of a penny on the dollar. Of *course,* they will be opposed. They will become completely unhinged at the possibility of American voters taking back control of their own government.

This is where you and I, the American people, come in. The ones *truly* in charge. The board of directors. The leaders of the leaders. Whether we know it or not, we have complete control over *all* our elected officials. We have the one thing our leaders want even more than money. The sparkling jewel that all this money is really intended to buy in the first place. The holy grail of every politician ever born.

Our vote.

This is our true currency. The key to the kingdom. The simple lever that can move a mountain. Our *precious*. So let's use it. Let's not throw away our shot! Here, then, is the solution approach for the first massive gnarled root cause of our ailing democracy. We the people must insist on public financing of campaigns for the House, the Senate, and the presidency. We must compel our leaders to pledge their loyalty to this proposition. And we must withhold our vote from any candidate who refuses to make this pledge.

More important, we must exact our revenge on any national officeholders who fail to *keep* the pledge. At the very next election cycle, we must unceremoniously toss them out of office. Again and again, we must reject the transgressors until they get the message. We the American people are determined to buy our government back, and we will withhold our precious votes until we get it. If we truly band together, no one can stop us!

Let's turn to our second massive root, gerrymandering. It is often stated that all politics is local. This is especially true of redistricting, which is left to the states according to Article I, Section 4, of the U.S. Constitution:

> The Times, Places and Manner of holding Elections for Senators and Representatives, shall be prescribed in each State by the Legislature thereof; *but the Congress may at any time by Law make or alter such Regulations*, except as to the Places of chusing Senators.

The Constitution does not even prescribe the arrangements of states into districts. The U.S. Congress does, however, have permission to regulate the process and has specified that congressional districts must be equal in population size (currently 711,000 voters) and may not be drawn in a way to infringe upon the voting rights of minorities.

In current practice, most states leave redistricting to their state legislatures and all the attendant biases therein. As such, political parties in power may engage in "packing" – consolidating blocs of like-minded voters into a single district to limit their impact in other districts, or "cracking" – breaking up blocs of like-minded voters into separate districts to dilute their strength. In either case, redistricting is designed to further the interests of the local party in power, which inhibits coalition-building at the national level.

The topic of redistricting is extraordinarily complex. The bad news is that the U.S. Supreme Court, when given a divine opportunity in 2019 to permanently cure this egregious system defect, fell breathtakingly, heartbreakingly, *headshakingly* short of the mark in the indelible moment that separates the ordinary from the great. The Justices, in a five to four ruling, passed this responsibility over to the legislative branch – the very ones who have an irresistible incentive to maintain their safe, gerrymandered districts exactly as they are. They might as well have put a stake in my heart!

The good news is that Americans can dictate what they want through electoral pressure. In fact, the surest way to rise above politics in this effort is to do what a handful of progressive states have already achieved – turn the process over to an independent non-partisan commission. Arizona, California, Idaho, and Washington are four states which have done so.

In 2000, for example, Arizona voters passed Proposition 106, which amended the state constitution to establish the Citizen's Independent Redistricting Commission to draw congressional district boundaries. In this effort, the enlightened voters of Arizona are worthy role models for the nation.

In following suit, the appropriate response by Congress would be to pass a federal law requiring independent commissions to draw district lines in *every* state. In a single, bold legislative act, Congress could slay the tenacious gerrymander once and for all.

But don't hold your breath. As noted above, House representatives have no personal incentive to cure this defect, which, after all, guarantees a safe seat in their next election. So, once again, the American people must rise up and insist that their elected officials do the right thing and repair our broken system – or be *sacked*. Once again, the ball is in *our* court.

And what about the factionalization of America, our *third* massive root? This unfortunate development is the consequence of our migration away from the political center toward the fringes. As we vacated the center, the new shape of the political landscape became a bimodal distribution – two hills divided by a valley. We have gone from being a one-humped dromedary to a two-humped Bactrian camel.

In his superb book, *The Checklist Manifesto*, Dr. Atul Gawande recounts an illuminating story about the construction of the Citicorp Tower, the iconic skyscraper in midtown Manhattan.[4] The tower has several unique architectural features, including a slanted roof and four base columns that support the entire building, which is raised high off the ground.

Because of these features, there was concern about the stability of the structure in high winds. The solution was ingenious. Inside the building on a high floor was suspended a 400-ton concrete block. When the structure begins to sway in high winds, the block serves as a counterweight, pulling the tower back to the center.

Our nation needs a counterweight like that concrete block, a large electoral mass that stabilizes our partisan leanings – a solid, weighty political center that dampens the swing of the pendulum from one election cycle to the next. In the 1960s and 70s we had such a counterweight. It was called the silent majority, and it always lay in waiting to counter the extremism that sometimes gained traction during an election year

Unfortunately, that 400-ton concrete block has disintegrated and our national tower is now constantly buffeted in the high winds of our political storms, especially the upper floors of our leadership hierarchy.

The net result is a hyperintense focus upon competition between the extreme forces in both political parties – an overwrought emphasis on hand-to-hand combat, trouncing the opposition, and running up the score.

It is up to the electorate to restore the counterweight by resisting extremism and repopulating the center. This may require some relaxation of cherished objectives and an openness to compromise – the currency of consensus that has been absent for the past two presidential election cycles.

This, then, is the solution approach for factionalization of American voters in both blue and red states: Relax. Ease up. Chill out. Stop turning every hot issue into its own Armageddon. Move toward the center of the bridge, away from the safety of the shores. Support candidates who build consensus so that our nation may advance on our collective goals of personal freedom, open opportunity, and broad-based prosperity.

If we the American people summon the will to mass on that bridge, we can restore the unity that permits us to advance our progress. If we remain on our respective shores to fight our endless battles, then buying back our government and slaying the gerrymander will leave us well short of our target state – necessary steps, but not sufficient to close the gap.

We have now addressed our three main roots: private campaign financing, gerrymandering and factionalization – three system defects that require behavior change by the electorate, all part of the solution approach. What am I forgetting? Ah, yes! I nearly overlooked the crucial counterpart to our system problem: the *people*. I admit that I have been emphasizing structural issues, but we must keep in mind that people are always part of the equation, even when the failing is primarily a system problem.

Remember when I forgot to write a prescription upon discharging an asthma patient? Recollect Natalie, the ICU nurse who failed to answer the alarm, and Stacy, the psychiatric nurse who failed to check two patient-identifiers? Recall the PwC representative who was not paying attention at the Academy Awards? We were all well-intentioned, but every one of us played a central role in the chain of unfortunate events.

Indeed, even after the cardboard boxes are piled up in the kitchen corner and oil-soaked rags are stuffed in the front closet, it still takes a careless visitor to flick a cigarette ash onto the shag carpet. Maybe we should pay more attention to the guests we invite into our home.

Our fourth and final fix, then, must reserve a component for misguided and incompetent leadership. The solution approach to this root, of course, must address the recruitment and oversight of our elected officials – presidents, senators, and representatives – who work in the faulty system and contribute to its failures. In short, we need a plan that improves the quality of our leadership team.

This is where our first nine lessons from the bedside come in. We expended many chapters-worth of effort to assemble the phenotype of a great leader. We must now return to this standard to review all applicants for higher office. Once we have made our selections, we must monitor their performance by continual surveillance, must encourage their progress through constant feedback, and must fire them if they fail to live up to our expectations. This is the *systematic* approach to our people problem.

If we rise up and take our role seriously, our leaders will straighten up and fall into line. Even better, our system changes will improve the desirability of political life so as to attract a better breed of office-seekers. With any luck, candidates with integrity, compassion, and belief in the truth will repopulate the forest. The system will practically select our leaders for us!

It is worth noting that the four elements of the solution approach are politically neutral; they favor neither Democrats nor Republicans. Indeed, I can now confess that I do not belong to either party as I have always been attracted to positive aspects of *both*. To Republicans for their commitment to free enterprise, fiscal discipline, and national defense. To Democrats for their dedication to compassion, fairness, and diversity.

In this way I have always been drawn to the political center, constantly seeking the equilibrium between two points of view. In fact, I could easily imagine the Republican Party as my father and the Democratic Party as my mother. Just one more duality, like art and science.

Now, here's the thing. I don't know what has happened to my father. I barely recognize him. He went off on a drinking spree and is lying in the gutter somewhere, having left me fully in the custody of my mother. To the leadership of the Republican Party, I say the following:

You walked out on your family. You poisoned the well of broad-based prosperity with your self-serving scheme of Supply-Side Economics. You betrayed the health of Americans by your bizarre hostility to the ACA. And you rejected the facts of science in your absurd denial of climate change. So let me be clear. I did not run from the party. The party ran from me.

To the Democrats, my mother, I have a different message. There are plenty of Republican voters who can be enticed back into the marriage, who can be wooed with the right message of inclusion, respect, and coalescence. Don't give up on them. Extend the olive branch. Call for a truce.

That would mean temporarily de-emphasizing divisive topics, such as abortion, gun control, and immigration. Better to start with unifying themes: redirecting tax cuts to the middle class, taking sensible first steps to address climate change, and adding Medicare as a choice on the ACA exchange. Seek the common ground and rebuild the marriage from there.

But even before that, even before you go for the win-win, you must fix the *system* – starting with campaign financing. Otherwise, to address tough issues will be like shoveling the sidewalk while it's still snowing. You might make temporary progress, but it will be all for naught after the blizzard of the next election. First things first. *Durable* progress calls for *system* change.

Once the relationship is back on solid ground, once the system has been repaired and you have rebuilt trust with some early wins, there will be time enough to address your fundamental differences, the hot-button issues that drove you apart. Time enough to find the sweet spot.

Most important, let's not forget that Trump was president for just four years and America's chronic disease has been brewing for *four decades*. In the final analysis, Trump was merely a *symptom*. Every doctor knows you can't cure a disease just by relieving a symptom.

So let me address a final piece of unfinished business – the truth that lies beneath. How did Donald Trump, whose leadership deficiencies were so clearly evident during the campaign, secure the presidency? Interestingly, I believe the answer lies in the same root causes that we have just addressed.

First, middle-class Americans have become deeply dissatisfied in the economic stagnation of their personal experience. Although the cause of this adverse outcome may be laid at the feet of corrupt campaign financing and Supply–Side Economics, Republicans have successfully attributed the plight of the middle-class to the out-group, the have-nots, the so-called *takers*, and many frustrated voters have accepted this perverted storyline.

Second, Trump successfully exploited the dark side of human nature – group bias. By tapping into the inborn tendency to discriminate that is latent in all of us, he harnessed factionalization for sinister purposes. To make matters worse, the electoral college system simulated gerrymandering by producing a perverse result in which a party prevailed with a minority of votes.

Finally, in our selection of Trump we ignored every one of the nine elements that make up the phenotype of a great leader. For whatever reason, many American voters did not care to consider Lincolnian attributes of humility, forgiveness, integrity, truth, compassion, or coalescence as prerequisites for filling the highest office in our land. In this way, Trump's 2016 election makes perfect sense within the framework of our broken system.

At this point, it is customary to bring our actors back onto the stage for their final curtain call. Please, everyone, give it up for Alec, Matt, and Candice, who portrayed my medical errors, for dear Natalie, who fell prey to alarm fatigue, and for well-intentioned Stacy, who failed to check two patient-identifiers just so that we might learn about the Just Culture.

More kudos to Nate, my behavioral health challenge, to Juan, my AIDS dilemma, and to Phil, my Munchausen fascinoma, for teaching us about trust. And, of course, a rousing hand for Faye Dunaway and Warren Beatty, *real life actors* who made cameo appearances.

Our Second Act featured a nuanced role played by the subtle whisper after a lub-dub – method acting at its best. But let's not overlook Stanley, whose myocardial infarction taught us a valuable lesson about the value of evidence. And props to Vigo, Apollo, and Seth for their heart-wrenching tales in Chapter 7, important lessons in compassion.

By special mention, Will Thomason deserves accolades for scintillating performances in two dramatic encounters 15 years apart, as do all the walk-ons in the stairwell of our gripping storm scene. Not to mention our favorite sleuths – Holmes, Poirot, and Marple – fictional characters who came to life in service to our message. Finally, a hearty hand for the debut of our uninsured trio: Debbie, Therèse, and Keith. Bravo!

By now the stage is crowded with so many extras – gun enthusiasts, abortion rights activists, and the medically underserved – that we barely have room for the real stars of our show, the American presidents: Washington, Lincoln, Roosevelt, Reagan, Obama, and Trump.

And finally, a special shout-out to Presidents Reagan, Clinton, and Bush (and now Trump) for their convincing portrayal of a classic three-phase historic experiment revealing the destructive consequences of Supply-Side Economics. Real presidents, we salute you all!

In conclusion, I must acknowledge the vital contribution of historic Bellevue, the grand matriarch of all public hospitals, as the perfect venue for our performance. For all of her warts, foibles, and blemishes, Bellevue has always stood tall as a house of healing, a mecca of learning, and a beacon of compassion, continuously ministering to the ailments of the humbly begotten, harshly downtrodden, and nearly forgotten castaways of New York's urban sea of humanity for nearly three centuries.

Of course, I do not mean to trivialize such serious topics. In truth, my hospital is a mighty crucible in which powerful forces engage to improve the human condition. A mystical palace of great pathos, of heart-wrenching suffering and life-affirming heroism. A deep receptacle of knowledge and sentiment, of timeworn memories that tickle the brain and tug at the heart.

But a touch of whimsy is a wonderful tool to keep us humble, to ensure that we do not take ourselves too seriously. Otherwise, we will be too puffed up with self-importance to see the simple truth. And yes, sometimes we must laugh in order not to cry.

As an encore, let's summarize the solution approach that must be carried out by the American electorate, the leaders of our leaders, for the nation – our patient. And let's not be distracted by *personalities*. This prescription for a cure is based on the methodical repair of *system* defects.

1. Americans must step up and buy their government back with all deliberate speed. We must meet this objective *before* proceeding any further. And we must repeatedly clean house until our elected leaders comply. No progress will be possible on income inequality, health care financing, or climate change until the keys are returned to their rightful owners, the American people.

2. Americans must rise up and slay the gerrymander. We must insist that Congress require independent commissions for redistricting within every state. And we must severely punish senators and

representatives who fail to deliver on this promise. We will not begin to solve sensitive issues touching on group dynamics until the gerrymander lies still in its grave.

3. Americans must ease up and move to the center. We must inch our way back onto the Bridge of Compromise to coalesce as a community. We must broaden our perspectives and bend our views. And we must place the collective success of our nation ahead of our biological drive to support the in-group. Not until we become a dromedary once again will it be possible to break up the gridlock.

4. Americans must wise up and select their leaders with care. We must seek attributes of great leadership in our candidates using our lessons from the bedside, qualities that promote self-reflection, trust, compassion, a Just Culture, sound decision-making, and unity among our electorate. And we must aspire to these same attributes in *ourselves*.

And for Pete's sake, let's stop blaming our elected leaders for our predicament. We picked them! And by now it should be clear that they are merely *symptoms* of our disease. Their behavior, after all, is the predictable consequence of the long sweep of American history, as ordained by the pioneers and pamphleteers and engineers who built our nation step by step, word for word, brick by brick, to craft a glorious, complex, and flawed edifice of rules, laws, and political culture, the cogs and gears and puppet strings of the *system, our* system, the one *we* own, operate, and maintain, the one that attracts candidates, elicits their responses, and inspires their practices, the one that is so perfectly designed to provoke the exact behaviors we fervently detest in those we seek to lead us, the one *we* must change once and for all.

As we contemplate the pros and cons of accepting this treatment, now is the perfect time to reflect upon our most eventful American life. Let us recall that we began with a violent birth as we were practically ripped from the womb in the emergency Cesarean section of 1776. We continued to battle our British parents in our childhood, then ourselves, as we nearly committed suicide in the Civil War of our turbulent adolescence. In young adulthood, however, we spread our wings, grew in stature, and flourished.

Many decades later, a prolonged period of deep Depression set in, requiring years of therapy. But we were resilient. We learned to cope and returned to a happy, productive life. Then, of course, we survived serious, acute, life-threatening conditions in our two World Wars, but we fully recovered from those as well. It wasn't until our midlife crisis of the 1960s that we did the long-overdue, deep reflection of a mature adult.

Now here we are, nearly forty years into a chronic illness that has resisted our best efforts at diagnosis. Is this the cancer of our advancing age, the long, slow, terminal decline that will defy the best approaches of modern Medicine? Our shadow at evening rising to meet us? Our fitful end?

Let me close with the prognosis, as promised. Is there any hope for this patient, our nation? Is this a life that can be saved? My answer to that question is a resounding *yes*. This is a treatable disease – a *curable* condition. As in most chronic disorders, the key to the cure is the patient.

If we the voters adhere to this simple prescription, we will not need to purchase costly medications, undergo a risky procedure, or endure an expensive inpatient stay that would likely be denied by the insurance company in any case. If we the electorate adopt the solution approach, we can fix the broken system that brings out the worst in our national leaders.

If we the American people rise up from our sick bed, surmount our differences, and coalesce as a nation, we can slice our way with the vorpal sword through the jaws that bite and the claws that catch. We can break free from the debilitating impact of dirty money and partisan politics. We can attract the finest and brightest to become our leaders and then bring out the best in them. Most important, we can pursue our mission with new-found fervor and resume our role as the world's oldest and best experiment in democracy. A nation healed. *Snickersnack.*

Postlude

"Like a golden braid, the art is woven tightly into the science and the two are mutually reinforcing."

As the reader might have surmised, the third and most important major theme of this book is "Coalescence." To that end, connectivity between microscopic cells, among specialized tissues, and across complex organs is an essential, life-sustaining feature of all higher beings. Likewise, relationships between individuals can foster healthy families, connections among families can generate vibrant communities, and coalescence across communities can create an extraordinary nation like ours.

In this way, coalescence can be seen as the epitome of the healthy state, and factionalization may be considered pathognomonic of the diseased state. This is true for ill patients, and I believe it to be equally true for our ailing nation. It is alignment that delivers vitality, vim, and vigor, and discord that sows disease, dysfunction, and decline.

Hence, my emphasis on dyads (art and science, diagnosis and treatment, right and left brain), which complement each other, and triads, which align in a weave as a braid to provide tensile strength. Accordingly, the principal structure of this book is the Rule of Three, which offers redundancy, resilience, and strength to sentences, paragraphs, and chapters.

Redundancy is further reinforced by fractals (e.g., triads of triads), alliteration (e.g., in the first two paragraphs above), and anagrams (e.g., *Natalie Ghintino*) – a meta-structure of wordplay that further binds *The Ailing Nation*.

The reappearance of words and phrases from the opening excerpts of each chapter in the text that follows is another example of an internal structure that strengthens the whole by imbedding art into the science, and this practice is reinforced by one extra layer of coalescence...

Within each chapter are words, phrases, and themes that are echoed by similar constructs in other chapters. These connections may collectively be considered a scaffold that adds strength and integrity to the text. But I prefer to think of them as direct channels, wormholes if you will, that expedite instant travel from one chapter to the next, bypassing the matrix much like the secret passage that connects the Study and Kitchen in the game of Clue.

By way of example from the first chapter, which has more than 30 echoes overall: My personal "backup generator" (p. 1) is echoed by the hospital's backup generators in Superstorm Sandy (p. 128). "Not to mention embracing my craft, Internal Medicine..." (p. 1) is echoed by the frigid ocean waters that "embraced" the "craft" of Donald Trump in my climate change fantasy (p. 239). The "speckled band" of light issuing from the doorway (p. 3) is echoed by the Sherlock Holmes reference: "The Adventure of the Speckled Band" (p. 147). Overall, there are more than 200 echoes crisscrossing the matrix of this book. A sample appears on the following two pages, and the complete list can be viewed on my website, *Snickersnack.com* – see Author Commentary under the Book tab.

In summary, the three major themes of "Art and Science," the "Systematic Approach," and "Coalescence" are the overarching lessons from my career in Medicine. They are fundamental to being a talented physician, vital to serving as an effective leader, and essential to becoming a great nation.

As my words come to a close, I am breathing a sigh of relief that America narrowly averted a tragic second term in the presidency of Donald Trump, the anti-hero of this book and my best example of how not to lead a nation. In this second printing, three months after the inauguration of Joe Biden, I am reassured by his focus on the COVID response, climate change, electoral reform, and the needs of the less fortunate. And I have happily changed Donald Trump to the past tense. For now.

But, as should be equally clear, the greater challenges facing our nation are the system problems that put Trump into office in the first place. Unless or until those system defects are repaired, the symptoms of our chronic illness will flourish, and we will fail to understand why our ailing nation continues to decline.

Echoes

1. The very first word of the text in Chapter 1, "Snickersnack" (p. 1), is repeated as the very last word of the text in Chapter 18 (p. 273) – the ultimate echo.
2. The triumphant diagnosis, "Colonel Mustard did it with a Lead Pipe in the Conservatory" (p. 54), is echoed by Philip DeSare, who had "mustered not a kernel of truth" (p. 44).
3. My first view of a major league baseball field, a "seemingly accidental collage of brilliant color" (p. 110), is echoed by Obama, who "entered Occidental College in Los Angeles" (p. 197).
4. The excess share of corporate income, industry's "false profits, if you will" (p. 153), is echoed by Donald Trump, "a tantalizing distraction. A false prophet." (p. 219).
5. The pajama-clad children who listened with pride to Neil Armstrong's words (p. 140) are echoed by the "convicts in horizontally-striped pajamas, bobbing up and down on the handle of the small railroad flatcar" (p. 175).
6. Donald Trump, who was the "free choice of an engaged electorate that was fully aware of his florid faults" (p. 218), is echoed by "Atlantic seawater gently lapping over asphalt Florida roadways" (p. 239).
7. The patient with alcohol withdrawal, who "would be disheveled, shaky, and agitated – in the delirious haze of severe alcohol withdrawal" (p. 55) is echoed by Vladimir Nabokov, "author of the highly praised novel, *Lolita*." (p. 145). The actual name for Lolita is Dolores Haze.
8. "A year later, as the project began to falter, visions of grandeur still danced in his head" (p. 217) is echoed by nursing leaders, who organized the thousand-plus registered nurses into their appropriate shifts and "settled down for a long restless night" as Superstorm Sandy approached (p. 133). Both are references to the holiday poem, *The Night Before Christmas*.
9. The dire situation during Superstorm Sandy, which "had now become a classic Hitchcock suspense thriller" (p. 129), is echoed *five* times: by the line, "I was imagining we were on a lifeboat, packed with survivors, while a sailor floundering in the sea petitions to come aboard" (p. 234), by Trump, who, during his first impeachment, became "a non-cooperator, a saboteur, an *obstructionist*" (p. 32), by the acute apprehension I felt "walking along the vertiginous catwalks coursing through the upper reaches of Cleveland Municipal Stadium" (p. 110), by the "perfect lens of the retrospectoscope" (p. 22), and by the line "Ironically, the only truth I knew in 1983 turned out not to be true after all!" (p. 92). *Lifeboat, Saboteur, Vertigo, Rear Window,* and *The Man Who Knew Too Much* were five films directed by Alfred Hitchcock.

10. The "chaotic cloud of electrical activity" in ventricular fibrillation (p. 88) is echoed by the "chaotic cloud of constant combat" in Donald Trump's presidency (p. 215).
11. Debbie Shault's emphysematous breaths, which were "oddly asymmetrical" (p. 165), are echoed by the "oddly symmetrical pattern of supply-side tax policy" (p. 248).
12. The sound of three pricks of the bubble, "Snap, crackle, pop!" (p. 147) is echoed by the sounds of climate change: "Flowing sheets of ice crisply snapping free from majestic Alaskan glaciers? The crackling burn of ancient Oregon forests? It does not matter. No one is listening. Nobody seems to care. Trump pops the cork." (p. 239).
13. The East River, which had "risen by at least a dozen feet and overflowed its banks - submerging the FDR Drive, which had now completely disappeared" (p. 134), is echoed by FDR's blood pressure, which, at 240/130, exceeded its limits and took out our 32nd president (p. 85)
14. The gun invoked by the department chair "patriarch" at the M&M (p. 8) is echoed by the gun owned by the matriarch in my gun control discussion (p. 183).
15. The approving murmur that rippled through the room in the M&M conference (p. 12) is echoed by the approving murmur that rippled through the room during the sepsis review (p. 71).
16. The aortic valve's "saloon doors" (p. 57) are echoed by Ronald Reagan's channeling of John Wayne "swaggering into the saloon" (p. 195).
17. Non-compliant patients with schizophrenia, "society's 'misfits' who have rejected all attempts at treatment" (p. 37), are echoed by "so many of my other Bellevue patients" who are "society's castaways. Its misfit toys." (p. 102).
18. "We have been outbid, outmanned, and outplanned" (p. 262) is echoed by "Let's not throw away our shot!" (p. 264). Both are lines from the musical *Hamilton*.
19. "Now that should have activated the flowsheet, right? Did we use the flowsheet?" (p. 71) is echoed by "Flowing sheets of ice crisply snapping free from majestic Alaskan glaciers?" (p. 239).
20. Nate Tomen, who lay still "with open eyes and an enigmatic smile" (p. 37), is echoed by Gerald Menard, who sported "horn-rimmed glasses, short brown hair, and a faintly bemused expression" (p. 55) and by Leonardo DaVinci's accomplishments, "From the Mona Lisa to flying machines" (p. 145).
21. "Indeed, it is nigh impossible to fully change a system from within – to paint the very spot one is standing on" (p. III) is echoed by "It is devilishly difficult to do this. To step completely outside our biased conceptual framework. To take a clean look inward with an open mind" (p. 27) and by Douglas Hofstadter's *Gödel, Escher, Bach: An Eternal Golden Braid*" (p. 145). The first two lines are references to Gödel's incompleteness theorem, which states that one cannot fully describe a logical system using terms within it.

Playbill
(Anagram Partners)

Character	Representing...
Alec Secceño	*Coalescence*
Matt Tener	*Treatment*
Candice Staner	*Art and Science*
Natalie Ghintino	*The Ailing Nation*
Stacy Hippocrates, MA	*Systematic Approach*
Nate Tomen	*Atonement*
Phil DeSare	*Leadership*
Juan Verdad	*One Truth*
Will Thomason	*The Will to Mass on the Bridge*
Gerry Menard	*Gerrymander*
Eugene Shaffertis	*Ease the Suffering*
Stan Loritan	*Translation*
Vigo Ferness	*Forgiveness*
Apollo Greene	*Apology*
Seth Feylend	*Deny the Self*
Debbie Shault	*Build the Base*
Therése Vorot	*Sever the Root*
Keith Tasker	*Take the Risk*
Thomas Spectes	*Set the Compass*

Chapter Notes

The Ailing Nation

1. The 1960s have an impressive resumé: 1961 - Expansion of Social Security; 1964 - Civil Rights Act; 1965 - Birth of Medicare and Medicaid; 1968 – Fair Housing Act; 1969 – Moon Landing; 1970 – Birth of the Environmental Protection Agency. Real GDP grew 51% in the 1960s but only 19% in the 2000s. Median family income grew 37% in the 1960s, more than the next 47 years combined! All this in one decade despite unsettling social upheaval and the awful pain and suffering of the Vietnam War.
2. NYC Health and Hospitals is the largest municipal health system in the U.S. In a given year, its facilities provide 225,000 inpatient admissions, 1 million emergency visits, and 5 million clinic visits. As a member of the system, Bellevue Hospital's official name is *NYC Health and Hospitals/Bellevue.*
3. Having raised two daughters, I am well aware that a braid requires a minimum of three strands. Not to worry. The underlying structure of the paragraphs and chapters of this book will rely heavily upon the rule of three.

Chapter 1: Atonement

1. The stories I am sharing are all true; however, I have changed some details – the name, age, and sometimes gender – of the patients to protect their anonymity. As a convention, I have referenced patients by their first name, although in real life I typically address older patients by their surnames. I have fashioned dialogue to fit the essence of the conversations that actually took place.
2. In the early 1980s, Alphabet City had fallen on hard times, with a high incidence of drug use and street crime. Nowadays it is a flourishing neighborhood with a vibrant nightlife.
3. The Manhattan VA is now known as VA New York Harbor Health Care System – Manhattan Campus. Together with Bellevue (the public hospital), and Tisch (the private one), it is one of a trio of contiguous teaching hospitals for NYU School of Medicine.
4. The Chief was none other than Lewis Goldfrank, MD, founder of NYU's Department of Emergency Medicine and iconic international leader in his field.

5. If you really want to know what it feels like for a physician to have a case unravel, watch the best example of this I have ever seen: "ER" *Love's Labor Lost* (Season One, Episode 19), in which ED physician Mark Green, MD, experiences a heartbreaking obstetrical case that falls apart minute by minute.
6. If a blood clot that that has formed in the veins of the arms or legs breaks free, it may travel to the chest and obstruct one of the main arteries leading to the lungs. We call this a pulmonary embolism. If the clot is large enough, it will severely impede blood flow leading to instant death of the patient. Not a risk to be taken lightly.
7. www.cbo.gov/system/files/2019-04/53651-outlook-2.pdf.
8. www.axios.com/trump-rnc-donors-apple-tim-cook-lie-2fd0b004-6fc3-4f81-9eb0-3b92f3264ef1.html.
9. www.hhs.gov/about/news/2017/09/28/hhs-secretary-price-statement-on-private-charter-airplane-travel.html.
10. www.washingtonpost.com/news/wonk/wp/2013/11/07/video-watch-obama-kinda-sorta-apologize-to-americans-losing-their-health-plans/?utm_term=.dbc8758dafcf.
11. www.cnn.com/ALLPOLITICS/1998/08/17/speech/transcript.html.
12. www.cnn.com/ALLPOLITICS/stories/1998/12/11/impeachment.vote/.

Chapter 2: Forgiveness

1. In this speech to the Women's Republican Club of Wheeling, McCarthy reportedly held up a slip of paper claiming to list dozens of communists that had infested the State Department. The claim of secret knowledge is a classic parlor trick of unscrupulous accusers and one that Trump employed in the Birther movement (see Chapter 15).
2. The three Senate votes on whether to accept the Tydings report ran strictly on party lines. The age-old custom of voting along party lines makes a mockery of congressional investigations.
3. Roy Cohn was a colorful figure in American history. He achieved notoriety as McCarthy's attack dog against communists and homosexuals in government, but he also contributed to McCarthy's downfall by his entanglement with David Schine. In 1986, Cohn was disbarred for multiple counts of unethical and unprofessional conduct.
4. Collins, Jim. *Good to Great: Why Some Companies Make the Leap... And Others Don't.* (New York, NY: Harper Collins. 2001). This, the best book on business leadership I have ever read, is remarkable for its evidence-based approach (see Chapter 6). *Every* assertion is backed up by facts.

Chapter 3: Trust

1. If a patient lacks decisional capacity, physicians must turn to a health care proxy or family member who is authorized to speak on behalf of the patient. If such a patient verbalizes refusal to undergo an invasive procedure, such as cardiac cath or surgery, a court order is generally required to ensure that the treatment is truly in the patient's interest.
2. A DNR (Do-Not-Resuscitate) order is entered into the chart by an attending physician if a patient requests not to be resuscitated in the event of a cardiopulmonary arrest. In other words, "If I die, don't try to bring me back." This is an appropriate choice for patients in the advanced stages of terminal illnesses. Nowadays, there are very strict protocols for how to establish and document this important decision between doctor and patient.
3. Blood clotting is a complex process that most of us take for granted. The liver makes clotting factors that circulate in the bloodstream, lying in wait for the moment of need. When an individual experiences an injury, the clotting factors kick into gear to stop the bleeding. But when the clotting system is overactive, it can cause unwanted clots to occur– resulting in obstruction of the blood vessels. To prevent this, we sometimes prescribe "blood thinners," which interfere with the activity of those clotting factors.
4. The blackball rule is derived from a voting process in which all the members secretly drop either a white ball or black ball into a container. If a single black ball appears, the proposal is defeated, thus ensuring unanimity of the vote.
5. In all fairness, there was nothing about Butler University per se that would have encouraged racism in a campus residence. Indeed, university leaders would have been appalled to learn that this event took place. Which just serves to make my point. Despite public and official prohibitions against discrimination, an act like this can occur in virtually any group in any setting.

Chapter 4: Diagnosis

1. This analogy is not perfectly accurate. The aortic valve normally has *three* saloon doors, known as valve cusps, or leaflets. They are shaped like triangles, and all meet at a point in the center. But the idea is the same. They swing open to let blood through and then slam shut to make sure it does not flow backward into the heart between heartbeats.
2. I am sorry I cannot provide a proper reference. I learned of this joke long ago and do not remember where it came from.
3. Lindsey, Rebecca. *Climate Change: Atmospheric Carbon Dioxide.* National Oceanic and Atmospheric Administration (NOAA). September 19, 2019. www.climate.gov/news-features/understanding-climate/climate-change-atmospheric-carbon-dioxide.

4. Lindsey, Rebecca and LuAnn Dahlman. *Climate Change: Global Temperature*. National Oceanic and Atmospheric Administration (NOAA). January 16, 2020. www.climate.gov/news-features/understanding-climate/climate-change-global-temperature.

Chapter 5: Treatment

1. Rhodes A, Evans LE, Alhazzani W, et al. *Surviving Sepsis Campaign: International Guidelines for Management of Sepsis and Septic Shock: 2016.* Critical Care Medicine 2017;45: 486-552.
2. The swat team consisted of Amit Uppal, MD, and Laura Evans, MD, from [illegible] from the Emergency Department; Douglas Bails, MD, Michael Janjigian, MD, and Alma Pamandanan, RN, from the Medicine Department; Ira Bader, Delande Auguste, and Yelisa Ferreira from Quality Management.
3. Office of the Medical Director, Office of Quality and Patient Safety. *New York State Report on Sepsis Care Improvement Initiative: Hospital Quality Performance.* New York Department of Health. March 2018 (page 28).
4. When compared to hospitals across the *nation*, Bellevue looked even worse. Our top-box score was in the 9th percentile of hospitals nationwide.
5. In all fairness, Thomas Jefferson, our third president, was an inventor with remarkable talents. But FDR seems to be the first president with a bent for the science of *leadership.*
6. Key to our success, our Patient Experience Officer was, and still is, Linda Lombardi, PhD. And I am delighted to note that, in the final six months of 2019, we finally got to our goal of 70%.

Chapter 6: Evidence

1. Feingold-Link M. *Heart Attack.* Journal of General Internal Medicine 2015. Web Version. August 18, 2015. https://www.sgim.org/web-only/medical-humanities/heart-attack.
2. Internal Medicine is best described as the non-surgical treatment of adults and comprises many subspecialties, such as Cardiology, Pulmonology, Gastroenterology, and Infectious Disease. A practitioner of Internal Medicine is known as an "internist," not to be confused with "intern," the generic term for a first-year resident trainee in any specialty.
3. Bellevue has a contractual relationship with NYU School of Medicine to staff the hospital with attending physicians, all of whom are on the medical school faculty and empowered to supervise and teach medical students, residents, and fellows.

4. ISIS-2 (Second International Study of Infarct Survival) Collaborative Group. *Randomized trial of intravenous streptokinase, oral aspirin, both, or neither among 17,187 cases of suspected myocardial infarction: ISIS-2.* Lancet 1988;332:349-360. The unfortunate acronym for this trial predated the Mideast fundamentalist group by nearly two decades.
5. Danchin N. *30-day mortality after AMI drops with improved treatment.* Presented at the European Society of Cardiology Meeting, August 28, 2012. Over 15 years, the in-hospital mortality rate for STEMI decreased from 13.7% to 4.4%.
6. MacMahon S, Collins R, Peto R, Koster RW, and Yusuf S. *Effects of prophylactic lidocaine in suspected acute myocardial infarction – an overview of results from the randomized, controlled trials.* JAMA 1988;260:1910-6. Although lidocaine reduced the risk of ventricular arrhythmias, it unexpectedly increased the risk of overall mortality. Myth busted.

Chapter 7: Compassion

1. Residency training refers to the 3 to 5 year period following medical school graduation, when a newly minted physician learns her trade under the supervision of attending physicians. The first-year residents are known as interns. Fellowship training refers to several additional (optional) years of post-residency training to prepare for an advanced specialty such as Cardiology. Residents and fellows are collectively known as housestaff.
2. In the early years of the Acquired Immune Deficiency Syndrome (AIDS), the prominent risk factors were the four H's: homosexuality, heroin use, hemophilia, and being of Haitian origin. The macabre joke at the time was that the biggest challenge in contracting AIDS was convincing your parents that you were Haitian.
3. Adrenalin, our "fight-or-flight" hormone, is released into the bloodstream during stressful situations. Studies have shown that adrenalin is a memory enhancer and probable contributor to post-traumatic stress disorder by facilitating vivid recall of those experiences.
4. The germ that caused my hand infection was Corynebacterium – an innocuous pathogen that was easily treated with the everyday antibiotic, erythromycin.
5. The intern who took care of Juan, was Edward Katz, MD, currently a senior cardiologist at NYU School of Medicine. Dr. Katz enjoys telling this story even more than I do.
6. Bellevue's grand history is best presented in David Oshinsky's masterpiece - *Bellevue: Three Centuries of Medicine and Mayhem at America's Most Storied Hospital.* (New York, NY: Penguin Random House, 2016).

Chapter 8: Acceptance

1. Tajfel H, Billig MG, Bundy RP, and Flament C. *Social categorization and intergroup behavior.* European Journal of Social Psychology 1971;1:149-78.
2. Sidanius J, Haley H, Molina L, and Pratto F. *Vladimir's choice and the distribution of social resources: a group dominance perspective.* Group Processes and Intergroup Relations 2007;10:257-65.

Chapter 9: Coalescence

1. As Medical Branch Director, I got to wear a so-titled command center vest, one of the "perks" of my role as Chief Medical Officer.
2. The leaders of the Medicine Service during this crisis included the Chief of Service - Douglas Bails, MD, Chief of General Medicine - Andrew Wallach, MD, and Director of Hospitalists - Michael Janjigian, MD.
3. The Director of Pharmacy who sustained his staff was Michael Blumenfeld.
4. Dr. Evans appears elsewhere in the discussion of sepsis (Chapter 5).
5. The Cardiovascular Surgery (CV) fellow in this story was Deane Smith, MD. Dr. Smith eventually completed his fellowship and became a CV surgery attending at Bellevue.
6. The Chief of Pediatrics was Benard Dreyer, MD, who went on to become President of the American Academy of Pediatrics (AAP) in 2016.
7. Our liaison at Central Office was Ross Wilson, MD, Chief Medical Officer of our entire system. Dr. Wilson capably led the system's coordinated response to Superstorm Sandy.
8. The Chief of Child and Adolescent Psychiatry who put her foot down was Jennifer Havens, MD.
9. The Chief of Adult Psychiatry who took a stand was Mary Anne Badaracco, MD.
10. My colleagues in the Command Center who held the fort for four consecutive days and nights included our Executive Director - Lynda Curtis; Chief Operating Officer - Steven Alexander; Chief Financial Officer - Aaron Cohen; Associate ED for Medicine and Ambula-tory Care – Marcy Pressman; Associate ED for Surgical Services – Linda Lombardi, PhD; Director of Facilities – Michael Rawlings; and Associate Medical Director - Joseph Carter.

Interlude

1. Turner, Justin G. and Linda L. Turner, eds., *Mary Todd Lincoln: Her Life and Letters*, p. 180. (New York, NY: Alfred A. Knopf, 1972). Letter from Mary Todd Lincoln to Abram Wakeman, September 23, 1864.
2. Brewster, Todd. *Lincoln's Gamble: The Tumultuous Six Months that Gave America the Emancipation Proclamation and Changed the Course of the Civil War.* (New York, NY: Scribner, 2014).

3. Lincoln may have mastered the art better than any other American president. His leadership skills are fully on display in Doris Kearns Goodwin's sublime biography, *Team of Rivals: The Political Genius of Abraham Lincoln* (New York, NY: Simon and Schuster, 2005).
4. Hofstadter, Douglas R. *Gödel, Escher, Bach: an Eternal Golden Braid.* (New York, NY: Basic Books, 1979).

Chapter 10: Curiosity

1. *Trends in the distribution of household income between 1979 and 2007.* Congressional Budget Office, October 2011. www.cbo.gov/publication/42729. Figures are derived from Table A-1, page 35, and converted to 2018 dollars. Income shares are reported on page 3.
2. Saez, Emmanuel and Gabriel Zucman. *Wealth inequality in the United States since 1913: Evidence from capitalized income tax data.* Quarterly Journal of Economics 2016;131:2.
3. Ariely, Dan. *Americans Want to Live in a Much More Equal Country (They Just Don't Realize It)*, The Atlantic. August 2, 2012.
4. www.census.gov/foreign-trade/balance/c2010.html.
5. *Corporate profits after tax (without IVA and CCAdj).* Federal Reserve Bank of St. Louis (FRED®) 2020. https://fred.stlouisfed.org/series/CP.
6. *Corporate profits after tax (without IVA and CCAdj)/Gross Domestic Product.* Federal Reserve Bank of St. Louis (FRED®) 2020. https://fred.stlouisfed.org/graph/?g=gt9.
7. *Wage Statistics for 2018.* Social Security On-Line. www.ssa.gov/cgi-bin/netcomp.cgi?year=2018. I derived the $1.22 trillion figure from the data table.
8. *National Health Expenditures, 2018.* Centers for Medicare and Medicaid Services, 2019. www.cms.gov/Research-Statistics-Data-and-Systems/Statistics-Trends-and-Reports/NationalHealthExpendData/NationalHealthAccountsHistorical.html.
9. *Employed full time: Median usual weekly real earnings: Wage and salary workers: 16 years and over.* Federal Reserve Bank of St. Louis (FRED®) 2020. https://fred.stlouisfed.org/series/LES1252881600Q.
10. *Real gross domestic product per capita.* Federal Reserve Bank of St. Louis (FRED®) 2020. https://fred.stlouisfed.org/series/A939RX0Q048SBEA.
11. Shapiro, Isaac and Joel Friedman. *Tax Returns: A Comprehensive Assessment of the Bush Administration's Record on Cutting Taxes.* Center on Budget and Policy Priorities. April 23, 2004. www.cbpp.org/research/tax-returns-a-comprehensive-assessment-of-the-bush-administrations-record-on-cutting-taxes.
12. *How the 2017 Tax Act Has Affected CBO's GDP and Budget Projections Since January 2017.* Congressional Budget Office. February, 28, 2019. https://www.cbo.gov/publication/54994.

13. *Distributional Analysis of the Conference Agreement for the Tax Cuts and Jobs Act.* Tax Policy Center, December 18, 2017. www.taxpolicycenter.org/publications/distributional-analysis-conference-agreement-tax-cuts-and-jobs-act/full. Technically the tax cuts are estimated for tax filing units (e.g., single and joint filers) which typically correspond to one per household.
14. *Updated Budget Projections: 2019 to 2029.* Congressional Budget Office, May, 2019. www.cbo.gov/publication/55151.
15. *All Employees, Total Nonfarm.* Federal Reserve Bank of St. Louis (FRED®) 2020. https://fred.stlouisfed.org/series/PAYEMS.
16. Federal Surplus or Deficit as Percent of Gross Domestic Product. Federal Reserve Bank of St. Louis (FRED®) 2020. https://fred.stlouisfed.org/series/FYFSGDA188S.
17. *Federal Surplus or Deficit.* Federal Reserve Bank of St. Louis (FRED®) 2020. https://fred.stlouisfed.org/series/FYFSD.
18. Watkins, Don and Yaron Brook. *Equal is Unfair – America's Misguided Fight Against Income Inequality.* (New York, NY: St. Martin's Press, 2016). A highly intelligent and thought-provoking presentation of the conservative argument. A must-read for liberals who spend all day on MSNBC.
19. Reich, Robert. *Saving Capitalism – For the Many, not for the Few.* (New York, NY: Penguin Random House, LLC, 2015). Nobody makes this case better than Robert Reich. This is required reading for conservatives who spend all day watching Fox News.
20. Krugman, Paul. *Arguing with Zombies: Economics, Politics, and the Fight for a Better Future.* (New York, NY: W.W. Norton & Co., 2020).

Chapter 11: Courage

1. These are three true stories of patients I cared for recently on the inpatient service. Stories like these are so common at Bellevue, I could have described a dozen more just like them. You can see why "safety net" is a great descriptor for hospitals like ours.
2. The subsidy is based on how the household income compares to the federal poverty level and what the costs of plans are on the available exchange.
3. Uberoi, Namrata, Kenneth Finegold, and Emily Lee. *Health insurance coverage and the Affordable Care Act, 2010–2016.* Department of Health and Human Services. ASPE Brief. March 3, 2016. https://aspe.hhs.gov/system/files/pdf/187551/ACA2010-2016.pdf.
4. *Table 1. National Health Expenditures; Aggregate and Per Capita Amounts, Annual Percent Change and Percent Distribution: Calendar Years 1960-2018.* Centers for Medicare & Medicaid Services. 2019. https://www.cms.gov/Research-Statistics-Data-and-Systems/Statistics-Trends-and-Reports/NationalHealthExpendData/NationalHealthAccountsHistorical.

5. *2016 Employer Health Benefits Survey: Summary of Findings.* The Kaiser Family Foundation and Health Research & Educational Trust, 2018. www.kff.org/health-costs/report/2019-employer-health-benefits-survey/.
6. *Private Health Insurance Premiums and Public Policy.* Congressional Budget Office. February, 2016. www.cbo.gov/sites/default/files/114th-congress-2015-2016/reports/51130-Health_Insurance_Premiums.pdf.
7. Holahan, John and Stacey McMorrow. *Slow Growth in Medicare and Medicaid Spending per Enrollee Has Implications for Policy Debates.* Urban Institute. February 11, 2019. www.urban.org/research/publication/slow-growth-medicare-and-medicaid-spending-enrollee-has-implications-policy-debates.
8. Poll: 'Obamacare' vs. 'Affordable Care Act,' CNN Politics. Posted online September 27, 2013. http://politicalticker.blogs.cnn.com/2013/09/27/poll-obamacare-vs-affordable-care-act/. When asked about "Obamacare," 46% of respondents were opposed to the law. When asked about the "ACA," only 37% were opposed.
9. Butler, Stuart. *Heritage Talking Points: A policy maker's guide to the health care crisis. Part II: the Heritage Consumer Choice Health Plan.* (Washington, D.C.: The Heritage Foundation, 1992)

Chapter 12: Compromise

1. It is well known that the brain is exquisitely sensitive to temporarily low oxygen levels, which may produce irreversible damage during the recovery period. It is customary to lower the patient's body temperature for at least 24 hours to mitigate injury following a prolonged period of CPR.
2. The data on cardiac catheterization laboratory mortality rates are publicly reported. This can have a chilling effect on a decision to perform a procedure on a patient with a low probability of survival. Fortunately, the Bellevue Cardiology Service, led by Norma Keller, MD, remains committed to giving every patient a chance, no matter how remote.

3. *Deaths: Final Data* for 2014. National Vital Statistics Reports. Centers for Disease Control, June 30, 2016
4. Jatlaoui, Tara, Lindsay Eckhaus, Michele Mandel, et al. *Abortion Surveillance – United States, 2016.* Morbidity and Mortality Weekly Report (MMWR) 2019;68(11):1-41.
5. *Public Opinion on Abortion: Views on Abortion, 1995-2019.* Pew Research Center, August 29, 2019. www.pewforum.org/fact-sheet/public-opinion-on-abortion/.
6. *Continued Bipartisan Support for Expanded Background Checks on Gun Sales*. Pew Research Center, U.S. Politics and Policy, August 13, 2015. www.people-press.org/2015/08/13/continued-bipartisan-support-for-expanded-background-checks-on-gun-sales/.
7. Agiesta, Jennifer and Tom LoBianco. *Poll: Gun control support spikes after shooting.* Reported by CNN Politics. CNN/ORC Poll. June 20, 2016. www.cnn.com/2016/06/20/politics/cnn-gun-poll/index.html.

Chapter 13. Reagan

1. *On the Record; Text of 1960 Reagan Letter.* New York Times. October 27, 1984. www.nytimes.com/1984/10/27/us/on-the-record-text-of-1960-reagan-letter.html.
2. Ronald Reagan, interview, Fresno Bee, October 10, 1965.
3. Schaller, Tom. *Ronald Reagan Redux*. FiveThirtyEight. Web. July 15, 2010. https://fivethirtyeight.com/features/ronald-reagan-redux/.
4. John Maynard Keynes, brilliant British economist of the 1930s, claimed that federal deficit spending was a way to provide a potent stimulus to economic growth
5. In a speech to the nation on March 4, 1987, Reagan acknowledged the sordid details of Iran-Contra and accepted responsibility for all that happened, but he did not actually directly admit he made a mistake, and he most definitely did not offer an apology. http://publicapologycentral.com/apologia-archive/political-2/ronald-reagan/.
6. Like most stereotypes, this one is outdated and overstated. The surgeons I know are thoughtful decision-makers who carefully weigh evidence from multiple sources.

Chapter 14: Obama

1. Dionne, E. J., Jr., and Joy-Ann Reid. *We Are the Change We Seek: The Speeches of Barak Obama*. (New York, NY: Bloomsbury, 2017), 1-4. The transcripts of all of Obama's speeches are freely available on the internet, but this book captures them in one place.
2. *Republicans strongly oppose Obama stimulus plan.* The Washington Times. January 27, 2009. www.washingtontimes.com/news/2009/jan/27/paul-warns-inflation-depression/.
3. *Federal Surplus or Deficit as Percent of Gross Domestic Product.* Federal Reserve Bank of St. Louis (FRED®) 2020. https://fred.stlouisfed.org/series/FYFSGDA188S.
4. *Unemployment Rate*. Federal Reserve Bank of St. Louis (FRED®) 2020. https://fred.stlouisfed.org/series/UNRATE.
5. Corporate Profits After Tax (without IVA and CCAdj). Federal Reserve Bank of St. Louis (FRED®) 2020. https://fred.stlouisfed.org/series/CP.
6. Fatás, Antonio. *What has the Eurozone Learned from the Financial Crisis*? Harvard Business Review. September 28, 2018. https://hbr.org/2018/09/what-has-the-eurozone-learned-from-the-financial-crisis.
7. Bergman, Ronen, and Mark Mazzetti. *The Secret History of the Push to Strike Iran.* New York Times Magazine. September 4, 2019. www.nytimes.com/2019/09/04/magazine/iran-strike-israel-america.html.

1. White House Office of the Press Secretary. *Remarks by President Obama at Strasbourg Town Hall.* April 3, 2009. https://obamawhitehouse.archives.gov/the-press-office/remarks-president-obama-strasbourg-town-hall.

Chapter 15: Trump

1. Trump, Donald. *Trump: The Art of the Deal.* (New York, NY: Ballantine Books, 1987), 72.
2. Trump, *Trump: The Art of the Deal, 213.*
3. Trump, *Trump: The Art of the Deal, 218.*
4. Trump, *Trump: The Art of the Deal, 248.*
5. Kranish, Michael, and Marc Fisher. *Trump Revealed: The Definitive Biography of the 45th President.* (New York, NY: Scribner, 2016). If you are going to read one book about Trump, this is the one. Based on the work of 20 investigative reporters from the Washington Post, this account is notable for comprehensiveness and objectivity.
6. Kranish, *Trump Revealed*, 135.
7. Buettner, Russ, and Charles V. Bagli. *How Donald Trump Bankrupted His Atlantic City Casinos, but Still Earned Millions.* New York Times. June 11, 2016. www.nytimes.com/2016/06/12/nyregion/donald-trump-atlantic-city.html.
8. Reilly, Steve. *USA TODAY exclusive: Hundreds allege Donald Trump doesn't pay his bills. USA TODAY.* June 9, 2016. https://www.usatoday.com/story/news/politics/elections/2016/06/09/donald-trump-unpaid-bills-republican-president-laswuits/85297274/.
9. Kranish, *Trump Revealed*, 190.
10. Kranish, *Trump Revealed*, 206.
11. Kranish, *Trump Revealed*, 207.
12. Kranish, *Trump Revealed*, 208. Trump's sixth bankruptcy came in 2009: Trump Entertainment Resorts.
13. Kurtz, Howard. *Kurtz: The Trump Backlash.* Newsweek. April 24, 2011. www.newsweek.com/kurtz-trump-backlash-66503.
14. MacNicol, Glynnis. *Donald Trump Has People in Hawaii Hunting for Obama's Birth Certificate.* Business Insider. April 7, 2011. www.businessinsider.com/donald-trump-today-meredith-hawaii-video-2011-4.
15. Johns Hopkins University Coronavirus Resource Center. Total cases reported as of May 20, 2020. US: 1,531,485. South Korea: 11,110. https://coronavirus.jhu.edu/map.html.
16. Biesecker, Michael. *US 'wasted' months before preparing for coronavirus pandemic.* AP News. April 6, 2020. https://apnews.com/090600c299a8cf07f5b44d92534856bc.

17. Hogan, Bernadette and Aaron Feis. *Cuomo says coronavirus may have infected around 25% of NYC residents.* New York Post. April 27, 2020. Random screening of New York City residents showed 24.7% were positive for coronavirus antibodies, suggesting that 2.1 million residents were infected. https://nypost.com/2020/04/27/cuomo-says-nearly-25-of-nyc-residents-may-have-had-coronavirus/.
18. New York City Department of Health and Mental Hygiene (DOHMH) Response Team. Preliminary estimate of excess mortality during the COVID-19 outbreak – New York City, March 11 - May 2, 2020. Morbidity and Mortality Weekly Report 2020;69:603-5. During the COVID-19 outbreak in New York City, there were 32,107 deaths, which were 24,172 more [illegible] lion infections (reference 17), the excess death rate was equal to 1.15% of COVID-19 infections. Applying this percent to 200 million infections nationwide produces an estimated total mortality of 2.3 million. https://www.cdc.gov/mmwr/volumes/69/wr/mm6919e5.htm.
19. Cohen, Patricia and Tiffany Hsu. *'Rolling Shock' as Job Losses Mount Even With Reopenings.* New York Times. May 14, 2020. https://www.nytimes.com/2020/05/14/business/economy/coronavirus-unemployment-claims.html.
20. "I've always known this is a real, this is a pandemic. I've felt it was a pandemic long before it was called a pandemic." Donald Trump, March 17, 2020.
https://www.politifact.com/factchecks/2020/mar/18/donald-trump/trump-says-he-always-felt-coronavirus-was-pandemic/.
21. "And we have it totally under control... It's going to be just fine." Donald Trump. January 22, 2020.
https://www.poynter.org/fact-checking/2020/we-have-it-totally-under-control-a-timeline-of-president-donald-trumps-response-to-the-coronavirus-pandemic/.
"It's going to disappear...like a miracle." Donald Trump. February 28, 2020.
https://www.politico.com/news/2020/03/17/how-trump-shifted-his-tone-on-coronavirus-134246.
"It's going to go away...The United States, because of what I did and what the administration did with China, we have 32 deaths at this point...it's pretty amazing when you think of it." Donald Trump. March 12, 2020.
https://www.politico.com/news/2020/03/17/how-trump-shifted-his-tone-on-coronavirus-134246.
22. Captain Brett Crozier, commander of the aircraft carrier USS Theodore Roosevelt.
Choi, David. *Trump reportedly wanted to fire the US Navy captain who pleaded for 'immediate' coronavirus help.* Business Insider. April 5, 2020. https://www.businessinsider.com/trump-wanted-to-fired-the-us-navy-captain-brett-crozier-2020-4.

23. Rick Bright, PhD., Director of the Biomedical Advanced Research and Development Authority (BARD).
    Florko, Nicholas. *Trump administration fires back at ousted vaccine expert as he testifies on his role in U.S. coronavirus response.* Stat News. May 14, 2020.
    https://www.statnews.com/2020/05/14/trump-fires-back-rick-bright/.
24. Christi Grimm, Principal Deputy Inspector General at the Department of Health and Human Services.
    Rein, Lisa. *Trump replaces HHS watchdog who found 'severe shortages' at hospitals combating coronavirus.* Washington Post. May 2, 2020.
    https://www.washingtonpost.com/politics/trump-replaces-hhs-watchdog-who-found-severe-shortages-at-hospitals-combating-coronavirus/2020/05/02/6e274372-8c87-11ea-ac8a-fe9b8088e101_story.html.
25. Martin, Jonathan and Maggie Haberman. *Trump Keeps Talking. Some Republicans Don't Like What They're Hearing.* New York Times. April 9, 2020.
    https://www.nytimes.com/2020/04/09/us/politics/trump-coronavirus-press-briefing.html.
26. Prose, Francine. *Will Americans ever forgive Trump for his heartless lack of compassion?* The Guardian. May 5, 2020. https://www.theguardian.com/commentisfree/2020/may/05/will-americans-forgive-trump.

Chapter 16: Mission

1. On January 10, 2020, our special pathogens team addressed the advisory and provided additional information about the coronavirus outbreak. On January 15, the team issued detailed guidelines about how we would handle such a patient at Bellevue.
2. Emory and Nebraska Medical Centers had each successfully treated Ebola patients in their federally-funded biocontainment units.
3. It initially seemed impossible to squeeze 56 patients into 25 beds but we were aided by one of the unfortunate outcomes of the pandemic - non-COVID patients stopped coming to the hospital. Over time the non-COVID census decreased to the point that we were 85% COVID-positive in our Medicine and Surgery units.
4. Plumbers adapted water intakes so that COVID-19 patients could be dialyzed in their inpatient rooms, electricians added power connections to expand the spaces that could accommodate ventilators, and carpenters fashioned window units to fit the exhaust ducts. Our employees in these trades deserve MD degrees for all they did to help our patients. No unit in the hospital escaped some form of adaptation.

5. During my nearly 40 years at Bellevue, I have seen a half-dozen inpatient units dismantled as we followed the national trend of decreasing hospital stays and shifting more care to the outpatient setting. The inpatient rooms on these units were typically converted into offices for a variety of programs, or even into outpatient clinics. By converting offices back into inpatient rooms, our facilities people were undoing the work of decades.
6. One Lean principle I have learned from experience is that good flow looks effortless. When admitted patients have no upstairs beds available, they back up in the ED, creating congestion. The crowded ED, with dozens of admitted patients lying on stretchers in every nook and cranny, appears to be incredibly busy with hardworking staff even if there are very few patients coming in through the front door. On the other hand, good flow clears out the space so the ED staff appear underworked even if they are highly productive with many ED visits of their own. During our COVID surge, the ED never seemed busy, even though the ILI's showed up in droves.
7. Mitchell Katz, MD, our system CEO, has transformed NYC Health and Hospitals in barely more than two years – a modern lesson in leadership. He has boosted revenue capture, fostered interhospital relationships, and promoted the Just Culture in ways that cemented our integration during the pandemic response. He could have written this book.
8. In my 37 years with Health and Hospitals, there has been no greater supporter of the public hospital system than our current mayor, Bill De Blasio.
9. Machelle Allen, MD, our system CMO, likewise embodies the Just Culture. The resulting transparent communication made it possible for our hospitals to help each other as they did for COVID-19. It was a luxury not to worry about supplies of staff, ventilators, and PPE, which were distributed fairly and transparently across our system.
10. Bellevue had many heroes in its COVID-19 response, but the nurses really stood out for their resilience, commitment, and ingenuity. At the height of our surge, nursing was stressed more than any other department, yet maintained its integrity.
11. While there is no way to determine how many of our employees became infected from their patients, and some undoubtedly were, it was reassuring to note that the overall infection rate in our hospital staff (20%) was somewhat less than the city overall (25%).
12. One aspect of COVID-19 that we were not fully prepared for was the high incidence of renal failure. At one point, we had nearly 70 COVID-19 patients in need of some form of dialysis. As we were challenged with having enough dialysis nurses, machines, and supplies, we eventually turned to peritoneal dialysis to keep our patients safe.
13. The workhorses of our COVID-19 response were the housestaff, the medical residents and interns who staffed the teams that provided 24/7 care of our 400 patients. Their dedication reminded me of Bellevue housestaff in the days of AIDS.

14. Over a six-week period, we took in 327 COVID-19 patients solely to relieve pressure on other hospitals, as well as another 300+ transfers (most with COVID-19) who needed some form of complex care that we alone could provide.
15. NYC Health (New York City DOHMH COVID-19 reporting website). https://www1.nyc.gov/site/doh/covid/covid-19-data.page.
As of May 22, 2020, there were 14,096 confirmed COVID-19 deaths among 50,776 COVID-19 hospitalizations city-wide. At Bellevue, there were 216 confirmed COVID-19 deaths among 1,107 hospitalizations as of this date.

Chapter 17: Revelation

1. Maslow, AH. A theory of human motivation. Psychological Review 1943;50:370-96. In Maslow's Hierarchy of Needs, each level must be achieved before we can move on to the next higher one. The need levels from bottom up are: Physiological, Safety, Love/Belonging, Esteem, Self-Actualization.
2. What is the difference between the mission and the target state? They are almost the same. The target state (stated as a noun) is the place we are trying to get to. The mission (stated as a verb) is the getting there. If broad-based prosperity is our target state, our mission is to achieve broad-based prosperity.
3. Gallup poll based on telephone interviews conducted on March 2-6, 2016, with a random sample of 1,019 adults living in all 50 states. https://news.gallup.com/poll/190010/concern-global-warming-eight-year-high.aspx.
4. The Center for Responsive Politics (CRP) as reported on opensecrets.org. CRP is a non-profit non-partisan research group that tracks campaign contributions. It was founded in 1983 by U.S. senators Hugh Scott, Republican, and Frank Church, Democrat.
5. Scheiber, Noam and Dalia Sussman. *Inequality Troubles Americans Across Party Lines, Times/CBS Poll Finds.* New York Times. June 3, 2015. www.nytimes.com/2015/06/04/business/inequality-a-major-issue-for-americans-times-cbs-poll-finds.html.
6. Confessore, Nicholas, Sarah Cohen, and Karen Yourish. *The Families Funding the 2016 Presidential Election.* New York Times. October 10, 2015. www.nytimes.com/interactive/2015/10/11/us/politics/2016-presidential-election-super-pac-donors.html.
7. *Distributional Analysis of the Conference Agreement for the Tax Cuts and Jobs Act.* Tax Policy Center, December 18, 2017. www.taxpolicycenter.org/publications/distributional-analysis-conference-agreement-tax-cuts-and-jobs-act/full.
8. Tankersley, Jim. *Trump's tax cut one year later: what happened?* New York Times. December 27, 2018. www.nytimes.com/2018/12/27/us/politics/trump-tax-cuts-jobs-act.html.

9. *An American Budget: Mid-session Review.* Office of Management and Budget. July 13, 2018. www.whitehouse.gov/wp-content/uploads/2018/07/19msr.pdf.
10. Severns, Maggie. *Big donors ready to reward Republicans for tax cuts.* Politico. January 29, 2018. www.politico.com/story/2018/01/29/big-donors-republican-tax-cuts-374842.
11. Tankersley, Jim and Michael Tackett. *Trump Tax Cut Unlocks Millions for a Republican Election Blitz.* New York Times. August 18, 2018. www.nytimes.com/2018/08/18/us/politics/tax-cuts-republicans-donors.html.
12. Jacobson, Brad. *Obama Received $20 Million from Healthcare Industry in 2008*. Raw Story. January 12, 2010. As identified by the Center for Responsive Politics and reported in an online article. www.rawstory.com/2010/01/obama-received-20-million-healthcare-industry-money-2008/.
13. The term gerrymander originated in 1812 when Governor Gerry of Massachusetts was favored by the shape of his voting district, which was seen to resemble a salamander.

Chapter 18: Solution

1. *The Lovesong of J. Alfred Prufrock* was the first literary piece I studied in college, and the subject of my first English paper - for which I earned a C. I hope I get it better now.
2. An estimate of annual campaign spending is provided by a report on the total amount spent by all candidates, parties, and third-party organizations combined in the 2016 elections for *all* the candidates in the presidential, Senate, and House races - $6.5 billion. Sultan, Niv. *Election 2016: Trump's free media helped keep cost down but fewer donors provided more of the cash.* Open Secrets. April 13, 2017. www.opensecrets.org/news/2017/04/election-2016-trump-fewer-donors-provided-more-of-the-cash/. Since the election cycle is biannual, this figure implies an annual cost of no more than $3.3 billion. To make sure we outcompete the private sector, I have generously rounded this number up to an even $5 billion. Nonetheless, early reports indicate that spending in the 2020 election cycle has well exceeded $10 billion!
3. Berr, Jonathon. *Election 2016's price tag: $6.8 billion.* CBS News, Moneywatch. November 8, 2016. Data originally compiled by the Center for Responsive Politics. This second reference on campaign spending confirms the first.
4. Gawande, Atul. *The Checklist Manifesto: How to Get Things Right.* (New York, NY: Metropolitan Books, 2009).

Acknowledgments

It is amazing to me how much help I needed to write this book. In response, I would like to thank the following friends and family members who read all or part of my manuscript and gave me advice and encouragement: Jon Woods, Lisa Maneval, Sally Lapiduss, Ellen Meyer Shorb, Mia MacCollin, my mother – Gladys, and my daughter – Lani. And special thanks to Mara, my daughter and muse, for reading the first draft of every chapter, to Jordan, my son, for helping me to hone my arguments, to Cynthia McFadden, for encouraging me to persist in my efforts, and to Kate Small, for teaching me how to tell my inner story. Also, a big thank you to my wife, Anat, for allowing me to plunge down this rabbit hole in addition to doing my day job and trying to be a good husband and father. More than anything, I needed encouragement, and I got that in spades from everyone.

The most important acknowledgments are to my colleagues at Bellevue and the thousands of patients we have cared for together over the past 37 years. Leadership is a team sport and I could not have asked for better teammates, many of whom I have named in the end notes. Health and Hospitals, New York City's safety-net hospital system, and Bellevue Hospital, its flagship, are led by a highly professional, yet humble, cadre of "servant" leaders who drive relentlessly to fulfill our mission. Although this book does not represent the views or endorsement of my health system or hospital, I learn every day from these great colleagues, and I am inspired and humbled by their personal commitment to our collective mission.

Finally, I must give a shout-out to my patients, who are the basis of my lessons and the source of my personal growth over a career in Medicine. I cut my teeth as an intern on Bellevue's storied wards at a time when AIDS ruled supreme over trainees like me. My patients with AIDS gave me my most valuable insights into humility and humanity, the core of the art of Medicine, and I can remember their names, faces, and medical presentations as if they were standing right in front of me today. Every one of them suffered unimaginable physical and emotional losses before succumbing to a premature death, but they left behind the valuable lessons that I hope I captured in the pages herein. In a manner of speaking, this is their legacy.

CPSIA information can be obtained
at www.ICGtesting.com
Printed in the USA
BVHW031302141021
618958BV00013B/137